EVERYMAN, I will go with thee,

and be thy guide,

In thy most need to go by thy side

Greek Poetry

TRANSLATED BY

F. L. LUCAS

DENT: LONDON

EVERYMAN'S LIBRARY

All rights reserved
Made in Great Britain
at the
Aldine Press · Letchworth · Herts
for
J. M. DENT & SONS LTD
Aldine House · Bedford Street · London
First included in Everyman's Library 1966

NO. *611*

To George Boas

CONTENTS

	PAGE
Preface	xv
Chronological table	xxi
Introduction	xxvii

PART ONE

HESIOD AND HOMERIC HYMNS

HESIOD	3
THE HOMERIC HYMNS	16
Hymn to Apollo	16
Hymn to Aphrodite	22
Notes	34

PART TWO

FROM ARCHILOCHUS TO ALEXANDER

ARCHILOCHUS	45
TYRTAEUS	47
ALCMAN	48
MIMNERMUS	48
Hymn to Dionysus	50
SEMONIDES	51
CLEOBULUS?	54
ALCAEUS	54
SAPPHO	55
SOLON	60
THEOGNIS	61
IBYCUS	68

	PAGE
HIPPONAX	69
PHOCYLIDES	69
ANACREON	70
XENOPHANES	71
HYBRIAS THE CRETAN	72
Hymn to Pan	73
SIMONIDES	75
PINDAR	78
BACCHYLIDES	84
PRAXILLA	92
EMPEDOCLES	92
PLATO	93
TIMOTHEUS	95
PARRHASIUS	96
ERINNA	96
CLEANTHES	97
PERSES	97
ADDAEUS	97
Notes	98

PART THREE

ALEXANDRIAN PERIOD

PHILETAS	117
ARATUS	117
CALLIMACHUS	118
THEOCRITUS	124
AUTOMEDON or THEOCRITUS	137
NICIAS	137
DIOTIMUS or LEONIDAS	138
LEONIDAS	138
POSEIDIPPUS	139
ASCLEPIADES	140
NOSSIS	141

	PAGE
ANYTE	141
APOLLONIUS RHODIUS	142
THEODORIDAS	149
DAMAGETUS	149
THYMOCLES	150
PHAEDIMUS	150
The Humbling of Sparta	150
DIONYSIUS THE SOPHIST	150
ANTIPATER OF SIDON	151
BION	152
Lament for Bion	153
Anacreontea	156
Notes	162

PART FOUR

ROMAN AND EARLY BYZANTINE PERIOD

MELEAGER	179
MELEAGER or PHILODEMUS	181
PHILODEMUS	181
ZONAS	182
THYILLUS	183
ERYCIUS	183
CRINAGORAS	184
ANTIPATER OF THESSALONICA	184
POMPEIUS	185
ALPHEUS	186
DIODORUS	186
SATYRUS	187
MARCUS ARGENTARIUS	187
BIANOR	188
MYRINUS	188
ISIDORUS AEGEATES	188
ANTIPHILUS	188

	PAGE
LUCILIUS	189
JULIUS POLYAENUS	190
ARCHIAS	190
GLAUCUS	191
RUFINUS	191
LUCIAN	192
PTOLEMAEUS	192
STRATO	193
OPPIAN	193
QUINTUS SMYRNAEUS	195
NONNUS	198
GLYCON	199
PALLADAS	199
MUSAEUS	201
DAMASCIUS	216
JULIANUS	216
MACEDONIUS	217
PAULUS SILENTIARIUS	217
AGATHIAS SCHOLASTICUS	219
ARABIUS SCHOLASTICUS	221
JOANNES BARBUCALLUS	221
Notes	222

Appendix I. Pieces of unknown date or authorship:

Hymn to Ares	231
Epigrams	231
Notes	237

Appendix II. The Palatine Anthology	239
Appendix III. The Oracle of Delphi	242

Index of Poets	250

PREFACE

It must be faced that the 'dead languages' are in some danger of dying a second death. It becomes harder and harder to find time for Greek or Latin in a world where knowledge grows ever more multitudinous, life more hustled—and more herded.

The Renaissance gave rebirth both to Classics and, thereby, to Science: today Science, like a giant cuckoo, pushes Classics more and more from the nest. To decry Science is senseless and thankless; we have misused its benefits; but without it we should starve. (Indeed mankind will need all its help to avoid starving in the next hundred years.) Yet intelligent scientists themselves deplore the narrowness produced by the study of Science alone. And it is curious that as the world grows more scientific, it now grows less scientific also. The twentieth century has shown, not less, but more besotted fanaticism than the eighteenth or nineteenth.

Yet Life itself still remains more an art than a science. And art, though it ceaselessly changes, has in the last three thousand years found it often hard to progress. The two greatest poems of western man are still, in many eyes, the two oldest. And the grace and sanity of Greece are not so common in our modern world that we can afford to forget them. Once already the West has forgotten Greek. That period we call 'the Dark Ages'.

Since, then, the place of Greek in higher education has declined, and seems likely to decline still more, what possible remedy is there but more translation and selection of the best Greek literature? Excellent books *about* it are produced every year; but books about books are no substitute for books—though many moderns seem to think so. All translations, indeed, remain inadequate. 'Everything', as Chesterfield said, 'suffers by translation except a Bishop.' Yet on translations Alfred the Great thought it worth while to spend some of his hard-won leisure a thousand years ago, to bring his England in touch again with the classic past; in our very different English-speaking world the need remains. Who, again, would burn our Bibles and demand that we read Hebrew literature in Hebrew or not at all? The Renaissance itself translated enthusiastically. The pity is that our Tudor and Jacobean translators did not render the great writers of the Hellenes, as of the Hebrews, into a collected volume of their admirable prose (for their verse-renderings are largely debased, like Chapman's overrated *Homer*, by tawdry efforts to be witty and ornate).

But that is a vain regret. There are now plenty of modern versions of Greek poetry; but not, to my knowledge, any attempt to combine all the best of that poetry in a single homogeneous book, with the introductions and notes needed by the non-classical.[1] If this work sends some back to the originals, so much the better.[2] It has been done at intervals over the

---

[1] *The Oxford Book of Greek Verse in Translation* contains versions by a hundred and twenty-four different translators and is, I feel, more suited to the classical than the non-classical reader. And, to be quite frank—though this is only personal taste, or lack of it—I find in some of its versions neither truth nor beauty.

[2] Those attracted by Greek need not be frightened off by the supposed difficulty of the language. Nineteenth-century educators took seven or eight years of boys' lives for Greek and Latin; after which most of their pupils never opened a classic author again, nor could have read him if they had. This was partly because many of these pedagogues planted the road to Helicon with grammatical prickly pears; partly because they chose to inflict on their victims classic authors who are either bores (there are plenty) or too difficult for novices to enjoy. Today, no doubt, teaching of the humanities has become more human; but the harm is done. In fact, the death of classical education, though partly from natural causes, was partly suicide. I have always cherished, for example, the memory of the pundit who at some conference objected to his boys reading Herodotus, because it spoilt their 'Attic style'. ('Quelle perte irréparable!' as Comte is said to have modestly observed on his own deathbed.)

Schliemann, on the other hand, being a practical business-man with no 'Attic style' round his neck, learnt Greek in four months. And in middle age. True, Schliemann was unusually gifted; but still . . . ! I believe that, equipped with the minimum of grammar, one should plunge straight into Homer and Herodotus, the two Greek writers who are still most vividly alive. Then perhaps the best of the *Anthology*, Hēsiod's *Works and Days*, and Theócritus. After that anyone should be able to pursue his own bent. (Plutarch's *Lives*, which I follow Montaigne —despite the purists—in thinking one of our most precious pictures of the ancient world, should certainly be also read; but in translation.) Admirably vital introductions to the life of Hellas will be found in books like Gilbert Murray's *Ancient Greek Literature* (though I cannot accept his Homeric theories), Livingstone's *Greek Genius*, and Zimmern's *Greek Commonwealth*.

last twenty-five years. I do not know if I have wasted my time. At least I have enjoyed it.

I have used verse, because modern prose translations, though often useful, remain for me unsatisfying. They seem like songs robbed of their music, or birds whose wings are clipped. Take, for example, the appeal of Elpēnor's ghost to Odysseus (*Od.* xi, 69–78):

> 'For well I know that, returning from Hades' house, awhile
> Thou wilt stay thy stout-built galley again at Aeaea's isle.
> There, O my lord, I charge thee, once more remember me,
> Nor leave me unwept, unburied, as thou sailest out to sea;
> Lest haply the wrath of Heaven upon thy head I bring.
> But burn me there and, with me, the arms of my warfaring,
> And heap a mound above me, beside the grey sea-flow,
> The grave of a man unhappy, for men unborn to know;
> Do this for me, I beg thee; and on my barrow raise
> The oar I pulled with my comrades, living, in other days.'

Put the same passage into prose: 'For I know that departing from the House of Hades you will bring your stout ship to land at the isle of Aeaea; there, my king, I charge you to remember me. Do not sail away again leaving me unwept and unburied, for fear I bring upon you the anger of the Gods; but burn me with the arms that were mine, and heap a mound above me on the shore of the grey sea, the memorial of a man ill-fated, for men to know hereafter. Do all this for me and set above my barrow the oar I pulled among my comrades while I lived.' Tastes may differ; but without metre it seems to me still harder to recapture some of that desolate sadness which catches at the heart in Homer's Greek. By the measure of verse this measureless sorrow is heightened and yet controlled. I know that some prefer prose versions; but the *Odyssey* is not *Robinson Crusoe*. To say that is not to undervalue Defoe. But the rhythm of verse can be like the movement of a horse that gathers its great limbs under one and devours the plain. If some find my horse lame, I am sorry. But here I prefer to ride.

Diction presents another problem. Too archaized, it becomes 'Wardour Street' English, a style to some so emetic that to avoid it they lurch into Cheapside, or beyond. That seems going further only to fare worse. Better King Lear in woad, even, than King Lear in a lounge suit. For two reasons at least. First, the society of Agamemnon or Lear was a primitive society; too modernized a setting inflicts constant jars of incongruity on anyone with a historic sense. This historic sense may itself be a modern thing. But it is there. To ignore it is not 'modern'; it is merely insensitive.

When in some film-script a spacious Elizabethan courtier replies to his sovereign 'O.K., Queen!', we smile; but there are modern translations on lines not very different.

These seem to me not only crude, but false. For, secondly, the Ancients believed that the higher kinds of literature demanded dignity. Much modern writing appears to have forgotten that such a thing even exists. But it did. And what the originals valued, it is not for translators to neglect. Accordingly I have tried to shun both aggressively ancient and aggressively modern words. After all, the English language is rich enough.

Then comes the vexed question of literalness. The first business of a translator is to be readable; if a translation reads like a translation, it must be bad. The literal jargon into which Browning turned the *Agamemnon*—as if in later life he had developed a sort of spite against beauty—seems to me worse than the wildest licences sometimes practised by FitzGerald. At least FitzGerald remains a pleasure to read. All the same I believe it is possible to be a good deal more literal than most verse translators.[1] It merely means a lot of trouble. On the other hand there is a tendency for those who pore over ancient texts with microscopes, forgetting that they were composed mainly to be heard—not read—and sometimes heard only through music, to insist on subtleties that no ancient audience could have noticed. (The same fallacy underlies much niggling modern analysis of what Shakespeare wrote for the noisy bustle of the stage.) There is a wise passage in a letter from Lawrence of Arabia: 'The worst of being a habitual translator is that one gets in the way of trying to squeeze every sponge dry—and so few authors really intend *all* the contents of their sponges.'

In short, as Pope says in that preface to his *Homer* which seems to me finer than his translation, 'a mere modern wit can like nothing that is not modern, and a pedant nothing that is not Greek'.

Lastly, there is the question of selection. Some snort at all anthologies. But here, for a large and important public, it is a case of anthologies or nothing. Much cant gets talked about 'artistic wholes', particularly by critics of that special psychological type which cares more for the form and organization of a work than for its spirit, its content, its supreme moments. Yet in practice we make automatic selections of our own from every book we read (if we remember them at all). Even before we turn the last page of *Iliad* or *Divina Commedia* or *Paradise Lost*, we have forgotten the greater

---

[1] One simple point is of importance: in Greek the emphasis tends to lie on the words at the beginning of the sentence; in English, on the words at the end. In translation this often entails changes of order.

part; all that we can hope to carry with us through life is an imperfect outline of the whole and an involuntary selection by our memories of the lines and phrases that moved us most. All ink is mixed with water of Lethe. And was it not the great Johnson who asked tartly, 'Sir, do *you* read books *through*?'

It may be recalled how one day a Sibyl came to King Tarquin in Rome and asked three hundred pieces of gold for nine volumes that she brought. Refused, she went away, burnt three, and came back to ask the same price for the rest. Again refused, she burnt three more; and the astonished king gave her for the remaining three the price of all the nine. Rome, we are told, did not regret the bargain. It seems to me that our own and future ages must more and more imitate King Tarquin.

Besides—why not face it?—much even of Greek poetry was, inevitably, minor; much has been superannuated by time. Some of Homer himself has lost savour—who wants *all* his battles? Sometimes, as Hēsiod already knew, 'the half is more than the whole'.

> Greece with calm eyes I see,
> Her pure white marbles have not blinded me,
>   But breathe on me the love
> Of earthly things as bright as things above:
>   There is (where is there not?)
> In her fair regions many a desert spot;
>   Neither is Dirce clear,
> Nor is Ilissus full throughout the year.[1]

'Of the Greeks,' wrote that master-critic, Sainte-Beuve, 'a page, an idyll from time to time suffices me. It is not deep knowledge of them that I require: it is their flavour.' Let those who love and believe in Hellas not make too extravagant claims on this hurried modern world. They will be refused. Let us ask less—only so can we hope for more.

Each author here is preceded by a brief notice and followed by a brief commentary. Both must ask the indulgence of the classical reader.[2] They

---

[1] Landor.

[2] On the same principle of consideration for the non-classical reader, I have marked the length of syllables in proper names, or their accentuation, wherever there seemed any possibility of mispronunciation. An accent on a syllable means that it is short, but *stressed* in English. (This has, of course, nothing to do with Greek accents, which marked *pitch*.) It need hardly be added that in Greek names a final *e* is pronounced, and pronounced long. Similarly with the spelling of Greek names I have been more concerned to be helpful than consistent.

are not meant for him, but for others less informed. *Ecce convertimur ad gentes.*

The present work was first published in 1951 by J. M. Dent and Sons (in U.S.A. by Macmillan and later, in paperback, by the Beacon Press). In its original form it included also a selection of outstanding passages from *Iliad* and *Odyssey*, linked by prose summaries of the intervening narrative. This Homeric section is here omitted, because the Everyman Library already contains complete versions of the two epics (*Iliad* by S. O. Andrew and M. J. Oakley; *Odyssey* by S. O. Andrew). Otherwise, apart from a few revisions and additions, this edition is reprinted unchanged.

The *Hymn to Aphrodite* was first published by the Golden Cockerel Press in 1949 and in a cheaper edition, along with the *Pervigilium Veneris*, by the Cambridge University Press in the same year under the title *Aphrodite*. The Golden Cockerel likewise produced *Hero and Leander* in 1950; and most of the epigrams in 1937, as *The Golden Cockerel Greek Anthology* (reprinted in enlarged and cheaper form, as *A Greek Garland*, by the Oxford University Press, 1939; second edition, Cohen & West, 1949). My thanks are also due to the Hogarth Press for permission to reprint several of the pieces of Theognis, which first appeared in *Time and Memory* (1929). Finally, I am deeply indebted to Mr A. S. F. Gow for allowing me in 1950 to see in proof the notes to his edition of Theocritus.

1965.

CHRONOLOGICAL TABLE

B.C.	Greek Literature and Art	Greek History	Events elsewhere
1500			Sixth city of Troy
		Destruction of Cnossus? (c. 1400)	
1400			Religious reform of Aknaton (c.1375) Tutankhamen (c. 1360)
1300			Ramses II (1292–1225) Israelite Exodus? (c. 1240)
1200		Fall of Homeric Troy ('Troy VII A') (c. 1260–1200)	Ramses III repels sea-raids on Egypt (c. 1190)
1100		Dorian invasion (c. 1100–1000)	Judges in Israel Samuel Saul (c. 1025) David (c. 1000)
1000			Solomon (c. 974)
900	Evolution of *Iliad* and *Odyssey* (c. 1200–750?)		Ahab (c. 876) Carthage founded (c. 820)
800	Hēsiod (c. 800–750)		
		Olympic Games founded (776)	
	Cyclic Epics and most Homeric Hymns (800–600)	Greek colonization in Black Sea, Sicily, and Italy	Amos (c. 760) Traditional founding of Rome (753)

B.C.	Greek Literature and Art	Greek History	Events elsewhere
		Sparta conquers Messenia (c. 736–716)	Assyrians take Samaria (722)
700	Archílochus (c. 700–650)		Midas, king of Phrygia (d. c. 693)
			Assyria conquers Egypt (681)
		Byzantium founded (660)	Gyges, king of Lydia (680–660)
	Tyrtaeus (c. 650–600)	Second war of Sparta with Messenia (c. 630)	
	Alcman (c. 650–600)		
	Mimnermus (c. 620)		Assurbanipal (Sardanapalus) (d. 626)
			Fall of Nineveh (606)
600	Semōnides		Nebuchadnezzar (605–562)
	Solon (c. 640–560)		
	Thales the philosopher (c. 624–546)		Nebuchadnezzar takes Jerusalem (597)
	Stesíchorus (c. 610–550)	Laws of Solon at Athens (594)	
	Alcaeus (b. c. 620)		
	Sappho (c. 610–565)		
		Peisístratus tyrant of Athens (561; d. 527)	Croesus, king of Lydia (560–546)
			Cyrus the Persian conquers the Medes (550)
	Ibycus (c. 535)		
			Cyrus conquers Lydia (546)
		Persia conquers the Greeks of Asia Minor (545)	
	Pythágoras (c. 530)		Takes Babylon (538)
	Thespis founds drama at Athens (c. 534)		

B.C.	Greek Literature and Art	Greek History	Events elsewhere
	Anácreon (c. 570–485)		
	Xenóphanes (c. 565–470)		
	Theognis (c. 540)		Cyrus slain by the Massagetae (529)
	Simōnides (556–467)		Cambyses conquers Egypt (525)
			Zerubbabel rebuilds the Temple (520–516)
		Hippias dethroned at Athens (510)	Tarquins dethroned at Rome (510)
		New constitution at Athens (507)	
500	Heraclītus (c. 500)		Confucius (551–479)
		Ionia revolts from Persia (499–494)	
		Persian defeat at Marathon (490)	
	Parménides (c. 520–455)		
	Aeschylus (525–456)	Thermópylae and Salamis (480)	
	Pindar (c. 518–438)		
	Bacchýlides (c. 510–430)		
	Anaxágoras (c. 500–428)		
	Temple of Zeus at Olympia finished (c. 456)		
	Sophocles (495–406)		
	Empédocles (c. 494–434)		
	Euripides (c. 485–406)		
	Heródotus (c. 484–430)		

B.C.	Greek Literature and Art	Greek History	Events elsewhere
	Parthenon finished (433)	Peloponnesian War between Athens and Spartan League (432–404)	
	Socrates (c. 469–399)		
	Demócritus (c. 460–370)		
	Thucydides (c. 455–400)		
	Aristophanes (c. 450–385)		
	Timótheüs, (c. 450–360)	Fall of Athens (404)	
		Thrasybūlus restores Athenian democracy (403)	
400			
		Socrates executed (399)	Ezra returns to Jerusalem (397)
	Plato (c. 427–347)		
	Aristotle (384–322)		
	Demosthenes (384–322)		
		Philip defeats the Greeks at Chaerōnēa (338)	
		Alexander invades Asia (334)	
		Alexander dies at Babylon (323)	
	Epicurus (c. 341–270)		
300			
	Philetas (c. 300)		
	Arātus (c. 315–240)		Pyrrhus invades Italy (280)
	Theócritus (b. c. 312)		
	Callímachus (c. 310–240)		
	Archimēdes (c. 287–212)		First War of Rome with Carthage (264–241)
	Apollonius of Rhodes (c. 280–200)	Sicily a Roman province (241)	Second (Hannibalic) War (218–202)

B.C.	Greek Literature and Art	Greek History	Events elsewhere
		First War of Rome with Macedon (214–205)	
200			
		Second War (200–197)	
		Third War (172–168). End of Macedonian kingdom	
			Rising of Maccabees (166)
	Bion	Rome destroys	Rome destroys
	Antípater of Sidon	Corinth (146)	Carthage (146)
100			
	Meleãger (c. 135–65)	Greece overrun by	
	Philodḗmus (c. 110–40)	Mithridates and reconquered by	
	Zōnas	Sulla (88–85)	
	Crinágoras		
			Death of Caesar(44)
	Antípater of Thessalonica		Octavian defeats Antony at Actium (31 B.C.)
A.D.			
I			
	Lucílius		Nero (54–68 A.D.)
	Plutarch (c. 46–126)		Titus takes Jerusalem (70)
100			
	Ptolemy the astronomer(c. 100–78)		
	Lucian (c. 115–85)		Marcus Aurelius (121–180)
200			
	Oppian (c. 200)		
300			
	Quintus of Smyrna	Constantinople founded (330)	

A.D.	Greek Literature and Art	Greek History	Events elsewhere
400			St Augustine of Hippo (354–430)
	Palládas		
	Nonnus		Romans leave Britain (c. 410)
			Alaric sacks Rome (410)
			Attila defeated near Châlons (451)
	Musaeus (*Hero and Leander*)		End of Western Empire (476)
500		Reign of Justinian (527–65)	Clovis makes Paris his capital (510)
	Julianus		
	Macedonius	Closes schools of	
	Paulus Silentiarius	Athens (529)	
	Agáthias	St Sophia dedicated (537)	
			St Columba brings Christianity to Scotland (563)
			St Augustine lands in Kent (596)
800–1000			
			Alfred the Great (871–901)
	Anthology of Cephalas under Constantine VII (912–59)		
1300	Anthology of Planudes (1301)		
	Manuel Chrysoloras begins teaching Greek at Florence (1396)		Dante d. (1321)
1400			
		Fall of Constantinople (1453)	End of Hundred Years War (1453)

INTRODUCTION

THE happy traveller who approaches Greece may enter, like most of her barbarian invaders, from the mountains of the north or, like the Roman, from the western sea. The sea-gate is perhaps even finer. And more sudden. Here at first sight stands revealed the character of Hellas, in full contrast to her richer sister, Italy. Yesterday the eye rested on the green hills of Samnium, the sun-baked flats of Apulia; but now, beyond the Straits of Otranto, dawn reddens on gaunt mountains towering like a rampart sheer from the Ionian Sea. No European coast I know, except Norway, stands up in such grim splendour. All day one's ship steams southward—past fertile Corcȳra (Corfu), perhaps the ancient Phaeacia that sent the sea-worn Odysseus home; past the death-grey ranges of Epīrus, where Acheron and Cōcȳtus, the infernal rivers of Woe and Wailing, wind through dark gorges down to the shore that rang with unseen lamentations one night two thousand years ago, at the news that Pan was dead; past the gulf of Actium, ringed with the mountains that watched Antony lose a world for Cleopatra; past the sheer white Leucadian headland of Sappho's legendary leap; past the rugged little Ithaca of Odysseus, nestling beneath Mount Nēritus, bare now of the 'tossing leaves' that Homer knew; past the low coasts of Cálydon and Misso-longhi, where Meleāger died for Atalanta and Byron for Greece—to anchor under Mount Panachaïcus in the harbour of Patras.

The northern land-gate through Jugoslavia brings contrasts of a different kind. In March the snowflakes may still be drifting down on that dreary Siberian plain south of the Drave, a muddy infinitude beneath a muddy sky, broken at last by the great mud-brown swirl of Save and Danube as they meet before Belgrade. South from Belgrade, gaunt and black on its height amid the snow, the train pants up the gorges of featureless hills towards Nish and the watershed of the Aegean; till beyond it, on a moorland desolate as Rannoch, watched from east-ward by the blue peaks of Thrace, winter vanishes and there comes a sudden sense of the approaching south, of the magic of the Mediterranean world. The same night at the frontier station of Ghevghelí the traveller would suddenly see shining out of the darkness a word in Greek charac-ters—ΑΙΘΟΥΣΑ. It was a word he had last encountered in Homer; but three thousand years had not killed it; it had merely changed its mean-ing from the 'vestibule' of an Achaean king to the 'waiting-room' of a modern railway. And one felt, suddenly, as if at last one had come home.[1]

Next morning, standing where Xerxes and St Paul stood long ago, on the shore of Salonika, one would vaguely glimpse, across fifty miles of blue Aegean, a far-off mist-capped whiteness—and cry, all at once, 'Olympus!' Beyond it, to southward along the sea, loomed the peak of Ossa; and then, dimmer still, the seaward ridge of Pēlion, the mountain of the Centaurs, where the little Jason and the little Achilles were once reared in Chiron's cave.

Thus, whether one comes from the land of the Latin or the Slav, Greece reveals itself at once (though one must see it to realize) as a country of endless mountains jostling mountains, till they fall at last into the sea. From Salonīka turn your back on the wind that shrieks down the Vardar valley, as blustering still as when men prayed to him as 'Bóreas', and take the southward road—past Pydna where Macedon went down before the legions (168 B.C.); through Piéria, the Muses' ancient home between the roots of Olympus and the sea; to where 'Pēneus rolls his fountains Against the morning star'. There the seaward crags of Ossa bar all progress, and the track turns west inland, between the precipices of Ossa and Olympus, through the forest-gorge of Tempe.[2] At its western end, where green grasses used to wave on the ruined mosque of Babá, for the only time in Greece proper a great plain opens—Thessaly. Like Lom-bardy beneath the Alps, it lies magnificently walled with mountains—Olympus to the north, Ossa to north-east, to westward the long white rampart of Pindus through which Caesar marched from the Adriatic in 48 B.C., to win the world at Pharsālus on the plain's southern edge. To southward, too, you must breast more mountain-bastions—Othrys; then Oeta above the deathless gate of Thermópylae; then Parnassus towering above the fatal field of Chaerōnēa—before you can look from the narrow

---

[1] Today, of course, it grows increasingly common, and convenient, to go by air. But though the aircraft may seem magical as a flying carpet, it seldom lends enchantment to the view. From Heaven the earth is dwarfed; mountains sink into molehills; and even if he is lucky enough not to be blocked by a wing, or blinded by a cloud, the traveller becomes a sardine in a flying box.

[2] When Alexander turned the pass of Tempe in 336 B.C. by scaling the side of Ossa, he had to cut steps in its crags.

ledge of Apollo's Delphi, across the blue Gulf of Corinth two thousand feet below, to the farther peaks of Arcadia and Argŏlis. All this land of tossing stone recalls Odysseus' words of his own Ithaca:

> Rugged, and yet a brave mother of men. In all wide earth
> No sight I know so lovely as the land of a man's own birth.

Such, then, is Greece: a labyrinth of sharp grey-white mountains, green valleys, all-embracing seas—mountains that hardened, valleys that gladdened, seas that widened the spirit of her race. Only one-fifth of the country is level: and, with an area one-sixth of Spain and Portugal, it has three hundred miles more coast. For first the land was crumpled upwards into ranges; then it sank downwards again, turning glens to fiords and peaks to islands.[1] Its mountain barriers bred individuality, but disunity; yet they made its sea more navigable by giving countless landmarks and harbours; and this sea, beautiful enough to have given birth to Beauty's Goddess, brought home to Hellas wealth and experience from other shores. It was the sea alone that prevented the mountain chains of Greece from becoming chains indeed.

A land in itself poor and barren. Yet, if crops were scanty save for vine and olive, its earth gave limestone and marble for builder and sculptor, clay for the potter's kiln. Its air is clear and brilliant as the Greek spirit at its best. The climate, with its summer drouth and glare, keeps the nerves tense, even over-tense; but its winds are bracing and its winters far from soft.[2]

Such a country was a fit cradle for its race; but men are not made only by their cradles. Greek greatness was brief. Through most of the two thousand years that followed, this remained an obscure and downtrodden land. Partly, perhaps, because in Europe the loveliness of the South seems to need ever and again to be reinvigorated by the energy of the North. That stands out from the history not only of Greece, but of Italy, France, and Spain. What these owed to Lombard, Frank, and Goth, early Greece received from Achaean and Dorian, as they swept down from the northern mountains on a decaying Minoan world. First the avalanche, then the flowers; and afterwards the autumn dust. A heroic age of splendid and passionate kings; then a dark period, after the Dorian invasion, of

---

[1] See M. Cary, *The Geographic Background of Greek and Roman History*.

[2] *c.* 1000–300 B.C. Greece may have been cooler in summer and wetter (and so less malarial), owing to a southward shift of the belt of cyclonic storms, which are believed to foster maximum human energy. (Ellsworth Huntington, *Civilization and Climate*, 3rd ed., 22 ff.)

oppressive landowners and grumbling peasantry; then a growth of cities, where the nobles slowly gave place to moneyed oligarchy, or popular dictatorship, or democracy, as the new bourgeoisie gained wealth by trade, colonization, and industry, with a perilously increasing exploitation of the slave. In the great conflict with Persia Hellas reached her height; in mad conflict with herself—Athens against Sparta, Sparta against Thebes—she fell. Partly through loss of wisdom and the simpler virtues, the city-states with all their brilliance went down before the rise of nations, of Macedon and Roman Italy. Yet even in this final phase, like an aloe in its supreme flowering before death, Hellenism could still conquer Asia with the sword of Alexander, and Rome by the force of her inspiration and her intellect. So was prepared the way for the spread of Roman Empire and Christian faith and for that thousand-year reign of Byzantium (A.D. 330–1453) which, with all its decadence and bigotry, yet preserved the seeds of Greek civilization for Europe's Renaissance.

Within seven centuries (c. 900–200 B.C.—and most of it was done in the last four) this race invented for itself epic, elegy, lyric, tragedy, comedy, opera, pastoral, epigram, novel, democratic government, political and economic science, history, geography, philosophy, physics, and biology; and made revolutionary advances in architecture, sculpture, painting, music, oratory, mathematics, astronomy, medicine, anatomy, engineering, law, and war. One need not be a frenzied philhellene to find this a stupendous feat for a race whose home was only half the area of England and Wales (with a third of it barren) and whose most brilliant state, Attica, was the size of Hertfordshire, with a free population (including children) of perhaps 160,000—less than Southampton.

But all this, however extraordinary, might be of merely antiquarian interest. It is not because they were ancient that the Greeks still matter, but because they are in many ways so modern. In science, indeed, they were children to us; one armed trawler could annihilate all their navies, one aircraft their armies. Even in art we can challenge them with Michelangelo and Mozart and Shakespeare. They were not more heroic; England in 1940 had a finer hour even than Greece at Salamis. They were more superstitious, more cruel than nineteenth-century Europe (we had better not speak of the twentieth); they took for granted a slavery which our modern age, with certain grim exceptions, has left behind. Their deepest fascination rests, I think, rather on our sense of the balance, completeness, and lucidity of their miniature world, our feeling that they had found a way of life where human beings could realize themselves with a grace, sanity, and freedom since attained only by a few favoured exceptions like Goethe. They had no anaesthetics, no medical or dental experts like ours, no aids for failing sight and hearing, not a hundredth part of our luxuries, toys, and pleasures in this world, little consoling faith in a world beyond. Their view of life was often tragic; their poets have cried again and again that it was better never to be born. And yet what vitality, what versatility, what vivid minds in vivid bodies! Their consolation lay not in divine, bu human grace. The transience and sadness of existence were made bearable by their splendour and their poetry. Tolstoy protested that it was bad Russian to use the same word (like our 'fine') for 'beautiful' and 'good': but it was very good Greek. From Homer onward their καλός means both. Many of them, I feel (like a few people one has known), carried into the art of living, consciously or not, a certain fineness, a certain sense of style, which redeemed them from the sterile futility of most human struggling. Such characters can suffer, grow old, be forgotten; but they were never ugly, nor squalid, nor ridiculous. If anything could justify the world, it would be its beauty; they were a part of that. Much Greek history, I know, is very different. Much medieval history is very different from the knightly ideal of Malory. If ideals were easy to realize, they would not be ideals. But in Homer and the best Greek writing, in the marbles of Olympia and the Parthenon, in the grave-reliefs of the Cerameicus, in many of the characters of Plutarch, this ideal seems to me to live.

It is curious to contrast their writers with those of the last two hundred and fifty years, since literature tended to become professionalized and specialized. Undeniable though modern genius has often been, what processions of eccentrics and neurotics, decadents and suicides!—figures like Swift, Rousseau, Gray, Collins, Chatterton, Blake, Coleridge, Byron, Shelley, Hölderlin, Hoffmann, Lenau, Musset, Baudelaire, Dostoyevsky, Carlyle, Poe, Rossetti, Swinburne, Nietzsche, Flaubert, Zola, Huysmans, Proust, D. H. Lawrence, Joyce (not to mention Surrealists and Existentialists). Our 'intellectuals' in their jaded restlessness, like haunted hypochondriacs scurrying from quack to quack, have genuflected before Negro mumbo-jumbos, or day-dreamed of Aztec atrocities, or adored the sombre decadence of Etruria, or sighed for the picturesque superstition of the Middle Ages once again—until this playing at barbarians helped to bring the grim earnest of two world wars.

There is a curious passage in the memoirs of Ethel Smyth: 'I even remember a few years later, when for the first time I saw Paestum, standing in the centre of the Neptune temple and suddenly being possessed with such an overwhelming horror of Wagner's art as compared to this, that it seemed as though one were physically seized and shaken by one of the ancient gods.' Much even of Greek art may be bad, much may be boring; but they did not crave blue wine—red was enough; they did not cultivate green carnations—enough the wild iris that Sappho saw trodden beneath the shepherds' feet upon the hills. There are human beings so anaemic that they need drink or drugs to feel alive; there are others so alive that, like Wordsworth, they can find intoxication in a mountain burn. There is no need to romanticize the Greeks in the style of Lord Leighton: the truth is remarkable enough. These men were much poorer than we; but they would have thought that most of us, rich and poor alike, lived the lives of slaves. They were much nearer to the primitive than we; but they were much further from the madhouse.

'First', says an old Greek poem on life's aims, 'is health'; in that—in uninhibited, clear-headed health of mind—lies perhaps no small part of their peculiar and enduring appeal.

This book contains extracts from the poetry of nearly thirteen or four-teen hundred years (eighth century B.C.? to sixth A.D.)—nearly as long a span as separates us from Roman Britain, or Hitler from Attila Natur-ally this is only a fragment of what survives; what survives is only a frag-ment of what existed once. But one need not too much regret what time has lost. Those who never revisit the past may become crude barbarians: those who stay too long there may become senile ghosts. It was the Greeks themselves who invented the maxim 'Nothing too much'.

There are books that give a couple of hours' pleasure, like fellow-travel-lers on a journey or fellow-guests at a party, and then pass out of our lives forgotten; there are books that satisfy mere curiosity—and die with it; and there are books that influence all our years. We may never reopen them; we may even forget them; but something in them has left its mark some-where in our brains. Such, for me, are Horace, Chaucer, Shakespeare, Montaigne, Johnson, Flaubert, Ibsen. These are the books that matter. Their authors have become our friends. I am not trying to introduce a few more modern readers to a few dead writings: I am trying to introduce them to certain living people who happen to have left their bodies, some time since, to mingle with the dust of Greece. Often it may be only a glimpse, through the haze of translation; and yet how much one reads sometimes even in a face that passes in the street! Whitman said that his readers would touch, not a book, but a man: here are many men—and women; and children even. They rise like the wraiths before Odysseus, by his pit of blood on the desolate shore of the Ocean-stream:

Young brides, and youths unwedded, and old men's weary years,
And maids in their tender girlhood, with young hearts new to tears,
And, from the grapple of Ares, many a mighty man
Slain with the bronze of battle—still red their armour ran.

It is not only a question of great poets; the minor writers are not always the least vivid—Hēsiod with his peasant grumblings (you can meet him

on Greek hillsides still); the laughing yet savage Archílochus; the embittered aristocrat Theognis, who could see no good in democrat or
merchant, yet could turn his bitterness into such passionate beauty that
even merchant and democrat must listen; Simōnides, that quieter, more
reticent man of the world who could undertake undismayed, where other
voices might have trembled, the task of saying for all Hellas the last
laconic words above the dead who had saved her from the Orient;
Theócritus, the returner to nature, hearing in the glare of Alexandrian
streets the sough of the sea-wind through the pines of Etna; Callímachus,
the Parnassian, irritable, pen-proud, pedantic, yet suddenly full of overmastering pity for child or friend laid in the tomb; his hated rival Apollonius, the bookworm who yet gave Europe its first clear picture of love's
blind stirrings in a young girl's heart; Musaeus who, when the Greek
world was dying, yet lent a new and lasting life to Hero and Leander;
and many another half-seen face of dimmer writers whom Meleāger and
later anthologists saved from the thickening dusk of time—Asclēpiades,
so passionately gathering his rosebuds; Leōnidas, singing of the rustic
and the poor; Ányte, the poetess of Tégea, whose lines on a Hermes by
the wayside seem to me a perfect symbol of what Greek poetry has
peculiarly to offer—not raptures, not rhapsodies, not even the Water of
Life—only the limpid purity of bright spring-water leaping beside a hot
and stony track.

> Beside the grey sea-shingle, here at the cross-roads' meeting,
>   I, Hermes, stand and wait, where the wind-swept orchard grows.
> I give, to wanderers weary, rest from the road and greeting:
>   *Cool and unpolluted from my spring the water flows.*

METRICAL NOTE
(Only for those interested in prosody)

The greater part of the Greek poetry here translated is either in hexa-
meters $\left(- \smile\smile \mid + \ - \ \smile\smile \mid \underset{-}{\underset{=}{\smile}} \mid \mid \ \mid - \ - \ \smile\smile \mid - \ \smile\smile \mid - \ \smile \right)$ or in that kindred metre,
which also flourished for over a thousand years, the elegiac, where
hexameters alternate with pentameters $\left(- \ \smile\smile \mid + \ - \ \smile\smile \mid \mid - \ \smile\smile \mid - \ \smile\smile \mid - \right)$.
What, then, is the best equivalent for Greek hexameters? Matthew

Arnold thought, English ones. But I cannot believe in English hexameters, except for semi-burlesque, as used by Arnold's friend Clough:

> But for the|funeral|train||which the|bridegroom|sees in the|distance
> Would he so|joyfully,|think you,||fall|in with the|marriage pro|cession?

The Elizabethan Nash has already summed the matter: 'The Hexa-
miter verse I graunt to be a Gentleman of an auncient house (so is many
an english begger), yet this Clyme of ours hee cannot thrive in; our speech
is too craggy for him to set his plough in: hee goes twitching and hopping
in our language like a man running upon quagmiers, up the hill in one
Syllable, and down the dale in another, retaining no part of that stately
smooth gate which he vaunts himselfe with amongst the Greeks and
Latins.' And surely Nash was justified by grotesqueries like—

> All travell|ers do|gladly||re|port great|praise of U|lysses
> For that he|knew many|men's||mann|ers and|saw many|cities.

Yet the last two centuries have seen persistent attempts to acclimatize this
alien growth, despite the scepticism of Swinburne and the protest of
Tennyson:

> These lame|hexamet|ers||the|strong-wing'd|music of |Homer!
> No—but a|most burl|esque||barbarous|experi|ment.
> When was a|harsher|sound||ever|heard, ye|Muses, in|England?
> When did a|frog coars|er||croak upon|our Helic|on?

Perhaps the most successful example is Cotterill's *Odyssey*; here is his
version of the prayer of Elpēnor quoted above (p. xvii):

> Well do I|know that de|parting||from|here, from the|mansion of |Hades,
> Back thou'lt|hold for the|isle||Ae|aea thy|well-built|vessel—
> Here when thou|com'st, O|bear me||in|memory,|prince, I im|plore thee,
> Neither un|wept and un|buried||ab|andon me|homeward re|turning,
> Parting in|haste—lest|aye||as a|curse from the|gods I shall|haunt thee.
> Burn me, I|pray, on a|pyre||with my|armour and|all my e|quipment;
> Also e|rect me a|tomb||on the|strand of the|grey-green|ocean,
> Haply for|ages to|come||of a|luckless|man a re|membrance!
> These my en|treaties ful|fil,||and my|oar set a|loft on the|barrow,
> Rowing with|which when a|live||so|often I|toiled with my|comrades.

The objections to this seem to me, first, that the whole movement is too
like a rocking-horse; secondly, that many of its spondees (– –) are really

trochees (‒ ⏑)—we do not say 'lŭck*lĕss*' but 'lŭcklĕss'; [1] thirdly, that
whereas Greek can vary the final rhythm of its lines between ‒ ⏑ ⏑|‒ ‒
and ‒ ⏑ ⏑|‒ ⏑, in English the monotonous 'jiggledy-jiggle' of the verse-
endings soon grows maddening. As for partly quantitative hexameters
like George Ernle's

> Queen Helen|a ex|cepted||a|lone, as|being an|Argive,

this does not seem verse at all. Despite Matthew Arnold, I find myself
still of Campion's mind: ' *Carmen Exametrum* doth rather trot and hobble
than run smoothly in our English tongue.'

What alternatives? Chapman's fourteener seems too lumbering; Pope's
ten-syllable couplet too short, too epigrammatic, too intolerant of extra
syllables to match the variety of a Greek verse that ranges, in practice, from
thirteen syllables to seventeen. Cowper, Lord Derby, Sir William Marris,
Maurice Hewlett, and others have used blank verse. But, without sharing
William Morris's view that blank verse should be banned by Act of
Parliament for at least two generations, I do feel with Goldsmith that it
tends to a 'disgusting solemnity' (as seen in bad Wordsworth); and that
it lacks that rapidity which Arnold stressed as one of the four key-qualities
of Homer. [2] It can march superbly; but it gallops ill.

We are driven back, then, to rhyme. And why not? As Johnson said
of Adam Smith, whom he did not much like; 'Sir, had I known that
he loved rhyme as much as you tell me he does, I should have HUGGED
him.' But what form of rhyme? Maginn's ballad-metre and Gladstone's
imitations of Scott are open to Arnold's charge of lacking Homer's
dignity. Worsley and Mackail tried the stanzas of Spenser and *Omar
Khayyám*; but stanzas break the rush of Homer's narrative and still more
of his speeches. What was a torrent becomes a river with locks. And
translating Greek epic is hard enough without shackling oneself to triple
and quadruple rhymes.

The obvious equivalent for a Greek verse of six feet might seem an
English verse of that number. But the pure iambic Alexandrine in
English (unlike French) develops a sort of gouty stiffness when used

---

[1] 'The translator', says Arnold, 'must learn to use spondees freely.' He
should. But how, when most such English 'spondees' are really trochaic?

[2] This quality specially struck Pope: 'His fancy . . . becomes on fire,
like a chariot-wheel, by its own rapidity'—'a tide of verse, the most
rapid, and yet the most smooth imaginable'—'Homer hurries and trans-
ports us with a commanding impetuosity.'

continuously. Drayton ruined his *Polyolbion* with it; and it does its full share in making Browning's *Fifine* intolerable. But suppose we try a freer six-foot line based on ballad-metre—just as the Greek hexameter may have grown from a shorter line (possibly four-foot) used in shorter lays now lost?

> They hae slain the Earl of Murray
> And hae laid him on the green.

Print both lines as one and you have the metre sometimes appearing in Tennyson's *Maud*, *Revenge*, and *Maeldune*, and employed by Morris for his *Sigurd* and his *Odyssey*. It is, roughly, as if the last syllable of a hexameter were simply shifted from the end of the line to the beginning. This slight change turns a falling rhythm of dactyl ($-\smile\smile$) and spondee ($--$) into a rising rhythm of anapaest ($\smile\smile-$) and iamb ($\smile-$), to which the natural run of English speech takes far more kindly.

Hexameter: $-\ -\smile\smile\ -\ -\smile\smile\ -\ \| \smile\ -\ -\smile\smile\ -\ \smile\smile\ -\ -$ (13–17 syllables)

This metre: $\smile\smile\ -\ \smile\smile\ -\ \smile\ -\ \smile\ -\ \| \smile\smile\ -\ -\ \smile\ -\ \smile\smile\ -$ (13–18 syllables)[1]

All the same, while my admiration for *Sigurd* is immense (an admiration I was delighted to find shared by T. E. Lawrence), I cannot feel Morris's *Odyssey* a success. The language seems too archaic, the metre too rough and too monotonous. To avoid that monotony I have tried to introduce more variety of both stress and pause; partly by occasional twelve-syllable Alexandrines, or by fourteeners (on the analogy of the Alexandrines that Dryden and Pope mingle with their decasyllables), or by triple rhymes (with similar precedent), or by shifting the main pause from the middle of the fourth foot to its end. And in rendering elegiacs I have alternated feminine and masculine rhymes to match the different endings of hexameter ($-\smile$) and pentameter ($-$).

One point, however, remains vital if this metre is to work. *As in the Greek, a just perceptible pause must be made at the central break or caesura in each verse.* If this is ignored, a line of this length just runs breathlessly off its feet.

But the only test is practice. Here are four strangely modern lines from the *Iliad* (xix, 221–4) on the grim waste of war:

---

[1] For, in practice, Greek lines *all* spondees (i.e. twelve syllables) or English *all* anapaests (i.e. nineteen syllables, with the extra syllable before the caesura) are too rare to need considering.

Αἶψά τε | φυλόπι|δος || πέλε|ται κόρος | ἄνθρω|ποῖσιν,
Ἧς τε | πλεῖστēν | μēν || κάλά|μēν χθόνῐ | χᾱλκὸς ἐ|χεύεν,
Ᾱμή|τος δ᾽ὀλῐ|γῐστος, || ἐ|πēν κλῐ|νēσῐ τά|λᾱντά
Ζεῦς, hὸς τ᾽|ᾱνθρώ|πōν || τάμῐ|ēς πόλέ|μōῐō τέ|τῡκταῑ.

In Chapman this becomes:

> We quickly shall have store
> And all satiety of fight, whose steel heaps store of straw
> And little corn upon a floor, when Jove, that doth withdraw
> And join all battles, once begins t᾽ incline his balances,
> In which he weighs the lives of men.

(Curious that Chapman, whose ear for blank verse was sometimes splendid, could perpetrate this jingle of 'store . . . store . . . straw . . . floor . . . withdraw'.) In Pope it runs (far better, though still very free as a translation):

> The bravest soon are satiate of the field;
> Though vast the heaps that strow the crimson plain,
> The bloody harvest brings but little gain:
> The scale of conquest ever wavering lies,
> Great Jove but turns it, and the victor dies!

In Cowper (who does not seem quite to grasp the meaning):

> Men, satiate soon with battle, loath the field
> On which the most abundant harvest falls,
> Reap'd by the sword; and when the hand of Jove,
> Dispenser of the great events of war,
> Turns once the scale, then farewell ev'ry hope
> Of more than scanty gleanings.

And in the metre that I have, rightly or wrongly, preferred:

> Soon of the shock of battle men surfeit and grow sick.
> There are no swathes so heavy as the sword reaps, nor so thick;
> But never a thinner harvest than men receive therefor,
> Weighed in the scales of God, that casts the account of war.

Of other Greek metres there is little to add. One can ask no better equivalent for Greek iambics than English blank verse (even though it is a foot or half a foot shorter); to turn them into rhymed couplets seems perverse. But in lyrics I feel the need for rhyme. No doubt the choruses of Swinburne's *Atalanta* and Murray's Euripides, despite their beauty, are too romantic for Greek. But far better that than the creaking boredom of Arnold's *Merope*, so inferior to Arnold's own rhymed verse. In any case their rhyme cannot be blamed for their romanticism. I have tried throughout not to romanticize the Greek. But I have *not* tried, except with Sapphics, to reproduce Greek lyric metres exactly—only to match their general structure as closely as I could without torturing English rhythm. Attempts to do more, though they seem always to give immense satisfaction to the writers, keep the reader in constant uncertainty which syllables to stress. It is like walking on cobbles. One cannot lose oneself in the poetry. And in poetry, unless one can lose oneself, one is losing one's time.

PART ONE

HESIOD AND HOMERIC HYMNS

8th–7th centuries B.C.

HESIOD OF ASCRA

(c. 800 B.C.?)

By such examples taught, I paint the cot,
As Truth will paint it, and as Bards will not.—Crabbe.

LESS impersonal and self-effacing than 'Homer', Hēsiod tells how his father had migrated from the Aeölic Cyme in Western Asia Minor to the village of Ascra at the foot of Mount Helicon in Central Greece—'evil in winter, in summer intolerable'. His *Works and Days*, a mixture of moral treatise and farmer's manual, is addressed to his idle brother Perses, who by bribing the 'gift-devouring princes' had gained an unfair share of their common heritage. Hēsiod is also credited with a theological poem, the *Theogony* ('Generations of the Gods'). As so often, this traditional authorship has been questioned; as so often, with little reason.

Hēsiod is a poet of superstitious but laborious peasants ('of Helots', said the contemptuous Spartan king, Cleómenes), while Homer is the poet of proud Viking princes. From Homer's glorious fictions Hēsiod turns to harsh and homely truths; he values the virtues, not of war, but of peace; not of the rich, but of the poor—hard work, prudence, honesty, thrift. There is, indeed, country life in Homer also—in the lovely similes, in the Shield of Achilles, in the cot of the swineherd Eumaeus; but it remains country life as seen by a spectator rather than a toiler—as Chaucer sees it, not Langland. Even Eumaeus turns out to be a kid-napped prince; just as in Malory even the hermits of the good old days are gentle-born. Homer too loved the rich damp blackness of new-ploughed earth; but on Hēsiod's hands we seem to feel the very blisters made by the handles of the plough. This poet has himself reaped, sweating, where the sun cracked the hillsides of Ascra; or shivered behind his team as the winds of winter whistled from the bleak forests of the North. Hēsiod is Europe's first realist.

On his *Works and Days* Virgil modelled the *Georgics*; but Virgil, like Homer, remains a court poet. He has an artistry, a refinement, a sensitive pity for the world, that are far removed from the sardonic old Boeotian. Yet each is admirable in his different way; if he has less imagination, Hēsiod has that blessed reality of writers—they are none too common —who really know the things of which they write; a reality more solid

*c   3

than Wordsworth's mystical rusticities, or the somewhat idyllic Berrichons among whom George Sand regained and matured her sanity.

But with all his realism Hēsiod remains a Greek—he feels the loveliness, as well as the harshness, of Nature. As we wander among his rock-strewn valleys, suddenly there comes the quiet benison of spring rain, or the cuckoo's call along the hills, or the peace of summer afternoons as he sits, for once at ease, in a great rock's shadow, gazing out across the blue distance of that sea he so distrusts. He has a sympathy of his own with the creatures of the wild, like another ploughman thousands of years later in the fields of Scottish Ayr. And he is not only a realist, like Tennyson's Lincolnshire farmers: in his dour way he is an idealist also. Two things he preaches tirelessly—Work and Justice. At times he recalls the strivings after righteousness of Amos, the herdsman of Tekoa, of our own Langland on his grey-misted Malvern Hills, of Crabbe among the muddy streams and harsh shingles of Aldeburgh. Shrewd, hard, close-fisted, this peasant who reveals at moments the wry humour of Hardy's country-folk, has also, like some of them, thoughts that scan questioningly the eternal Heavens and this Earth that seems only to worsen with the years. So that, while in one direction he is an ancestor of the artificial poets of pastoral, in another he foreshadows the philosophic poets of later Greece with their more reasoned cosmologies.

True, his *Theogony* seems a far more shadowy work than the *Works and Days*. Its war in Heaven has not the marble dignity of Milton, who trod the purple heights of Helicon, not its foothills; nor the elaboration of Keats, whose *Hyperion* is a far-off descendant of Hēsiod as well as of Milton. For us, it is Hēsiod's picture of the Farmer's Year that remains vividly alive; recalling, to all who have known them, the barren limestone ridges that are still Greece, the hum of bees among their prickly scrub and pallid asphodel, the oxen ploughing far below, the rhythmic rise and fall of the peasants' mattocks among the young-leaved vines—that blending of grey mountainside and blue-shimmering sea that still makes Hellas one of the poorest, yet loveliest, of European lands.

WORKS AND DAYS
SUMMARY

1. *There are two kinds of emulation—one evil, that breeds war and strife; one good, that toils for excellence.* (1–27.)

2. *Do you, Perses, follow the good emulation, and exert yourself; instead of pursuing the evil and cheating me, your brother, in lawsuits.* (28–41.)

4

3. *The evil of all unrighteousness, the universal necessity of toil, are witnessed by the tale of Pandora and the past Ages of the World. Now in our Age of Iron, alas, might is become right, as the hawk said to the nightingale. (42–212.)*

4. *None the less it is better for kings and commoners alike to keep justice; as for you, foolish Perses, work and honesty are the only way. Then there follow precepts for agriculture; precepts for navigation; precepts for living; and precepts about lucky and unlucky days. (213–828.)*

The Fall of Man and The Early Ages of The Earth

We have shared already our father's goods; and beyond thy share,
Thou hast robbed me richly, brother, by speaking false and fair
To gift-devouring princes. Such suits delight their soul,
The fools!—that have never learnt how 'Half is more than whole',
Nor know that life can be happy on mallow and asphodel.
For, alas, the Gods keep hidden the way to wealth too well;
For else, one day of labour easily could have brought
Food to last thee a twelvemonth, lying and doing nought;
Idle above the chimney might hang thy steering-oar,
And neither ox nor patient mule need toil for evermore.
But God hath taken such ease away, and hidden it,
Angry that He was cheated by Prometheus' cunning wit.
So Zeus ordained us sorrow, and fire He hid from men.
Yet the hero-son of Iápetus stole it again
For mortals' sake, in a fennel-stalk, from Zeus the wise;
Then spake the Lord of Thunder, whose wrack benights the skies,
In wrath: 'O soul most subtle, Iápetiónides,
Thou hast stolen fire, and tricked me—thy heart it well may please.
Yet sorely shalt thou repent it! And men unborn! In vain!
Such a curse will I send to requite them—a curse they shall rush to gain,
Embracing in their blindness the thing that is their bane.'
So spoke the Sire of Gods and men. Loudly His laughter rolled;
And the glorious Hephaestus He bade with speed to mould
Clay and water together—to shape them, and mingle there
The voice and might of a mortal, and a face divinely fair,
To form a sweet maid's loveliness. 'But all the art
Of the loom, and the weaver's cunning, Pallas shall teach her heart;
And golden Aphrodite about her brow shall set
Grace, and the pangs of passion, that pines men with regret;
And last the Argus-slayer, God's herald, shall compound
The soul of a thief therewith, and the heart of a shameless hound.'

5

Such was the word of Crŏnus' son. The Gods obeyed;
And straight the glorious Haltfoot in the form of mortal maid
Fashioned an earthen image, as the Lord of Heaven planned.
Bright-eyed Athene decked her with robe and girdleband;
And then the heavenly Graces and sovran Peitho dressed
Her beauty with chains all golden; and the Seasons lovely-tressed
Wreathed around her forehead all the flowers of spring:
But in her heart, by the counsel of Zeus loud-thundering,
The Argus-slayer planted the faith that still must fail,
The stealthy soul of a thief, and the crooked and cunning tale;
The power of speech he gave her, and called the woman's name
'Pandora', because to her making all the Olympians came
With gifts—for the undoing of all the sons of earth.

But when this snare escapeless, this pit, was come to birth,
Her the glorious herald, the Argus-slayer, bore,
By the will of Zeus, as a gift, to Epimetheus' door,
In whose heart *then* the warning of Prometheus lay forgot—
To turn from his door all gifts of Zeus, and take them not,
For fear some doom of evil befall the sons of men.
He took her; and once the curse was his, too late he saw it *then*.

For hitherto all mortals on earth were living still
Unvexed by bitter labour, untouched of any ill,
Free from the pains of sickness that lays life in the dust;
But *now* from the jar that held these plagues, the hands of the woman thrust
The lid, and let them scatter, for the ruin of humankind.
Only Hope was left there, a captive still confined,
Caught in the mouth of the vessel. For ere she escaped—the last,
Once more the hands of Pandora had shut the jar's lid fast
(Thus the Aegis-wielder, the Lord of Tempests, willed).
But those other, infinite curses roam loose in the world; and filled
Is all the earth with evils, with evils filled the sea.
Maladies stalk at noonday, bringing men misery,
And maladies steal through the darkness, unlooked-for and unheard
(Zeus made them, in His wisdom, to wander without word).
And so no man may avoid it, whatever He ordain.

But here is another story, if thou wilt listen again,
And well my tongue can tell it—of the years when first began
The race of Gods (heed thou my words) and the race of Man.

First of all, the Immortals, who high Olympus hold,
Created that earthly race which bears the name of Gold.
Those were the years when, still, in Heaven Crŏnus reigned
And men lived happy as Gods, with hearts that no cares constrained,

Free from all toil and travail. Never upon them hung
The burden of age—with hands and feet for ever young
They revelled and made merry, till Death, like a gentle rest,
Ended those lives untouched of pain, in all ways blest.
Ever the kindly cornlands, that no man toiled to till,
Brought forth their harvests' bounty; and all men lived at will,
Crowned with every blessing, on their own fields quietly.
Long since the dust has hid them; but still, by God's decree,
They haunt the world as spirits, that guard men and befriend,
Bringing us wealth and plenty.   This glory crowns their end.
    Next, the Lords of Olympus fashioned in their place
A second breed, of Silver—but theirs was a meaner race,
Neither in flesh nor spirit like to the men of Gold.
The infants in their houses were a hundred winters old
Ere they could leave their mothers, or cease their childish play;
Yet once they had reached the years of youth, then brief their day
And evil, by their folly. For, with infatuate pride,
They outraged one another, and to the Gods denied
Worship, and sacrifices, such as all men have laid
On Heaven's holy altars. Therefore, because they paid
No honour to the Immortals who hold Olympus' height,
Zeus in His anger smote them—and earth hid them from sight.
And yet 'Blest souls' men call them still, in the world below;
Lesser are these in honour—yet honoured even so.
    Then from the hand of Zeus, in turn, a third race came,
Far changed from the breed of Silver; from Bronze it took its name.
Grim, strong men, sprung from ash trees—*they* had no other care
But War, with its pain and outrage. Bread for their daily fare
These would not eat; their hearts of adamant were made,
Ruthless—and vast their vigour, and from their shoulders played
Great brawny arms, with hands resistless and untamed.
Bronze were their weapons; bronze their tools; of bronze they framed
Their dwellings (for unknown yet was black iron in the world).
Yet, to extermination by their own violence hurled,
They passed to the house of Hades, its chill and mouldering gloom,
Nameless—their fury faded in the blackness of the tomb,
And they left behind for ever the glorious light of day.
    But when the dust had hidden this race in its turn away,
Then Zeus, the son of Crŏnus, created in their stead
A fourth upon the kindly earth—more nobly bred,
More just—the godlike Heroes, as demigods revered,
The last that dwelt in the boundless world, before our race appeared.

7

But evil strife destroyed them, and the grim battle's roar—
Some before Thebes of the Seven Gates, as they made war
For the flocks of Oedipus, in the Cadmeian land;
And some in the host that sailed, far off, to the Trojan strand
Across the sea's abysses, for fair-haired Helen's sake:
There they found the slumber that nothing more shall wake.
But on some the Almighty Father another home bestowed,
Another life, at the world's far end, where no men find the road;
There dwell the happy Heroes, with hearts for aye at rest,
Beside deep-eddying Ocean, in the Islands of the Blest,
Where thrice in the passing seasons from bounteous earth is born
The harvest in its splendour—and honey-sweet its corn.

But ah, that I were not living in this fifth age of the earth!
Would I had died aforetime, or later come to birth!
For now is the Race of Iron. Never shall these by day
Find rest from toil and trouble; and the night-time shall not stay
Their ruin; but the Gods shall give them sorrows without cease
(Though *some* good with their evils be mixed for even these).
And yet for this race also hath the will of Zeus prepared
Doom—in the days when their children shall come to birth grey-haired.
For then indeed all concord of son with sire shall end,
And the host shall hate his guest, the friend shall hate his friend;
The ancient love of brothers in those days shall not hold,
And children shall dishonour their parents growing old.
Yea, they shall revile them with bitter words and rude,
And hardened hearts, that fear not God—small gratitude
Shall aged sire and mother receive for all their care.
Might shall be right, and city shall plunder city bare.
But they that are keepers of faith, and just, and of good intent—
To these shall none give honour; nay, to the insolent
And doers of all outrage. For men shall lose their shame,
And in force of hand shall their justice be—they shall defame
The noble with crooked speeches, and seal them with perjury;
And to all such as suffer shall cling implacably,
The hateful joy of malice—ill tongue and evil face.
Then to rejoin the Immortals, quitting the human race,
Quitting the wide-wayed earth, once more, for Heaven's height,
With snowy mantles veiling their beauty from men's sight,
Honour at last, and Righteousness, shall flee away,
Leaving but pain, and anguish, and griefs that nought can stay.

But now will I tell our princes (they have wit enough) a tale—
The words the hawk once uttered to the dapple-necked nightingale,

As in his claws he gripped her, and towered through the cloudy skies.
Pierced by those curving talons, his prey with piteous cries
Lamented; but her captor rated her rudely—'Now
Why squeaking, wretch? There holds thee a stronger far than thou.
Where I take thee, thou must follow, for all thy minstrelsy.
For my dinner I can eat thee, if I will, or set thee free.
Fools struggle with the stronger. Defeat is all they gain,
And to humiliation they add but bitterer pain.'
Such were the words of the falcon, with swift wings quivering wide.
But thou—heed justice, Perses, and puff not up thy pride.

(*Works and Days*, 37–213.)

Worldly Wisdom

Evil to choose is easy, of her thou canst find thy fill;
For close she dwells beside thee, and smooth the road to ill.
But the way that leads to Goodness the Gods made full of sweat,
Long is the path, and steep, for those whose face is set
Towards *her*; and the start is stony. Yet once thou hast gained the height,
Although before so painful, at length it groweth light.

(287–92.)

Bid him to dine that loves thee, leave him that hates alone,
But him be sure to summon, whose house stands near thine own.
When trouble comes in the village, the neighbours run at sight;
But thy kin at a distance linger, to pull their girdles tight.

(342–5.)

Drink deep when the winejar's opened, or when 'tis running low;
In the middle, spare. Too late, when the dregs begin to show.
What to thy friend thou owest, pay it him full and fair.
When thy own brother borrows, smile—but have witness there.
By trust alike and *dis*trust has many a man sped ill.
Let no hip-wagging woman cajole thee to her will
(When 'tis thy barn she covets) with her flattering, fond deceit;
Who puts his trust in woman, trusts himself to a cheat!
Thou art wise if thou begettest but one son to sustain
Thy father's house—then the plenty within its walls shall gain.
And a second son thou mayest leave, if thou die old;
Nay, for still more, if He will, can God find wealth untold.

(368–79.)

Wed, above all, a woman that dwells not far away;
And look well ere thou leapest, lest thou make thy neighbours gay.

9

For a good wife is the fairest prize that life can bring;
But as for a wife that is evil—there is no grislier thing—
Some greedy slut that, goodly although her husband be,
Roasts him, without a fire, to raw senility.

(700–5.)

Take care to keep thy name untouched by ill report.
For evil reputation—easily it is caught,
But heavy it is to carry, and hard to cast away.
Nothing perishes wholly, that many have come to say.
Ay, Reputation also is a Goddess, in her way.

(760–4.)

One carpenter hates another, potter hates potter still,
The beggar envies the beggar, the singer the singer's skill.

(25–6.)

A small ship—thou mayst praise her; but set thy goods in a great.

(643.)

Rustic Wisdom

Autumn Ploughing

Take heed, what time thou hearest, high in the clouds, the crane
Calling her yearly call, for plough-time come again,
Crying that the rains of winter once more are nearing now—
Bitter her voice to his hearing, that hath no team to plough.

(448–451.)

Spring Ploughing

But if thou art late with ploughing, remedy thou hast still;
When, from the leaves of the oak, the cuckoo calleth shrill
For the first time, and gladdens all men to the wide earth's end,
Then on the third day after, if Zeus vouchsafe to send
Good rain that fills the hoofprint of an ox—just fills, no more—
Late ploughers then shall prosper as they that ploughed before.
But note these things with a mindful heart—mark in their hour
The signs of the grey spring's coming, and the seasonable shower.

(485–92.)

Summer

But when up stalks from the ground House-carrier turns to climb,
Fleeing from the heat that the Pleiads bring, past is the time
For digging vines—with sickles keen, call out thy men to the corn,
And shun the seat in the shade, and lie not late till morn.
Now, in the days of harvest, when the hot sun tans the skin,
Now is the time to be stirring forth, thy sheaves to win;
Rise with the very daybreak, that thy life pass free from need;
A third part of thy labour those hours of Dawn shall speed.
Dawn is the toiler's, the traveller's friend—she that each day
Sets forth so many a wanderer, world over, on his way,
And on so many an ox's neck once more the yoke doth lay.
But when the artichoke flowers—when with quick-quivering wings
Through the heavy heat of summer the shrill cicada sings
And, perched in a tree's green leafage, pours out his piercing notes,
Then wine is at its finest and fattest then are goats;
Women, most wanton; and weakest, men. For the Dog-star's heat
Scorches the skin on their bodies, and parches head and feet.
Then in a great rock's shadow, with milk-bread, let me lie,
And Biblian wine, and milk from goats just going dry,
And flesh of an uncalved heifer, fed in a forest-glade,
Or kids first-born of their mother. *So* let me sit in the shade,
With a bellyful within me, sipping at my ease
The fire-red wine, and turning to face the western breeze.

(571–94.)

Autumn

After the sun has turned him, for the space of fifty days,
While summer draws to its ending and men sweat in his blaze,
Then is the time for sailing. For never a tempest then
Shall shatter the timbers of thy ship, nor drown her men,
(Unless the heart of Poseidon, the Shaker of the Land,
Or Zeus, the Lord of Heaven, their certain doom hath planned;
For all good hap, and evil, lies lastly in God's hand).
Then steady blow the breezes, and the sea's wrath lies asleep;
So fear not—trust thy vessel to the winds, and on the deep
Launch her, and see her cargo tightly stowed aboard.
Yet turn with thy best speed homeward, linger not abroad
Till the new wine, and the tempests that break the summer's drouth,
With winter hard behind them—when grim gales from the south

Lash the deep to fury, and earthward heavily
Zeus hurls his rains autumnal, and savage grows the sea.
There *is* another season, for sailing, in the spring,
When on the fig-tree's summit the first leaves opening
Stretch as wide as the footprints a crow sets on the earth;
'Tis then the springtime sailing comes. But little worth
I hold it—for such ventures full little love I bear.
They are but snatched occasions. Perilous. Yet men dare
These also, in the folly of their infatuate mind.
For money is very life to hapless humankind.
Yet death at sea is a bitter thing. So heed me well,
Store in thine inmost heart these counsels that I tell;
And trust to no hollow ship all that thou callst thine own—
Keep most ashore, and venture the lesser part alone.
'Tis ill to find in the wave the grave of thy happiness,
Ill to o'erload thy wagon with weight so merciless
That the axle splits, and thy lading is spilt and spoilt with the fall.
Keep to the mean, Due measure is always best of all.

(663–94.)

Winter

But beware the month of Lēnaion, ill days of bitter frost,
Days that would flay an ox, when the wide seas are tossed
By Boreas, blowing hard from the horse-pastures of Thrace,
And land and woodland bellow, as he wrenches from their place,
Amid the glens of the mountains, many an oak high-crowned,
Many a stalwart fir, and flings them to the ground,
Till the multitudinous forest shouts with a single cry.
Shivering under their bellies the tails of the wild beasts lie,
For all the fur that warms them—through the shaggiest breast it goes,
Through the hide of the ox himself that icy tempest blows,
And through the goat's lank hair—the fleece of the sheep alone
With its thick wool can baffle that blast from the northward blown.
It sets an old man running; and yet it cannot come
To the tender maiden sitting by her mother's side at home,
Of the golden Aphrodite as yet all unaware.
Ay, warm in an inner chamber—soft limbs new-bathed, and fair
With olive oil—she lays her down and slumbers sweet
Through the winter days, when No-bones must sit and gnaw his feet

Alone in his fireless house, and the depths of his dismal den;
For never forth to pasture the low sun lights him then.

(504-26.)

But pass thou by the smithy and the warm seat in the sun,
In winter, when for the cold no work in the fields is done,
(E'en then a stirring fellow can still increase his store);
For fear the bleak December bring misery to thy door
And thou press, with a vagrant's hand grown thin, a foot grown fat and
    sore.

(493-7.)

Religion

First, of the Heliconian Muses be my song,
To whom the great and holy heights of Helicon belong;
Whose soft feet sway for ever by the violet-shadowed spring
And round about the altar of Crónion the King.
With lovely bodies newly bathed in Hippocrēne's fount,
Or Olmeius the holy, or Permessus, on the mount
Of Helicon at its highest they gather for the dance—
Ay, beautiful past telling their rushing footsteps glance.
Thence 'tis their way to wander, wrapt in a mantling cloud,
Across the night, with voices choiring sweet and loud,
In praise of the Aegis-wielder and in Queen Hēra's praise
Who passes, Lady of Argos, gold-sandalled on her ways;
In praise of bright-eyed Athene, daughter of Zeus most high,
In praise of Phoebus Apollo, and Her whose arrows fly
Swift in the chase; of Poseidon, that girds and shakes the earth—
Grave Thĕmis—Aphrodite with her dancing eyes of mirth;
Of fair Diōne, and Hēbe, with forehead golden-crowned,
Of Dawn, and the Sun's great circle, and the Moon's fair-shining round;
Of Lēto, of Iápetus, of Crŏnus subtly wise,
Of Earth, and boundless Ocean, and Night in her sable guise,
And the rest of the race of Heaven, the race that never dies.
Fair too was the song they taught, one day, to Hēsiod,
Feeding his flock on Helicon, the Mount of God.

Thus on the mountain-silence the Olympian Muses broke,
The Aegis-wielder's daughters, and thus to me they spoke;
'Shepherds of wild and wasteland, ill-famed, ye bellies blind,
Many a falsehood like to truth our tongues can find,
Yet many a true word also, when truth is to our mind.'
    So spake the Daughters of Zeus, whose words are verity,
And a wondrous staff, of deathless bay, they plucked and gave to me.
                                                    (*Theogony*, 1–31.)

Daemones

To spirits thrice ten thousand by God's will 'tis assigned
Through all the fruitful earth to watch o'er humankind.
Deathless, hidden in darkness, wandering everywhere,
They watch all judgments given, all evil that men dare.
                                            (*Works and Days*, 252–5.)

Poetry

For it is the Archer Apollo, and the Muses, that inspire
All minstrels upon earth, all players of the lyre,
Just as of Zeus come princes. Blessed is he among men
Whom the Muses love—like honey the words flow from him then;
And if with a heart new-burdened by sorrow overstrong
Some man sits bowed, and a servant of the Muses lifts his song
To tell of the ancient heroes, or hymn with praise the blest
Immortals, that have their dwelling on high Olympus' crest,
Swiftly even the mourner casts off the load that lay
Upon his heart—by the Muses' gift his cares are smoothed away.
                                                    (*Theogony*, 94–103.)

Mountains

Earth bore the long-ridged mountains, within whose fair depths dwell
The Nymphs divine, in the valleys that run 'neath peak and fell.
                                                    (*Theogony*, 129–30.)

14

The Coming of Aphrodite

And by her side went Eros, and Passion followed fast,
As the new-born Aphrodite to the host of Heaven passed;
For her kingdom and her glory she holds for aye assigned
Both among Gods in Heaven and among humankind—
The maiden-whispers of love, its smiles, and its deceit,
And all its loving-kindness, its fulfilment honey-sweet.

(Theogony, 201–6.)

THE HOMERIC HYMNS

ALTHOUGH other poets of the early period also wrote epics

> Presenting Thebes, or Pelops' line,
> Or the tale of Troy divine,

not one of them seems to have shown the greatness of *Iliad* and *Odyssey*, and only a few fragments remain. Like the civilization of Ionia, on the western edge of Asia Minor where life was softer than in the Greek motherland, the Homeric epic was a spring flower; first to bloom and first to fade. Yet even in its decline this Homeric tradition could still produce most of the so-called 'Homeric Hymns'. They are not comparable with *Iliad* or *Odyssey*. Mortals, indeed, are usually better subjects for poetry than gods. But the six best of these poems deserve far more readers than they have usually found.

In all, our collection of 'Homeric Hymns' contains thirty-four pieces. Four of them—those to Apollo, Aphrodite, Demeter, and Hermes—are of some length (290–580 lines); two—those to Pan and Dionysus—are briefer (49 and 59 lines); the rest are very short (3–22 lines) and presumably mere preludes to longer recitals.

The four longest seem the oldest. Indeed the Hymn to Apollo is assigned to Homer himself by Thucydides, who quotes its old poet's final farewell to the daughters of Dēlos. All, however, must be later than *Iliad* and *Odyssey*. *Aphrodite* and the Dēlian section of *Apollo* seem perhaps as old as the eighth century; *Demeter* and *Hermes* probably seventh-century; and the rest younger.

HYMN TO APOLLO

The first half of the *Hymn to Apollo*, here translated, seems composed for the God's festival on Dēlos.[1] We have to imagine ourselves on a little

---

[1] The rest of the hymn (177–546) deals with the Delphic Apollo and seems a later, inferior addition.

islet of yellow sand and granite, three miles long, with, in its midst, the low granite hill (370 feet) of sacred Cynthus. It is crowded with pilgrims for the festival; as they still crowd to the neighbouring isle of Tēnos for the festival of the Virgin, during which the Italians treacherously torpedoed the Greek cruiser *Helle* in 1940. Round the horizon of Mediterranean blue stretches one of the most marvellous seascapes in the world—mountain-island after mountain-island, east and west and south and north—Sȳra, Gýaros, Tēnos, Mýconos; Paros, with its veins of marble; Naxos, where Theseus left Ariadne; Serīphos, where Dánaë drifted ashore in her floating chest with the baby Perseus, who was one day to sever the Gorgon's head. And now among the white-robed pilgrims from Attica and Ionia an old blind poet takes his stand to sing of the nativity of the Sun-god, whom his mother Lēto, despite the jealous persecution of Hēra, the Queen of Heaven, bore at last to Zeus, here on the isle of Dēlos.

This Nativity of Apollo presents a vivid contrast to the Bible story of the Nativity of Christ. In both, indeed, there is the jealous persecutor—Hēra or Herod; in both there is the mother's hard search for shelter before the divine child is born. But where the Hebrew thinks of ethics—of the blessing of the humble, of the peace for men of good will—the Hellene turns to aesthetic beauty, to the dazzling splendour of the youthful God of Song. Here is no poor inn, no hay-filled manger, no shepherds with their flocks in the cold midnight; instead, the sunlight beats on golden Dēlos and blue-dancing Aegean, on the radiant grace of Olympian Goddesses, on the proud, wilful splendour of eternal youth. None here invites the weary and heavy-laden with the promise of rest; the Gods of Greece are like Nature, as modern man sees her—often divinely beautiful, but often amoral, often indifferent, or ruthless, to the ephemeral sufferings of mortality. 'How comfortless!' some may cry; but I suppose a Greek might have answered—'Comfortless, yes; but profoundly true. It is not just because of their beauty that our Gods of Olympus still haunt your European mind; it is because of their strange symbolic truth to the ways of the Universe. We loved life, but without illusions; as a man may love a woman who is beautiful, splendid even, but—in the end—cruel.'

Hymn to the Delian Apollo
(8th century B.C. ?)

Now shall my song remember Apollo, Lord of the Bow,
At whom the Immortals tremble, what time they see him go

17

Through the house of Zeus. To their feet they spring, each from his
   throne,
As Phoebus comes with his bright bow bent; and Lēto is left alone,
By the Son of Crŏnus sitting, the Lord of the thunder-rack.
Then she closes her dear son's quiver, and makes his bowstring slack,
And off his stalwart shoulders she lifts his bow in her hands
To a peg of gold, on the pillar that by his father stands.
Last, to his place she leads him. Now Zeus upon the board,
To welcome his son, the nectar in a golden cup hath poured;
Then the Immortals take their thrones; and the heart of Lēto stirs,
To think that such an archer, so mighty a son, is hers.
Hail to thee, blest among mothers! For children of glory are thine,
O Lēto—our lord Apollo and the Maid of the bow divine.
In Ortygia thy daughter, on Dēlos' rocks thy son
Thou barest, by the palm tree, where Inōpus' waters run.
On the ridge of Cynthus resting, till thy travail-time was done.

   But how shall I praise thee, Apollo, whom songs so many praise?
For all the ways of songcraft—O Lord, they are thy ways,
Through all the meadowed mainland and the islands of the sea;
All high hills, too, thou lovest, all peaks are dear to thee,
That tower amid the mountains, all streams that seaward sweep,
And beaches that slope to the breaker, and havens of the deep.
Shall I tell how Lēto, resting on Mount Cynthus, gave thee birth,
There in the rocky islet, to thee, the joy of earth,
Alone in sea-girt Dēlos, while round on beach and cove
Before the piping sea-wind the dark blue billow drove?
There she bore thee, master of all men near or far.
For lord thou art of the Cretan land, of Attica,
Of Aegīna's isle, and Euboea, with her ships far-famed at sea,
Of wave-washed Peparēthus, Aegae, Eirésiae;
Lord of the Thracian Athos, of Pēlion towering tall,
Of Sámothrace and Ida, where the forest-shadows fall,
Of Scyros and Phocaea, of Autócane capped with cloud,
Lord of the smoke-topped Lemnos, and Imbros deeply ploughed
Of Lesbos the fair, where Măcar dwelt, of Aeŏlus' race;
Of Chios, that most fruitful of isles that the seas embrace;
Lord of the craggy Mĭmas, and Claros glittering bright,
Of Córycus' beetling headland, and of Aeságea's height;
Lord of well-watered Samos and Mýcale soaring bold,
Milētus, and that city of the Méropes of old,
Cos, and the lofty Cnīdus, and Cárpathus tempest-blown,
Of Naxos, and of Paros, and Rhēneia's isle of stone.

So far, when travail seized her, world over, Lēto passed—
Where should her son find refuge, find him a home at last?
For all these feared and trembled—there was not one to dare
Shelter the babe Apollo, however rich they were;
Until at last to Dēlos the Lady Lēto came,
And words from her lips flew winging, and she called the islet's name:
'Dēlos, wilt *thou* give welcome to my son? Upon thy ground
Wilt *thou* let Phoebus Apollo his golden temple found?
For no man else (thou knowest) will build amid thy rocks,
And small hope thine to be rich in kine, or white with flocks;
From *thy* soil shall no harvest, no orchard come to be.
But, if the Archer Apollo once sets his shrine on thee,
Hither shall all the nations gather with sacrifice
And from thine earth for ever the smoke of incense rise,
Measureless. Thou shalt nourish with fruits of *other* lands
All those that dwell within thee, though barren lie thy sands.'
    She spoke, and Dēlos gladdened, and swift came her reply:
'Lēto, great Coeus' daughter, most glorious!—glad were I
To be in truth the cradle of thy son, the Archer-king—
For ill indeed is my name on earth; and *he* would bring
Glory to me, past telling. And yet my fears are stirred—
I will not hide it, Lēto—by a rumour I have heard.
'Tis told me that Apollo shall be one proud of heart,
That he shall bear hereafter a proud and princely part,
Alike among Gods and mortals, through all the fruitful earth.
For *that* my mind misgives me. I fear when he comes to birth
And looks upon the sunlight, *I* shall but wake his scorn,
Who am but a rocky islet, barren and forlorn.
I fear he may spurn me beneath him and tread me under the foam,
And the depths of the weltering surges be mine eternal home;
That he may seek some fairer land, more worth his love,
Wherein to build his temple and plant his hallowed grove,
While polyps breed within me, and black seals make their den
Upon me at their pleasure, left desolate of men.
But if, of thy grace, great Goddess, thou swear an oath to me,
That here his first fair temple, his oracle, shall be,
Throughout the earth thereafter let him turn on other ways,
For I know that his names are many, and wide shall be his praise.'
    Then Lēto swore that mighty oath the Immortals swear—
'Witness the Earth beneath me, and the Heaven's upper air,
And the down-dropping stream of Styx—the deadliest,
The holiest thing that ever Immortal lips attest—

19

Here shall the grove of Phoebus and his fragrant altar stand,
And he shall honour Dēlos like no other land.'
     When Lēto thus had sworn it and her oath had found its close,
Dēlos rejoiced for her new lord's birth. But bitter throes,
And passing expectation, on Lēto fell; in pain
Nine days, nine nights she travailed. Beside her sat, in vain,
Rhea and Diōne, the mightiest powers to save,
Thĕmis and Amphitrīte from the deep-moaning wave,
And others still. (Yet Hēra, the white-armed, came not nigh,
Throned in the hall of Zeus, whose rack benights the sky.)
One only—Eileithyia, who soothes the agony
Of mothers, still knew nothing; 'neath the golden clouds sat she
On Olympus' height, by Hēra in her jealousy beguiled,
Who knew that the fair-tressed Lēto should bear a peerless child.
     But to seek for Eileithyia the Immortals in their need
From that fair isle sent Iris, and promised for her speed
A necklace of nine cubits, all strung on threads of gold;
Bidding her go in secret, lest Hēra's word withhold
The coming of Eileithyia. Then on her wind-swift feet
Iris arose and hastened, far off, to that high seat
Of the Gods on the sheer Olympus. And straightway from its hall
She summoned Eileithyia, and with winged words told her all,
As the Immortals bade her—quickly she gained her prayer
And like frightened doves, together, they darted through the air.
But soon as Eileithyia touched Dēlos, suddenly
The birth-pangs fell on Lēto, and the longing to be free.
On the soft grasses kneeling, tightly her arms she cast
About the palm of Dēlos. And all at once there passed
A smile across the face of earth—and forth he sprang
To the light of day, Apollo! Loud through the island rang
The cry of the Immortals; and then, O Archer-lord,
Over thy limbs the water, stainless-clear, they poured,
And wrapped a robe of the fine-spun wool, snow-white, around,
And about thee for a girdle a band of gold they bound.
But the golden-sworded Apollo knew not his mother's breast;
Ambrosia sweet, and nectar, unto his lips were pressed
By the deathless hands of Thĕmis. And Lēto's heart grew glad
To think what a mighty archer, and stalwart son, she had.
     But, at the taste of that food divine, no girdling gold,
No swaddling bands, O Phoebus, thy quivering limbs could hold.
And as thy limbs were loosened, in the Immortals' ear
The voice of Phoebus Apollo on a sudden rang out clear:

'Let me love the cry of the lyre, let me love the bended bow,
And the will of Zeus, that fails not, through *me* mankind shall know.'
Then up he leapt, far-striding o'er earth's immensity,
The Archer-god Apollo, with his tresses tossing free;
And the Goddesses marvelled at him, and in Dēlos' heart was bliss
That the son of Zeus and Lēto had chosen her for his,
Before all lands, all islands. Yea, Dēlos flowered with gold,
As on some mountain-summit the woodland flowers unfold.

But thou, far-shooting Apollo, Lord of the Silver Bow,
Now upon craggy Cynthus up and down didst go,
Now through the isles and nations didst wander to and fro.
For many thy sacred groves, many thy temples be,
And all high hills and headlands were ever dear to thee,
All peaks amid the mountains, all seaward swirling streams;
Yet Dēlos, O Apollo, to thy heart the dearest seems.
There gather to thy glory the long-robed Ionians,
They and their honoured wives, their daughters and their sons:
There, when the lists stand ready, faithfully they throng
To gladden thee with boxing, and with dancing, and with song.
A man might dream them ageless and deathless evermore,
Who sees the Ionians gather upon the Dēlian shore,
And marks with what grace they bear them, and rejoices there
In the glory of their manhood and their women girdled fair,
Their swift ships, and the riches of the proud Ionian race.
And there, too, is a wonder that the years shall not efface—
The mustered maids of Dēlos, who serve the Archer-king.
For first the praise of Apollo their lips in chorus sing,
The praise of Lēto his mother, and his sister's deadly bow;
Then, of men and women that lived long years ago
They chant, till all who listen their life's own cares forget;
And last their quick tongues mimic the dancer's castanet,
Or the speech of many a country, till each man seems to hear
His own tongue calling to him—so subtle-sweet their ear.

Now the grace of Apollo upon us, and the grace of Artemis;
And so farewell to you, maidens; and in days after this
Remember, whenever a stranger and wanderer over earth
Hither shall come and ask you—'What minstrel is most of worth,
Of all that sail to Dēlos? Whose songs have sweetest fall?'
Then shall ye make this answer to his question, one and all—
'A blind man; craggy Chios is his homeland—and 'tis he
Whose songs of all are noblest, for all the years to be.'

And *I* will spread your glory, wherever I shall go
Among earth's teeming cities, as I wander to and fro;
And verily they shall believe me, for indeed the truth is so.

(1–176.)

HYMN TO APHRODITE

Just as the *Hymn to Apollo* is full of the wind of Greek seas, so is the *Hymn to Aphrodite* of the wind of the Greek mountainside, that keen wind of Ida which still blows two centuries later through the pages of Bacchý-lides, when Hēracles beholds the wraiths of the dead in Hades—'many as the dry leaves the wind tosses up the sunlit ridges of Ida, among the grazing sheep.'[1] Of its kind, I think, Greek poetry has produced nothing finer.

The poem begins with a vision of Aphrodite, symbolizing the repro-ductive force of Life; as in Lucretius, and in Tennyson's *Lucretius*:

> The all-generating powers and genial heat
> Of Nature, when she strikes thro' the thick blood
> Of cattle, and light is large, and lambs are glad
> Nosing the mother's udder, and the bird
> Makes his heart voice amid the blaze of flowers.

For ultimately the legend of Anchises and Aphrodite seems to belong to the familiar type of ancient tale that symbolizes, under the brief loves of Goddess and mortal (Cýbele and Attis, Aphrodite and Adonis, Demeter and Iásion, Selēne and Endymion), the beauty of spring's awakening, the brevity of summer's pride, the sadness of the swiftly declining year.

So here the poem tells how Aphrodite's power dominates alike Gods and men, birds and beasts and creatures of the sea. Only three of the Immortals are proof against her—Artemis, who embodies that other virginal side of Nature which the hunter or the shepherd meets, in the silence of the forest or on the lonely ridges of the hills; Athene, who incar-nates the mind of man in wisdom and in war, in art and craft; and Hestia, the Goddess of hearth and home, where the wildness of passion is tamed and sanctified. All others the Goddess of Love can bow to her will. And so, to humble her pride in her omnipotence, Zeus ordained that she

---

[1] p. 87.

should fall in love herself—in love with a shepherd-lad on Ida, Anchises the cousin of Priam, King of Troy.

Then the tone grows gay, ironic, mischievous, to tell how 'the Laughter-lover' was thus snared in her own net, and how by woman's wit she gained her end. But suddenly upon this smiling sensuousness there breaks the cry of human passion—as if a child at play had loosed a wild thing from its cage. And now, as love finds fulfilment, there sounds the deeper note of human tragedy:

Mortal beside the Undying he lay—and knew it not.

For a moment the tension relaxes, while through the hush of evening the herds on Ida turn their heads towards home. Then a new climax, as the Goddess who had seemed but a girl resumes her godhead, and her fair imperious figure towers to the very roof, and she wakens her sleeping lover to the anguish of her own pride and shame at the infatuation by which Zeus made her fall. This mood in its turn yields to a quieter sad-ness, as she calls up before Anchises the vision of Age and Death—the decrepitude that palsies the bright limbs of Tithōnus, the doom that awaits, after many a generation, even the half-immortal Dryads whose green arms wave in the winds of Ida. And so to the close, with its mingled hope and warning—the promise of the child unborn that shall uphold the House of Troy, the menace that awaits him who betrays in his folly the secrets of the Gods (as one day Anchises was to do).

It is hard to guess a writer's intentions across so many centuries; but hard also to believe that these swallow-swift turns and wheelings of the poet's mind are merely fortuitous caprice. In half an hour's space he has passed from Heaven to earth, from earth back to Heaven, from Olympus to Cyprus, from Cyprus to Mount Ida, from youth to age, from Love to Death. So the builders of the tiny Ionic temple of the Wingless Victory on the Acropolis of Athens did not find even a frieze less than eighteen inches high too small to hold, on three sides the swaying tides of battle, on the fourth the conclave of the Olympian Gods.[1]

Europe has other poems like this in theme; but the difference of treat-ment remains more striking than the likeness. 'The machinery of the Pagans', says Johnson, 'is uninteresting to us: when a Goddess appears in Homer or Virgil, we grow weary.' But not here. And, again, Paul Valéry: 'Vénus est bien difficile à peindre. Puisqu'elle porte toutes les

---

[1] For a discussion of the technical subtleties of the Greek original see H. N. Porter, 'Repetitions in the Homeric Hymn to Aphrodite' in *Amer. Journal of Philol.*, lxx, 249 ff.

perfections, il est à peu près impossible de la rendre vraiment séduisante. Ce qui nous captive dans un être, ce n'est pas ce degré suprême de la beauté, ni des grâces si générales: c'est toujours quelque trait particulier.' Yet here that individuality comes to life. The frivolous lay of the loves of Ares and Aphrodite sung by Demódocus in the *Odyssey* at the court of Phaeacia shows no such feeling for the beauty of Nature or the tragedy of Man; it is a mere occasion for cynical court-jests. Ovid's tale, where Venus openly flings herself at Adonis, is neat, light-hearted, and heartless as a *Conte* by La Fontaine. Shakespeare's *Venus and Adonis*, fleshy as a Rubens painting, and spotted all over with foolish cleverness, is only saved by its occasional lovely lines, and by its dumb creatures—hare and horse, boar and snail, dive-dapper and lark:

> My sighs are blown away, my salt tears gone,
> Mine eyes are turn'd to fire, my heart to lead.
> > Heavy heart's lead, melt at mine eyes' red fire!
> So shall I die by drops of hot desire.

Not even the molten lead can warm the frozen reader. Fortunately Shakespeare found other styles than this.

Yet these three far cruder poems have been much more read than the Homeric Hymn: ignored by the ancients, it has been hardly more noticed by the moderns. The only worthy trace of it known to me in English literature is Tennyson's *Tithonus*. Already in the pages of *Oenone* Tennyson had visited the glens of 'many-fountain'd Ida', with their fawning panthers. His *Tithonus*, though it owes little in style to Aphrodite's telling of that legend in her Hymn, yet echoes—with a difference—the world-sadness of the Greek; that 'immeasurable sadness' nearer to the real heart of Tennyson himself than any 'larger hope':

> The woods decay, the woods decay and fall,
> The vapours weep their burthen to the ground,
> Man comes and tills the field and lies beneath,
> And after many a summer dies the swan. . . .

> Yet hold me not for ever in thine East:
> How can my nature longer mix with thine?
> Coldly thy rosy shadows bathe me, cold
> Are all thy lights, and cold my wrinkled feet
> Upon thy glimmering thresholds, when the steam
> Floats up from those dim fields about the homes
> Of happy men that have the power to die,
> And grassy barrows of the happier dead.

It remains one of Tennyson's finest poems. And yet its grey gloom lacks that dancing changefulness of light and shade which makes the Homeric Hymn so radiantly alive. The English poem closes with a prayer for death: but the Greek with a promise of birth. The English seems autum/ nal as its dank, mist/bound woods: the Greek as springlike, despite its sense of human sorrow, as the wind of an April morning. Each time I read these Hymns to Aphrodite or Apollo, which even for Thucydides were already ancient, they bring back this sense of flushed and unspoilt youth. The page grows dim; the walls turn air; the wind and sun of other years in Greece return. Once more, at the tale of Lēto's travail upon Dēlos, round the horizon loom the blue mountain/shapes of the Cyclades above the glitter of the Aegean, as once from a surf/tossed boat I watched them dancing round the little yellow islet where the God of Light was born:

> Alone in sea/girt Dēlos, while round on beach and cove
> Before the piping sea/wind the dark blue billow drove.

Is it merely the graceful fancy of a bygone race, this vision of the mysterious power of Love that can bow the loftiest and noblest in suppli/ cation to the young and unknown; that masters alike the Lord of Olym/ pus and the lad who keeps his cattle on the hills; that brings ecstasy, and falls asleep, and passes on the winds like a morning dream—yet leaving behind it the seed of the eternal future, as well as the sorrow for the irre/ vocable past; that reigns in resistless domination not over mankind alone, but over the wild things also of earth and sky and sea? Call her 'Aphro/ dite', or 'Nature', or 'the Life/force', or 'the Will to Live'—names may alter, the reality endures—tender yet wanton, beautiful yet pitiless, immortal yet amoral. And no less living here is that other side of Nature —the virginal, the aloof, the lonely—the Nature that watches us across the unsullied snow of the high peaks or amid the bracken of the whispering forest—her whose stern splendour our poet calls "Ἀρτέμιδα κελαδεινήν" —'Artemis of the hunting/cry'—as she halloos her hounds upon their endless chase. The same two powers, Aphrodite and Artemis, the Nature that is love and the Nature that is loneliness, meet again face to face in the *Hippolytus* of Euripides, in the *Pervigilium Veneris* of the declin/ ing Empire. Both are here: both are eternal. Only yesterday an English poet uttered anew, in some of the most perfect lines in English poetry, the same bitter cry of the mortal lover of Nature forsaken by his cold immortal mistress—as Artemis forsook the dying Hippolytus, as Aphro/ dite left Anchises on the sunset slopes of Ida:

25

Tell me not here, it needs not saying,
  What tune the enchantress plays
In aftermaths of soft September
  Or under blanching mays,
For she and I were long acquainted
  And I knew all her ways . . .

Possess, as I possessed a season,
  The countries I resign,
Where over elmy plains the highway
  Would mount the hills and shine,
And full of shade the pillared forest
  Would murmur and be mine.

For nature, heartless, witless nature,
  Will neither care nor know
What stranger's feet may find the meadow
  And trespass there and go,
Nor ask amid the dews of morning
  If they are mine or no.[1]

To all mankind she comes, whether on Ida or Cithaeron, Brocken or
Bredon, or under the Eildon Tree; from all, at last, she goes.

Hymn to Aphrodite

Of the Golden Aphrodite tell to me, Muse, the ways,
Who sends on the Gods in Heaven love's sweet desire, and sways
All races of men that perish, and the fleeting fowls of air,
And the myriad beasts the lands bring forth, and all that the oceans bear.
The fair-crowned Cytherēan, they heed her one and all,
But three there are she snares not, three that contemn her call.
  First, the bright-eyed Athene, the Aegis-bearer's child—
On the golden Aphrodite *her* heart has never smiled.
For *her* delight is the clash of fight, where Ares stands,
Battle, and war, and the splendour that springs from the master's hands;
Hers is the craftsman's cunning, whom first her wisdom taught
To fashion the wagon's timbers and the chariot bronze-inwrought;

---

[1] A. E. Housman, *Last Poems*.

26

And the skill that quickens maidens' wit, to broider fair,
As soft they sew by the fireside's glow—'twas she that set it there.
Next, Artemis of the hunting-cry, Queen of the shafts of gold—
Her too no Aphrodite, with all her smiles, can hold.
She loves but the bow of the hunter and the beasts she smites on the hills,
And the harping, and the dancing, and the cry of the Nymphs that thrills,
And the shadows of the forest, and the cities of righteous folk.
And a third there is whose maiden heart Love never woke,
Nor the deeds of Aphrodite—Hestia, eldest daughter
Of Crŏnus the crooked in counsel. Although for bride there sought her
Poseidon and Apollo, queenly she said them nay,
And with a vow she sealed her word, that never shall pass away,
Laying her hand in witness on the Aegis-bearer's head,
To abide through the years for ever inviolate and unwed.
To her, instead of wedlock, Zeus gave another grace—
Hers is the hearth in the heart of home, for her abiding place,
And of sacrifice the fairest, and honour in every shrine,
And in human hearts the dearest praise of all the host divine.
These three, then, Aphrodite has never the power to move,
These three the sweet cheat snares not. Else from the might of Love
Nothing escapes—not mortal men, not Gods above.
Yea, Zeus, the Lord of Thunder, Almightiest, Prince of Praise,
She has beguiled his wisdom and led him wandering ways,
Oft as she would, and laid him by many a mortal's side,
Forgetting the love of Hēra, his sister and his bride,
The noblest child of Rhea and the subtle Crŏnus bred,
The true wife and the queenly, whom Zeus the all-wise hath wed,
Of all Immortal faces herself the loveliest.
So, in return, Zeus wounded the Cyprian's own white breast
With sweet desire for a mortal's love. Once she had lain,
She too, at last in a mortal's arms, then never again
Should she vaunt in the halls of Heaven with sweet, disdainful smile,
The laughter-loving Cypris, how oft she could beguile
High Gods to seek the kisses of the daughters of the earth,
And from their seed immortal bring mortal sons to birth,
Or daze the daughters of Heaven with love for mortal men.
Therefore in Aphrodite Zeus awakened then
Sweet longing for Anchises, fair as the Heaven's kings,
As he kept his kine on Ida, mount of the many springs.
The laughter-loving Cypris, she saw him, and her heart
Maddened with measureless longing. Swiftly she fled apart
To her fragrant shrine in Paphos, far on the Cypriot shores,

Tree-girt, asmoke with incense, and shut its shining doors.
Round her the Graces gathered, and bathed her beauty there
With water, and oil ambrosial, that makes more fair
Even the Gods undying. New-clad and golden-bright,
Once more the Laughter-lover soared through the cloudy height—
From the sweet airs of Cyprus to Troy and Ida's head,
Mount of the many waters, mother of beasts, she sped.
Over the hill, to the neatherds' byre, she passed; and as she came,
The grey wolves followed, fawning, and lions with eyes aflame,
And bears, and lightfoot leopards, devourers of the deer.
The Goddess smiled to see them; and on all, both far and near,
She cast her lure of longing—back to their forest-dens,
Pair by pair, they vanished, down the darkness of the glens.
But herself to the herdsmen's huts she came, built well and fair,
And alone she found Anchises, left by his comrades there
In his god-given beauty. For all the rest were gone
With their herds to the mountain-meadows; and he was left alone,
Striding forth and backward, while the cry of his harp rang clear.
Then Zeus-born Aphrodite stepped forward and drew near,
Changed to the form and stature of a young unwedded maid,
Lest his eyes discern her godhead and the hero grow afraid.
Then Anchises saw and wondered—so beautiful she seemed,
So tall she towered before him, so gay her garments gleamed.
For the robe that rippled round her, shone like a fire ablaze;
Richly her twisted armlets, her earrings flashed their rays;
Round her soft throat fair chains of gold glanced fitfully;
Light from her soft breasts shimmered, like moonlight, strange to see.
Then passion gripped Anchises. Swift was his greeting given—
'Hail to Thee, Queen, whoe'er Thou art among the Blessed in Heaven!
Whether the bright-eyed Pallas, or Thĕmis high of heart,
Or Lēto, or Aphrodite, or Artemis Thou art,
Or one of the deathless Graces come earthward, it may be,
Who walk, men say, in Heaven in the high Gods' company;
Or one of the Nymphs that harbour in springs whence rivers rill,
Or deep in the lovely woodland, or up the grassy hill.
Now on some far-seen summit that looks across the lands
For Thee will I build an altar, and bring Thee with my hands
Fair gifts through the circling seasons. But Thou—in the Trojan town
O Goddess, of Thy goodness grant me to win renown.
Let me leave good sons behind me. Long let my own days run,
Happy among my people, seeing the light of the sun.
Let me come, at last, to the door of eld, before I die.'

Then the Aegis-bearer's daughter, Aphrodite, made reply:
'Nay, Anchises, noblest of men that are born of earth,
Why liken *me* to a Goddess? Mine is no Heavenly birth.
I am but a mortal woman, that of earthly mother came,
Daughter of famous Otreus—if ever you heard his name—
Lord of the well-walled cities of all the Phrygian land.
Yet the tongue of the Trojans also, like mine, I understand;
For my nurse at home was a Trojan born. My mother dear
Gave me, a little child, into her hand to rear.
But now the Argus-slayer has caught me away unseen,
The God of the Golden Sceptre from the Golden-shafted Queen,
From Artemis of the hunting-cry, round whom we danced and played,
Many a Nymph, past number, many a long-wooed maid.
The Argus-slayer seized me, God of the Golden Wand—
O'er many a tilth and ploughland he bore me, and beyond
Many a waste and wilderness, untilled of men,
Where beasts devouring wander, deep in the shadowy glen—
I thought that never again should I feel the kindly ground.
For the bride-bed of Anchises, the God said I was bound,
To be the wife you wedded and bear strong sons to you;
He said it, and pointed towards you, then swiftly away he flew,
The mighty Argus-slayer, back to the Heavenly Gate—
And to you I came—for upon me hard lay the hand of Fate.
But now, by Zeus and the noble hearts that gave you birth,
I beg you (for, sure, no dastards bred such a son of worth),
Take me a maid as I am, that nothing know of love,
Home to your noble mother, home to your sire, to prove;
And to your brothers show me, bred of the selfsame race—
Let them judge if this bride before you will bring your blood disgrace.
Then to my land of glossy steeds, to Phrygia,
Send word at once to my father, to my mother that mourns afar—
Much gold, and woven dresses, they will send you back again.
The noble gifts they offer, let not your hand disdain;
But make the banquet ready for the lovely bridal-day,
The feast that all men honour, and Gods that live for aye.'
So in his heart she made the sweet love-longing stir,
And passion gripped Anchises, and swift he answered her:
'If you are a mortal maid indeed, of woman bred,
And the great Otreus is your sire, as you have said;
If Hermes, the Herald of Heaven, truly has brought you here,
To be my wife for always, unto my latest year,
Then there is no man living, there lives no hand divine,

29

Shall have the power to hold me before I have made you mine,
Now!—no, not even Apollo, though from his silver bow
The Archer-king should slay me with the arrows of his woe.
Face fair as the Immortals, once let me share your bed,
And then the House of Hades may close above my head!'

Hard by the hand he gripped her. With eyes cast down for shame
Upon the earth, and bending her face away, she came,
The laughter-loving Cypris, to the bed of the prince spread fair
With many a fleecy mantle, and furs of the forest bear
Above them, and hides of deep-mouthed lions, that his own hand
Had stricken to death aforetime, high in that mountain-land.
But when they two together in that fair bed were laid,
He drew the gems aglitter from the body of the maid,
Brooches and twisted armlets, earrings and chains of gold;
And loosed the girdle round her, and drew off fold by fold
Her garments in their glory, and laid them, soft and still,
On a seat with silver studded. Then, by the high Gods' will,
Mortal beside the Undying he lay—and knew it not.

But at the hour's returning when the herdsman seeks his cot
With his fat sheep and his cattle, home from the flowery field,
Then the eyes of Anchises deep in sweet sleep she sealed.
Once more she clad her body, a Goddess glorified,
In the beauty of her raiment, and stood at his bedside.
But now to the rooftree rose her head, and from her face
Shone in its deathless splendour the Cytherean's grace.
Out of his sleep she roused him and called him clear by name—
'Up!—wilt thou never waken? *Now* do I seem the same,
Dardanides, to thy vision as in the morning light
When this face for the first time dawned upon thy sight?'
With that cry in his ears on a sudden he started in surprise;
Then, at the sight of that proud neck, those flashing eyes,
He shrank away, in his mantle hiding his comely face,
And the words came winging from him, and he begged the Goddess'
        grace:
'I knew it in that first moment, when I saw Thee—well I knew
That Thou *wert* indeed a Goddess. 'Twas *Thy* tongue spoke not true.
But, by the Aegis-bearing Zeus, have mercy Thou—
Leave me not, I beseech Thee, on earth to linger now
A feeble, strengthless shadow! For that man wastes away
Who once in the arms immortal of a daughter of Heaven lay.'
Then the Aegis-bearer's daughter, Aphrodite, made reply:
'Courage, Anchises, noblest of men that are born to die.

Fear not too much—from me thou hast no ill to fear,
Nor from the other Immortals. For Heaven holds thee dear.
And now a loved son shall be born thee. He shall reign as the Trojans'
    king,
And children of thy children, years without end, shall spring.
His name shall be called "Aeneas", for deep and bitterly,
When I sank to the bed of a mortal, the heart was shamed in me.
But indeed, of all earth's peoples, the children of thy race
Have ever stood next the Immortals in comeliness and grace.
So Zeus the all⁄devising for his beauty skyward bore
The fair⁄haired Ganymēdes, to dwell there evermore,
Honoured among the Blessed, glorious to behold,
As he draws the deep⁄red nectar from the mixing⁄bowl of gold.
Fathomless was the sorrow that on Trōs his father lay,
Mourning the loss of his vanished son, long day by day,
Not knowing whither had whirled him the storm⁄blast from on high.
But the heart of Zeus was softened, hearing that father's cry,
And he bade to King Trōs in requital a team of steeds be given—
Such steeds as draw, high⁄prancing, the chariots of Heaven—
And sent the Argus⁄slayer, his messenger, before
To tell how Ganymēdes god⁄like evermore
Should live—unaged, undying. That word came not in vain;
The Trojan ceased from weeping, glad grew his heart again,
As his steeds with the feet of the tempest swept down the Trojan Plain.
Of your race too came Tithōnus, fair as the high Gods are,
Whom Eos gold⁄enthronéd bore from your land afar,
Then came to Zeus, whose storm⁄rack benights the skies with gloom,
To beg that her love for ever might live, nor see the tomb.
So the Son of Crŏnus nodded to her prayer, and grudged it not.
Ah fool, the Queen of Morning, there as she prayed, forgot
To ask for Youth eternal and shear grim Age away!
So, while his lovely youth endured, rejoicing, gay,
With Eos gold⁄enthronéd, the Daughter of the Morn,
He dwelt by the Stream of Ocean, at the round earth's utmost bourn.
But, when on that fair countenance, that noble head,
To grey the first hair faded, the Goddess left his bed,
Yet lovingly still she cherished him, within her hall,
With glory of fair raiment and food ambrosial.
Then, when the hateful course of age had run its length
And even to lift his limbs her lover lost the strength,
Best in her heart the Goddess deemed to set at last
The old man in a chamber with shining doors shut fast.

There still his voice chirps ceaseless on, but dead and cold
The manhood lies that quickened in those lithe limbs of old.
Not like to him would I wish for *thee* to live for aye,
Immortal among the Immortals. If, as thou art this day
In comeliness and beauty, thou couldst for ever be,
To have thee for lord and husband were then no grief to me.
But now—without any pity, swift on thine head shall draw
The doom that waits on all men, that the very Gods abhor,
Old age, the grim, the weary. And, as for me, my name
Always henceforth in Heaven must bear its bitter shame
Because of thee. Aforetime, my power held all in dread,
For all the Gods in Heaven to women of earth I led
With my love-wiles and love-whispers. But now, the name of love—
Never my lips dare speak it, henceforth, in Heaven above,
Since this folly came upon me, past utterance, terrible,
That to the bed of a mortal, infatuate, I fell.
And now beneath my girdle I bear, I too, a child.
But him, when he sees the sunlight, the Nymphs of the mountain-wild
Shall take to their deep bosoms. This high and holy peak
Is theirs, and no haunts of mortals, no haunts of the Gods they seek.
Long are their days of living, ambrosia is their bread,
And in the Gods' fair dances their whirling footsteps tread.
By the keen-eyed Argus-slayer, alone, their love is won,
Or by the wild Silēni, where under the mountains run
Fair caverns deep in the darkness. But with them, at one birth,
For each an oak, or a pine-tree, springs from the nurturing earth,
Towering green and lonely, high on the mountainside,
In groves no woodman touches, by the high Gods sanctified.
But when at last for the Dryad draws near the doom of death,
First, where it grows on the hillside, each fair tree withereth.
Down from the trunk the branches fall, the bark grows dry,
And the life of the Nymphs, too, passes from the sunlight, and they die.
These, then, shall be the nurses to watch and tend my son.
And when to lovely childhood he grows, as the seasons run,
The Nymphs shall lead him hither, for thine own eyes to see:
And again in his fifth summer will I bring him back to thee,
And thou shalt learn my purpose. At sight of that young face
In the first flower of its springtide, fair as the Gods in grace,
Thy heart shall leap rejoicing. Then shalt thou take the boy
And bring him down beside thee to the windy walls of Troy.
But as for thy dear son's mother, if thou art asked of men,
"Who bore him under her girdle?"—beware, Anchises, then!

This be thine answer (remember!)—"They say he was the child
Of a flower-faced Nymph of Ida, where wave the woodlands wild."
But if, with the mind of a madman, thou boast vaingloriously
That the fair-crowned Cytherēa once gave herself to thee,
Then Zeus shall loose in his anger his reeking bolt on thy head.
Therefore take heed what I tell thee. My latest word is said.
Mind well thy mouth, nor name me. Of the wrath of the Gods beware.'
She ceased, and vanished, soaring, through the windy wastes of air.

Lady of fair-tilled Cyprus, O Goddess, fare thee well.
My tale of thee is told now, of another will I tell.

[p. 5] *Gift-devouring princes.* Homer's heroes have now dwindled to petty local oppressors—more like the Suitors in Ithaca.

[p. 5] *Half is more than whole.* Cf. *Ps.* xxxvii, 16: 'A little that a righteous man hath is better than the riches of many wicked'; *Prov.* xv, 16–17: 'Better is little with the fear of the Lord than great treasure and trouble therewith. Better is a dinner of herbs where love is, than a stalled ox and hatred therewith.' But Hēsiod's adage is of wider scope and allied to the fundamental Greek moderation of 'Nothing too much'.

[p. 5] *Mallow and asphodel.* The poor ate mallow-shoots and asphodel-bulbs. Asphodel, despite its poetic name, is a pallid, scraggy plant, common on barren patches throughout Greece.

[p. 5] *Prometheus* ('Forethought'), the Titan, son of Iápetus and brother of Epimetheus ('Afterthought'), was originally a trickster like the Norse Loki, but later idealized as a champion of man against Heaven's harshness. The *Theogony* tells how he tried to dupe Zeus by dividing the sacrificial ox into two portions—the flesh covered with the paunch, and the bones within a rich roll of fat. Though seeing the trap, Zeus chose, as Prometheus had hoped, the fat and bones (the part that Greek ritual in practice gave the Gods); but he punished the deceiver by depriving him and mankind of fire.

[p. 5] *Iápetus.* Father of Prometheus, Epimetheus, and Atlas the upholder of the sky. Perhaps an ancient figure of Asiatic mythology, as his name seems to recur in the Biblical Japhet.

[p. 5] *Fennel-stalk.* Giant fennel-stalks, some 5 feet long and 3 inches thick, with hard rind, and pith that burns slowly like a wick, were still used for carrying fire in Greek lands as late as the 19th century.

[p. 5] *His laughter.* 'He that sitteth in the heavens shall laugh' (*Ps.* ii, 4). Homer smiles sometimes even at Zeus; but in Hēsiod it is Zeus that grimly laughs. This grave Boeotian is less at home on Olympus.

[p. 5] *Argus-slayer.* The meaning of *Argeiphontes* as title of Hermes was obscure to the later Greeks themselves. It may mean merely 'bringer of brightness'. But it was often associated with the legend that when Io, beloved of Zeus, was turned into a cow, the jealous Hēra set as guard over her the many-eyed Argus (the starry sky?); then Zeus in his turn sent Hermes to lull Argus asleep and kill him.

[p. 5] *Soul of a thief.* . . . It is curious how constantly this strain of misogyny recurs in world literature—in Semōnides (p. 51 ff.), for instance, Euripides, the Old Testament, the Early Fathers, the *Roman de la Rose*, Chaucer, Milton, Pope, Strindberg, Tolstoy. Whereas the corresponding term *misandry* does not even exist. Nor, on the other hand, do women or women-writers seem to idealize Man as men have often idealized Woman. Probably no poet has ever expressed *both* attitudes towards the feminine with more vehemence than Euripides. For example:

> Fearful the violence of the raging sea;
> Fearful the force of torrent and of flame;
> Fearful is penury, and a thousand ills
> There are beside; but none so fell as woman—
> No written word has power to say how evil,
> No tongue has power to tell it. If any God
> Created *them*, He was an evil genius—
> That let Him know—and hated all mankind.
>
> (Fr. 1059.)

And yet, in a famous women's chorus of the *Mēdēa* (410–30), it is as if he were answering such passages as this in Hēsiod:

> Backward the Streams of Righteousness are driven—
>   All things lie confounded, Justice overborne.
> Men are turned to traitors and their solemn pledges given
>   In Heaven's sight forsworn.
> 'Tis time earth's songs were altered, to sing of Woman's fame—
> Ay, honour shall be rendered, at last, to Woman's name;
>   No more the ancient slanders shall hold us up to scorn.
>
> And *they* shall be silenced, the bards of old that chide us,
>   Harping still their stories of false wives that fell.
> Well for men that Phoebus, the Lord of Song, denied us
>   The poet's godlike spell!
> Else *we* had sung our answer, and loud our lips had rolled
> To men a chant of challenge. For Time, from years of old,
>   Many a tale of the dealings 'twixt us and men could tell.

[p. 6] *Peitho.* Persuasion, Allurement, Temptation.

[p. 6] *The Seasons lovely-tressed . . . all the flowers of spring.* Misogynist though he is, Hesiod makes the creature very fascinating.

[p. 6] *Pandora.* Originally an epithet of Earth—'all-giver'; though here she becomes the primeval *femme fatale*.

[p. 6] *The jar*, which Pandora had brought with her (cf. Homer's twin jars of good and evil in the house of Zeus). Hēsiod here seems to assume his hearers' knowledge and tells his story in allusive and abbreviated form. Frazer (*Pausanias*, 1, 24, 7 and note) compares an ancient Peruvian legend that the Creator sent to the Inca Huayna-Capac a box containing all maladies in the shapes of butterflies which, when the box was opened, infected the whole world.

[p. 6] *Only Hope*. Commentators have debated whether Hope is one more plague (cf. p. 236) or a consolation-prize. But allegories, though seldom delicious as peaches, like them should not be pressed. Hēsiod seems simply to mean that, in a world filled with evils, Hope yet abides persistently with man. In Pope's words:

> Hope springs eternal in the human breast;
> Man never is, but always to be blest.

[p. 6] *Race . . . of Gold*. Like other dreams of Golden Ages, this seems psychologically a reflection of man's nostalgia for the happy days of childhood. But it would, perhaps, be over-fanciful to see in the hundred-years childhood of the Silver Age that follows, a reflection of the not uncommon psychological resistance to growing up.

[p. 7] *Sprung from ash trees*. The wood used for spear-shafts.

[p. 7] *Of bronze . . . their dwellings*. Cf. beehive tombs like the Treasury of Atreus at Mycenae, with its bronze doors and roof-rosettes; and the legends of Dánaë shut in her brazen tower, of Eurystheus hiding from Hēracles in his brazen pot.

[p. 7] *The godlike Heroes*. Hēsiod has not done badly in dating the heroic era of the sieges of Thebes and Troy at the close of the Bronze Age and on the eve of the Iron.

[p. 8] *All concord of son with sire shall end*. Cf. *Mark* xiii, 12; 'Now the brother shall betray the brother to death, and the father the son; and children shall rise up against their parents and shall cause them to be put to death' (after all, we have ourselves seen such things in our own century) and the still grimmer Sibyl's Prophecy from the *Edda* (Vigfusson and York Powell, *Corpus Poeticum Boreale*, II, 625):

> Brother with brother shall grapple in battle,
> Kin that are closest, shall couple and care not,
> Harsh shall the world wax, and heedless of whoredoms—
> An axe-age, a sword-age, when shields shall be shattered,
> A storm-age, a wolf-age, ere the world's ending.

[p. 8] *Honour . . . and Righteousness*. Aidōs and Nemesis—roughly, the

36

self-condemnation pronounced by the individual conscience, and the general condemnation pronounced by the public conscience.

[p. 8] *Hawk . . . nightingale*. The first European fable. The hawk, though Hēsiod leaves it unsaid, corresponds to the 'gift-devouring princes'. Cf. the fable of cat and ratons in *Piers Plowman*, equally veiled and equally directed against insolent barons. (Those interested will find a parallel between Hēsiod and Langland in my *Studies French and English*, 2nd ed., pp. 28–76.) Here the point is: 'The great are ruthless as the hawk. But let us follow justice. God pays in the end.' Cf. the Latin distich quoted by Salimbene (1221–c. 1288):

> Milvus ait pullo, dum portaretur ab illo,
> 'Cum *pi pi* faris, non te tenet ungula talis.'

'In vain "Peep-peep!" you squawk,' to the chicken quoth the hawk,
As through the air he bore it; 'these claws of mine ignore it.'

[p. 8] *Dapple-necked*. Ordinary nightingales apparently are not 'dappled'. But Ovid likewise (*Met.* VI, 669) speaks of the nightingale's neck as still bearing traces of her murder of her child Ítylus.

[p. 9] *Worldly Wisdom*. Sainte-Beuve justly compares some of this shrewd but prosaic prudence to the homely precepts of Benjamin Franklin (*Poor Richard's Almanac*).

[p. 9] *Evil to choose is easy*. Cf. the Delphic oracle, p. 245.

[p. 9] *Long is the path and steep*. A famous passage, imitated by Simōnides, referred to by Plato and Xenophon. Cf. *Matthew*, vii, 13–14: 'Wide is the gate, and broad is the way, that leadeth to destruction ... strait is the gate, and narrow is the way, which leadeth unto life'; and Donne, *Satyres*, III: 'On a huge hill Cragged, and steep, Truth stands.'

[p. 10] *Crane*. See p. 62 and compare Aristophanes, *Birds*, 709–12:

For first we show how the seasons go, autumn and winter and spring,
And *then* ye know it is time to sow, when the crane flies chattering
Towards Libya's shore; then the skipper can snore, by the chimney his
   his rudder leaving,
And Orestes takes note to get him a coat for his winter nights a-thieving.

[p. 11] *The heat that the Pleiads bring*. They rise with the sun in May.
[p. 11] *House-carrier*. The snail.
[p. 11] *Biblian wine*. Not known. Possibly 'Biblian' does not mean 'brought from Biblis', but indicates a *type* of wine, made locally in Boeotia.
[p. 12] *Wave . . . grave*. Corresponding to a jingle in the Greek: 'meta kūmasi pēmati kursai'.

[p. 12] *Lēnaion.* Late Jan.–early Feb.

[p. 12] *No-bones.* The cuttlefish. Aristotle (*Hist. of Animals,* VIII, 2) says this vulgar error that they eat themselves arose from the finding of tentacles that had really been bitten off by congers. Cf. the old idea of the bear sucking his paws in winter:

> And when these fail'd, he'd suck his Claws,
> And quarter himself upon his Paws.
>
> (Butler, *Hudibras.*)

[p. 13] *Helicon.* The Muses' mountain (5,800 feet), N. of the Corinthian Gulf and SE. of the far more imposing Parnassus (8,200 feet). Hēsiod's Ascra topped a high conical hill ENE. of Helicon.

[p. 13] *Violet-shadowed spring.* Aganippe, supposed to give inspiration to the drinker. Perhaps a source near the monastery of St Nicholas in the Valley of the Muses, at the N. foot of Helicon, close to the River Archontitza, which seems the ancient Permessus.

[p. 13] *Crónion.* Zeus.

[p. 13] *Hippocrēne.* 'The Horse's Fount' (because produced by a blow of Pegasus' hoof) lies in a firwood-glade near one summit (Zagara) of Helicon. On the summit itself, 100 paces E., stands a chapel of St Elias, probably on the site of the altar of Zeus mentioned here (Frazer, *Pausanias,* v, p. 158).

[p. 13] *Olmeius.* River flowing from Helicon to the Copaic Lake.

[p. 13] *Diōne.* Daughter of Heaven and Earth, and at Dōdōna the consort of Zeus; sometimes given as the mother of Aphrodite.

[p. 13] *Hēbe.* Youth, daughter of Zeus and Hēra; cupbearer, like Ganymede, of the Gods; and wife of Hēracles in Heaven.

[p. 13] *Hēsiod.* Some have argued that 'Hēsiod' here is not the same person as 'me' below; i.e. the *Theogony* is not Hēsiod's. But it seems much more like a Greek poet to sign his own work by putting his name at its beginning than to name a predecessor while himself remaining modestly anonymous.

[p. 14] *Many a falsehood . . . many a true word also. . . .* Here in two lines is the scope of all poetry. Herrick made them the motto of his *Noble Numbers.*

[p. 14] *The mourner casts off the load. . . .*

> Qui chante
> Son mal enchante.

Compare Montesquieu's astounding statement that he had never had a grief which an hour's reading could not cure.

[p. 18] *Ortygia:* 'Quail-island'. Probably here Rhēneia, severed from Delos by a narrow channel.

[p. 18] *The Cretan land, etc.* Roughly the poet circles the Aegean—S., W., N., and E. Peparēthus is an island E. of Mt Pēlion; Aegae, perhaps an island off Euboea; Eirésiae, perhaps an island in the Thermaic Gulf near Thessalonica; Autócane, opposite Lesbos; Mĭmas, the mountain facing Chios, with Córycus at its S. end; Claros, on the Asiatic coast, NE. of Samos. (Aeságea is unidentified.)

[p. 19] *All these feared.* Because of Hēra's jealousy.

[p. 19] *Coeus.* A Titan, son of Heaven and Earth.

[p. 20] *Rhea*, daughter of Heaven and Earth, wife of Crŏnus, mother of Zeus, Poseidon, Hades, Hēra, Hestia, and Demeter; in origin, one of the many Mother-goddesses of the ancient Levant.

[p. 20] *Diōne.* Likewise daughter of Heaven and Earth (see p. 38).

[p. 20] *Thĕmis.* Justice. Another daughter of Heaven and Earth; in fact, the Goddesses of the old order here gather to the birth of the radiant deity of the new.

[p. 20] *Amphitrīte.* Goddess of the Sea, wedded to Poseidon.

[p. 20] *Eileithyia.* Goddess of Childbirth.

HYMN TO APHRODITE

[p. 27] *From the might of Love Nothing escapes.* Cf. Sophocles, Fr. 855:

> My children, Love is more than Love alone,
> For Love hath also many another name.
> Ay, Love is Death; Love is a power eternal;
> 'Tis passion's heady wine, 'tis wailing anguish,
> 'Tis frenzy at its starkest. Love hath all—
> Strong purpose, utter peace, wild violence.
> It melts its way into the hearts of all
> That breathe on earth—what does not yield to Love?
> It moves the plunging fishes of the deep,
> Seizes the four-foot creatures of the land,
> Flutters its wings among the birds of air:
> Nor beasts nor men escape, nor Gods in Heaven.
> With Love what God that wrestled hath not found
> A triple overthrow? If I dare say it—
> And why may I *not* say what is the truth?—
> Love masters Zeus Himself.
> Love needs no spear, no swordblade, to confound
> The wisest plans alike of God and man.

Ida. Source of the Scamander, Granīcus, and Aesēpus, and still a 'mount of many springs', lies south of Troy, along the north shore of the Gulf of Adramyttium, and rises in its highest point, Mount Gargărus, to nearly 6,000 feet. Still each summer, like a Swiss alp, its uplands are grazed by herdsmen from the country round. In late May, when the lower lands are already beginning to parch, they begin driving up their beasts to the new grass that springs, starred with crocus and hyacinth, in the wake of the receding snows. Indeed Leaf found a stone cattlefold on the very summit. The mountain, he says, was still held holy by the local Mohammedans and still covered with forests of pine and oak.

It is also of interest that, while the Troad, north of Ida, has severe winters with deep snow and fifteen to twenty degrees of frost, the coast south of Ida is a sort of Riviera, free from lasting snow, rich in olives, and famous in antiquity for its fertility (Leaf, *Troy*, pp. 11, 202, 218)—as if the two sides of the mountain still symbolized the meeting of the lovely Aphrodite and the hardy Anchises.

[p. 29] *Argus-slayer*. See p. 34.

[p. 29] *Otreus*. King of Phrygia and brother of Priam's queen, Hecuba.

[p. 30] *That man wastes away*. Probably because of the jealousy of the Gods. Thus Orion was slain by Artemis for having loved Eos, or by Apollo for having loved Artemis. Zeus slew Demeter's lover Iásion; and in his own arms perished Sémele by the guile of the jealous Hēra.

[p. 31] *He shall reign as the Trojans' king*. The Homeric idea (*Iliad* xx, 307-8) was that the House of Aeneas was to rule in the Troad. Strabo locates them at Scepsis, north of Ida. The legend of Aeneas' voyage to Italy seems to begin with Stesíchorus (6th century B.C.). Later still came the tradition that Aeneas founded Lavinium and his son Iūlus (Ascánius) Alba Longa, whence in its turn sprang Rome. The belief that the Julian Gens in particular descended from Iūlus was sufficiently living in Caesar's day for him to give 'Venus Genetrix' as the password at Pharsālus and Munda.

[p. 31] *Aeneas*. An imaginary derivation of 'Aineias' from *ainos* ('terrible'). The true etymology is unknown.

[p. 31] *Ganymēdes*. This story of his being carried off by a whirlwind is earlier than the familiar version in which he is borne away by Zeus in the shape of an eagle, or by the eagle of Zeus.

> Or else flush'd Ganymede, his rosy thigh
> > Half-buried in the eagle's down,
> Sole as a flying star shot thro' the sky
> > Above the pillar'd town.
>
> > > > Tennyson.

[p. 32] *His voice chirps ceaseless on*. Later versions definitely state that he was turned into a grasshopper or cicada, emblem of garrulous age. When we recall that Memnon, son of Tithōnus and Eos, was identified by the Greeks with the colossal statue of Amenhotep III, near the Egyptian Thebes, which uttered a musical cry each dawn, it seems conceivable that the withered immortality of Tithōnus himself may have been suggested to the Greek imagination by the wizened eternity of the Egyptian mummy in its shining sarcophagus.

[p. 32] *Silēni.* Wild men depicted in early art with *horse*-ears and, often, *horse*-legs and tail. They are much confused with Satyrs; who, however, by association with Pan, tend to become *goat*-like.

[p. 32] *For the Dryad draws near the doom of death.* Hēsiod (Fr. 171) gives the following table of expectation of life for nymphs:

> 1 crow = 9 generations of men
> 1 deer = 4 crows
> 1 raven = 3 deer
> 1 phoenix = 9 ravens
> 1 nymph = 10 phoenixes.

Clearly, however, this fantastic version bears no relation to the comparatively brief life of a tree.

[p. 33] *Zeus shall loose in his anger his reeking bolt.* Legend told that, despite this warning, Anchises (by one account, when flushed with wine) could not keep his secret and was accordingly paralysed, blinded, or even killed by the lightning of Zeus. Many sites are assigned to his grave, from Ida to Arcadia and Italy. Virgil makes him share the wanderings of Aeneas as far as Trápani in Sicily: there he died and was buried, with a hero's shrine, on Mount Eryx.

PART TWO

FROM ARCHILOCHUS TO ALEXANDER

7th–4th centuries B.C.

ARCHILOCHUS OF PAROS
(earlier 7th century B.C.)

'HOMER' had been as impersonal as Shakespeare in his plays: Archílochus becomes as personal as Shakespeare in his sonnets. But personalities easily grow bitter—Archílochus is the father of European satire. He was, too, the illegitimate son of a noble father and a slave mother; that may have helped to make him feel at war with the world, like Shakespeare's illegitimate Edmund, and scoff at it, like Shakespeare's Bastard Falconbridge.

His questionable birth (says tradition) caused another Parian noble, Lýcambes, to break off the betrothal of his daughter to the poet; who retaliated with lampoons so savage that Lýcambes and both his daughters hanged themselves. He took part in the colonization of the North-Aegean island of Thásos, which he hated; fought the Thracian natives of the mainland—his flight from whom on one occasion he celebrated in a poem of famous irony, which caused him to be banned from Sparta; and finally fell in battle against the men of Naxos. (It is not the worst soldiers that own laughingly to being afraid.) Tradition adds that the Delphic oracle cursed the man who had slain 'the servant of the Muses'.

Time has left us only fragments that do not make it easy to understand why some ancient critics should have ranked Archílochus next to Homer himself; though they justify Quintilian's praise of his style as 'vigorous, terse, vibrating—full of blood and sinew'. He remains the type of poet who has more strength than sweetness, hate than love, passion than wisdom—like Juvenal, Villon, Skelton. Theirs is not the highest type of poetry: yet literature would be poorer without them. And so Archílochus too finds his place in that garland into which Meleāger, in the first of European 'Anthologies', gathered the infinitely diverse flowers of Greek poetry:

> Sweet as the honeysuckle that springs from its own sowing,
>> Here is Anácreon's singing, his nectared elegies,
> And Archílochus' thorny blossoms, in their tangled thicket growing,
>> Bitter as the spindrift that drives across the seas.

Life and Art

A henchman sworn of Ares, Lord God of war, I live,
And a master of that beauty the Muses' hands can give.
(E. Diehl, *Anthologia Lyrica Graeca*, I, p. 211.)

The Freelance

For me my spear is kneaded bread; wine from the Thracian land
My spear is; and, to drink it, I lie with spear in hand.

(p. 211.)

The Better Part of Valour

Some Thracian now goes strutting with the shield I left behind me,
Under a bush—a peerless shield—regretfully.
However—I came home living. Plague take it! I will find me
Another one hereafter—and just as good to me!

(p. 213.)

Girlhood

A branch of myrtle in her happiness
She held, and a rose's beauty; and her hair
Fell shadowing deep her shoulders and her back.

(p. 218.)

Too Versatile

Many a trick the wise fox knows;
But the hedgehog has *one*, worth a lot of those.

(p. 241.)

Sursum Corda

Heart, my heart, with cares past curing thou that liest sore opprest,
Lift thee up now and defend thee. Grapple closely, breast to breast,
Foes that lie in ambush for thee—undismayed and undistrest!
When thou winnest, let not all men see thee too triumphant stand;
When thou losest, hie not homeward there to lie and mourn unmanned.
Grieve in sadness, joy in gladness, not past measure—thine to know
How the tides of human fortunes must for ever ebb and flow.

(p. 230.)

TYRTAEUS OF SPARTA
(later 7th century B.C.)

Legend described Tyrtaeus as a lame Athenian schoolmaster sent at the request of the Spartans to raise their morale in the Second Messenian War (*c.* 630 B.C.?). It may indeed be true that, like Alcman of Lydia, he was no Spartan born. Patriotic war-poetry, however, like hymns and other *too* purposeful art, seldom reaches the heights. Few would name Campbell as a favourite poet, or wish to multiply the *Marseillaise*. Tyrtaeus' work shows, too, some of the monotonous grimness of Sparta, with her iron laws and her iron money, her black broth and her barrack communism. When he copies Homer, he shows his own inferiority. Homer's Priam laments the unsightliness of an old man butchered in contrast to the grace, even in death, of the young; as an appeal to Hector to pity him and not defy Achilles single-handed, this becomes moving poetry. But Tyrtaeus twists it round into propaganda for the young to fight—even dead they will be handsome; and what was pathetic becomes slightly morbid and disgusting.

Still Tyrtaeus remains a characteristic figure; and his picture here of the miseries of the refugee has an only too modern bleakness.

'Dulce et Decorum'

It is a fair death, fighting in the front of battle
    For the cause of country like the brave to fall;
But to flee his city, his fields of corn and cattle,
    And beg!—among man's sorrows *this* is worst of all.
A banished wretch, with aged sire and her that bore him,
    With his little children and the wife he wed,
To all men he is hateful, wherever he comes, and o'er him
    Beggary is master, and the cry for bread.
A brand he brings upon his fathers; ay, disgraces
    His body's grace; and with him all blame and shame must live.
Therefore, since dishonour and scorn in all men's faces,
    Both for him and his children, wait on the fugitive,
For our sons, for Lacedaemon, for this land that gave us birth,
Fight and die, accounting mere life of little worth.

(E. Diehl, Anthologia Lyrica Graeca, I, p. 9.)

ALCMAN OF SPARTA
(later 7th century B.C.)

Alcman, perhaps a Greek of Sardis in Lydia who migrated to Sparta, wrote choral songs, especially for maidens—the earliest Greek lyrics, apart from a few lines of Terpander, that survive.

The Old Poet to his Maiden Choir

Ah voices sweet as honey, ah maiden songs divine,
Faint grow my limbs and fail me! Would the halcyon's lot were mine!—
Wherever the white foam flowers, with my fellow-birds to fly,
Sea-purple bird of the springtime, blithe heart where no cares lie.

(Diehl, II, p. 34.)

Vesper

Now sleep the mountain-summits, sleep the glens,
The peaks, the torrent-beds; all things that creep
On the dark earth lie resting in their dens;
Quiet are the mountain-creatures, quiet the bees,
The monsters hidden in the purple seas;
And birds, the swift of wing,
Sit slumbering.

(p. 27.)

MIMNERMUS OF COLOPHON
(later 7th century B.C.)

You promise heavens free from strife,
Pure truth, and perfect change of will;
But sweet, sweet is this human life,
So sweet, I fain would breathe it still.

W. Cory, *Mimnermus in Church.*

In temperament, Mimnermus is an even completer contrast to Tyrtaeus than Rossetti to Meredith, or Pater to Carlyle. The softer Greek cities on the Asiatic riviera had been the first part of Hellas to flower: they were to be the first to fade. Mimnermus turns like Ovid, or Omar Khayyam, or Herrick, to gathering rosebuds, and the sadness that it brings. A flute-player himself, he loved a flute-girl, Nanno, who inspired much of his poetry. Despite a fine fragment on courage, he may perhaps be called the first European decadent. But, like many decadents, he remains a brilliant minor artist.

'Gather ye rosebuds'

Ah, what is life?—what is joy?—but Aphrodite the golden?
    Let me die, when I am gladdened no more by things like these—
Her gifts honey-sweet, and the bed of love, by none beholden,
    And all the flowers of youth, that are so sweet to seize,
For the hands of man and woman. But he who is once o'ertaken
    By grim old age, that makes him ugly at once and base,
With misery and anguish his heart without cease is shaken,
    No more to the sun rejoicing, thenceforth, he turns his face.
Hateful he grows to boyhood, a scorn to women's gaze—
Such is the bitter burden God made life's latter days.

(Diehl, I, p. 39.)

'The Sated Guest'

I would that free from sickness, untouched by cares and tears,
The doom of death might take me at the end of sixty years.

(p. 41.)

The Labours of the Sun

No day released from labour to the Sun-god's self is given;
    No hour of rest for his horses, no hour of rest for him,
From the moment when there rises, across the height of Heaven,
    Dawn the rosy-fingered, leaving Ocean's rim,
Till he sinks to the bed all golden, fair-fashioned for his sleeping,
    That bears him back to eastward, round the circling seas,
Wrought by the hand of Hephaestus with wings that, swiftly sweeping,
    Waft him over the wavetops, from the Hesperides
To the Ethiop shore, where his horses, his headlong chariot wait
Once more, till mounts the Morning again through her eastern gate.

(p. 42.)

HYMN TO DIONYSUS
(7th–6th century B.C.?)

Despite a certain vividness, this piece seems markedly inferior to the best 'Homeric Hymns', such as *Apollo* or *Aphrodite*. At moments the hand of the poet shakes; and in general Dionysus himself is less attractive than many of the Olympians. There clings about him too much of that decadent romanticism and fanaticism of which his worship remains the eternal symbol. It is characteristic that 'Homer' hardly mentions him; yet Greek wisdom realized that it is perilous too much to repress the instinctive and impulsive forces of human nature. The Puritan Pentheus is torn in pieces by the Bacchanals; the wiser Apollo grants his tumul-tuous younger brother a share in the Delphic sanctuary. All the same Dionysus remains to this day one of the supreme dangers to the civiliza-tion so laboriously and precariously built by man.

Hymn to Dionysus

Of him that had for mother the glorious Sémele
I will sing, of Dionysus—how by the barren sea
Upon a jutting headland he stood revealed once, fair
As a stripling in his flower of youth, with raven hair
Tossing about his shoulders, and a mantle purple-wove
Round his broad chest. But, swiftly, in sight a tall ship hove,
Manned by Tyrsēnian pirates, cleaving beneath her stem
The waste of wine-dark waters—ill hour it was for *them* !
Seeing him they nodded each to each, and speedily
They sprang ashore, and seized him, and dragged with savage glee
Aboard their ship. For they deemed him a prince that they had caught,
Son of some king by Heaven blest; and bitter gyves they brought.
But lo ! not a thing could hold him—the bonds all slid away
From his hands and feet and, before them, he sat there, smiling gay
With eyes of blue. Then the steersman, seeing such things befall,
Cried aloud in warning to his comrades one and all:
'Madmen, what God is this that ye seize and bind in vain !—
A mightier one is here than *our* ship can contain.
Zeus it must be, or Poseidon, or the Lord of the Silver Bow,
Apollo ! For only Immortals were ever fashioned so,
That dwell on high Olympus—and none of mortal birth.
Come, let him go in freedom across the dark-loamed earth,
Delay no more, **un**hand him !—for fear that in wrath he cast
Some great gale loose against us, some tempest's raging blast.'

But angrily the captain made answer: 'Keep an eye,
Fool, on the wind behind us, and hoist full sail on high.
This lad is for *men* to handle. If it go as I have planned,
To Cyprus, or to Egypt, or the Hyperborean land—
Or farther yet—I will ship him. He shall tell us in the end
The names—ay, and the riches—of family and friend,
Seeing that fate was minded to throw him in our way.'
    With that he hauled at mast and sail; and every stay,
As the breeze swelled out the canvas, they stretched taut to the blast.
But suddenly before their eyes strange wonders passed—
First of all, through their swift black ship gushed streams of wine,
Sweet to the taste and nostril, while a fragrance all divine
Floated around—the seamen stood gaping at the sight.
All up the sail went climbing a vine to left and right,
Loaded with hanging clusters; and high aloft the mast
Dark coils of winding ivy, bright with its flowers, clung fast,
All beautiful with berries; and the thole-pin of each oar
Stood wreathed in green. To the helmsman, they cried to steer for shore;
But, from the prow of the galley, the God's self met them there,
Like a grisly lion, with thunderous roar; and a shaggy bear,
Rising erect in her fury, by his wonder-working power,
Amidships stood, while forward they saw the lion lour,
Terrible. Then to sternward they huddled, shuddering,
Around the righteous steersman. But, with a sudden spring,
The lion seized the captain; and the crew, all mad to flee
That evil end, plunged headlong into the sacred sea
And changed at once to dolphins. But, apart from all the rest,
On the helmsman the God took pity, and held him back, and blessed:
'Courage, thou noble heart! I am well pleased with thee.
But *I* am Dionysus, the Lord of Revel—he
Whom Zeus begot on Cadmus' child, His own loved Sémele.'

Son of fair Sémele, farewell! No man shall raise
Sweet song, save he remember to yield thee too thy praise.

SEMONIDES OF AMORGOS
(*c.* 600 B.C.)

Semōnides 'of Amorgos' (in the Cýclades), so called to distinguish
him from his greater namesake, Simōnides of Ceos, was by birth a

Samian and took part in colonizing Amorgos about 600 B.C. His iambics provide an early example of the satire that attacks, not individuals like the lampoons of Archílochus, but a whole class or type. Characteristically, he here takes for his subject (like Juvenal, Chaucer, Dunbar, Skelton, Pope, and so many others) that eternal topic—woman. It is, indeed, curious that satire—not wholly to our credit—seems a verse-form almost exclusively cultivated by men; though perhaps men might retort that women make up for this in conversation—not to mention novels like Jane Austen's.

Women

God from the first created diversely
The minds of women. One from a bristly sow
He made, within whose house the goods and chattels
Lie filthy, tumbling higgledy-piggledy,
While she, the slattern, dressed in dirty clothes
Sits in her muck and fattens.
  Another kind, God made from a vicious vixen—
Omniscient. There's nothing, good or bad,
Escapes *her* comprehension.
Evil she'll twist to good, and good to evil,
Just as, from day to day, the whimsy takes her.
  Another has a dog's soul—nimble mongrel,
That needs must know all, hear all, everywhere
Nosing, and scurrying, and giving tongue,
Though none be there to bark at. Nothing stops her,
Not threats, not gentleness—not though in rage
One lifted up a stone and dashed her teeth out.
Even as guest, sitting at others' tables,
Still, unabashed, she plies her futile yapping.
  Then there's another sort the Olympians made
From simple clay—a half-wit, knowing nothing—
Nor good, nor bad—all that *she* understands
Is eating—*that* apart, she has not sense,
In the depth of the worst winter God can send,
Although she's shivering, to pull near the fire.
  Another was created from the sea,
Two persons in one body—one day laughing,
So gay that any stranger seeing her
At home, will sing her praises—'Never woman

So sweet in all the world, so lovable!'
Let a day pass—and she's insufferable,
To come near or to look at; in a frenzy,
Like a bitch with puppies, snapping at everyone,
To friend and foe a universal shrew.
Just as the sea will often lie so calm
And gentle—sheer delight to all that sail it—
Through summer days; and no less often rages
In a convulsion of deep-thundering breakers.
Nothing in all the world's so like such women.

    Another's made from a dusty, stubborn ass
That only blows and endless objurgation
Can make consent to labour.
And all the while, day long, night long, she eats—
Eats at the table, eats in a private corner.
In love, no less, she is omnivorous.
Greedy to grasp whatever lover comes. . . .

    Another's born of a dainty, long-maned filly,
Shying away from trouble and drudgery—
Never ask *her* to grind flour, or to finger
Dishes, or empty slops.
As for an oven—lest a smut fall on her,
She'll not go near it. *Her* love's tyranny.
Never a day but twice or thrice she washes,
And daubs herself with perfume; and her hair,
Flows deep, smooth-combed, all shaded o'er with flowers.
A lovely thing to look at, such a woman,
For other men; but a curse to him that has her—
Unless he be a king or a dictator,
To glorify his fancy with such toys.

    Then there's the ape. *She* is, beyond compare,
The deadliest pest of all that Zeus has sent us—
A sort of woman that's so foul to look at,
She's the laughter of the town, as she goes by—
Short-necked, and wooden-jointed; limbs like sticks,
And skimpy-hipped—poor miserable man,
That has this monster for a bed-fellow!
But every trick she knows, and every cunning,
Just like an ape—she cares not who may laugh.
She does no kindnesses, her only thought,
Her study, all day long, is simply this—
To vent her utmost malice.

53

Last there's the bee—and lucky he that finds her!
For she alone is a woman without reproach
And in her hands life blossoms and bears fruit.
Beloved and loving, she grows old beside
Her husband, mother of children fair and honoured;
Her name shines out among all womankind,
And on her ways a grace lies, like the Gods'. . . .

A man can gain no prize on earth that's better
Than a good woman, nor grislier than a bad.

(Diehl, i, p. 248.)

CLEOBULUS OF LINDUS?
(6th century B.C.)

Cleobūlus of Lindus in Rhodes, perhaps a Carian by birth, was counted among the 'Seven Sages'. A fragment of Simōnides reproaches him for impiously comparing in this poem the duration of a mere mortal monument with that of the eternal forces of Nature.

Midas' Tomb

Here, a maiden of bronze, I stand on Midas' grave,
And as long as runs the water, as long as tall trees wave,
As long as the sun, to light us, and the bright moon mount the sky,
As rivers flow, and the breakers along their beaches cry,
Beside this tomb of sorrow my shape its vigil keeps,
To tell the traveller passing, that here King Midas sleeps.

(*Homeri Opera*, ed. T. W. Allen, v, p. 157.)

ALCAEUS OF MYTILENE
(born *c.* 620 B.C.)

Alcaeus was a Lesbian aristocrat, driven into fifteen years of exile by his political opponents, whose extreme democracy, as so often in history, tended to throw up dictators. Finally his enemy Pittăcus, before laying down his power in 580 B.C., forgave the poet and allowed him to return home. A great fighter (though, like Archílochus, he once threw away his shield and wrote a poem about it) and a great hater, he took for his main themes love, wine, and war. But most of his work is lost, and his chief memorial remains that Alcaic stanza which Horace was to adopt in many of his finest odes. With Alcaeus the lyric becomes as passionately personal as elegy and iambus had been in the hands of Archílochus; but here, for us, he is overshadowed by his contemporary and country-woman, Sappho.

The Footsteps of Spring

The flowery spring—I heard her, coming upon her way.
A bowl of honey-sweet wine! And mix it fast as ye may.

(Diehl, 1, p. 431.)

To his Brother in the Service of Nebuchadnezzar

Homeward from earth's far ends thou art returned
With gold-and-ivory swordhilt—ay, and well
By service to thy comrades *that* was earned,
The men of Babylon; who saw thee quell
So stout a champion, in single fight.
Of five royal cubits, in his giant height,
    But one span short he fell.

(p. 412.)

A Country's Greatness

It is not streets where proud-roofed mansions stand,
Nor masonry of ramparts deftly planned,
    It is not dockland, quay, or jetty,
    That, in themselves, can make a city—
But *men*, with hearts to use what comes to hand.

(J. M. Edmonds, *Lyra Graeca*, 1, p. 339.)

SAPPHO OF MYTILENE
(born *c.* 610 B.C.)

Yea, they shall say, earth's womb has borne in vain
New things, and never this best thing again;
Borne days and men, borne fruit and wars and wine,
Seasons and songs, but no song more like mine.

Swinburne, *Anactoria*.

Like Alcaeus, Sappho—or Psapho—belonged to the aristocratic party in Lesbos; and like him suffered exile, perhaps in Sicily. One of her poems reproached her brother Chăraxus because in Egypt he fell into the toils of the courtesan Rhŏdōpis or Dōricha, whom he ransomed and married (see the epigram on p. 140); though she afterwards forgave him. On the other hand later stories of her own vain passion for Phăon, which drove her to hurl herself from the Leucadian headland, seem pure myth. She appears on the contrary to have married and had a daughter Kleïs, 'fair as the golden flowers, dearer to me than all the Lydian land'. Tradition makes Sappho herself small, dark, and not beautiful.

That towards other women she felt passions perhaps in her eyes 'passing the love of men', has given rise, like the similar background of Shakespeare's *Sonnets*, to much learned cant and hysteria. In some Greek communities feelings of this kind were accepted and honoured; if modern psychology knows better the danger of such departures from the normal, that is no reason for trying, like many modern scholars, to garble the plain language of the past.

Sappho remains a supreme example of the Greek gift, so lamentably rare today, of combining subtlety and simplicity, plainness and dignity, in a style so tense, yet terse, as to defy the translator. It rings as naturally as the spoken word—yet here are words such as few lips ever spoke. Perhaps its nearest modern counterparts are to be found in some lyrics of Musset, Heine, Christina Rossetti, and A. E. Housman. It may recall, too, that natural grace of language which has enabled some women (like Dorothy Osborne, for instance, or Julie de Lespinasse) to write better letters, even when they could not spell, than far greater male masters of literature. True, Sappho's poetry is as narrow as it is intense; her one subject is love; none the less her poems remain, in the phrase of Meleāger, 'few—but roses'.

Like the 'Alcaic', the 'Sapphic' stanza has become familiar through the odes of Horace; it has even been one of the few Greek metrical forms to bear, in some degree, transplantation into English, in the hands, not indeed of Isaac Watts or Canning, but of Swinburne.

To Aphrodite

Aphrodite, daughter of Zeus, undying
Goddess, throned in glory, of love's beguilements,
Do not now with frenzy and desperation
    Utterly crush me.

Hear and come!—if ever before Thou heardest
Cry of mine, that called from afar Thy succour;
Then, in haste, with chariot swiftly harnessed,
    Forth from the golden

Hall of Zeus Thy father, to me Thou camest—
Then Thy lovely sparrows from Heaven swept Thee
O'er the dark-loamed earth, through the ether beating
    Swift wings together.

Fast they brought Thee hither; and Thou, most blessed,
With a smile of heavenly lips didst ask me,
What it was I suffered; and why I called Thee
    Hither to aid me.

'Tell me what it *is*, then, that most thou cravest,
Heart so full of madness?—who *is* it, Sappho,
Passion must awake to desire and love thee?
    Who is it wrongs thee?

'For, although she shun thee, she soon shall seek thee;
Though she scorn thy presents, herself shall bring them;
Though she love thee not, yet she soon shall love thee!—
    Yea, though she would not.'

Come again today, then, as once Thou camest.
Save my soul from sorrow, that grows too bitter—
Grant my heart's desiring—be Thou my helper,
    Thou, Aphrodite!

                    (Diehl, 1, p. 325.)

The Beloved

Him I hold as happy as God in Heaven,
Who can sit and gaze on your face before him,
Who can sit and hear from your lips that sweetest
    Music they utter—

Hear your lovely laughter, that sets a-tremble
All my heart with flutterings wild as terror.
For, when I behold you an instant, straightway
    All my words fail me;

Helpless halts my tongue; a devouring fever
Runs in flame through every vein within me;
Darkness veils my vision; my ears are deafened,
    Beating like hammers;

Cold the sweat runs down me; a sudden trembling
Sets my limbs a-quiver; my face grows paler
Than the grass in summer; I see before me
    Death stand, and madness.

(p. 327.)

The Lost Friend

Atthis, our own loved Anactória
In Sardis dwells afar,
And yet, there too, of us her memories are;

Recalling other days—how once you were,
To her, divinely fair,
And with your song no singing could compare.

Now among Lydia's daughters that dear head
Shines, as when day is fled
The risen moon, with fingers rosy-red,

Outshines the stars, and flings her glory wide
Across the salt sea-tide,
Across the many-flowered countryside,

While fair her dew falls on the flowering rose,
And where soft anthrysc grows,
And where in bloom the melilōtus blows.

Yet, Atthis, still, of *you* her memories wake,
Where'er she goes, and make
That gentle heart grow heavy for your sake.

'Come back!' she cries. We know. For many be
The ears of Night; and She
Brings us that cry across the sundering sea.

(p. 371.)

To a Rich Uncultured Woman

Dead you shall lie, for ever, a name that none recall;
  For never you gathered roses upon the Muses' tree.
Dim as you were in living, there too in Hades' hall
  You shall drift where only phantoms faint and forgotten flee.

(p. 354.)

Forsaken

Moon 's set, and Pleiads;
  Midnight goes by;
The hours pass onward;
  Lonely I lie.

(p. 368.)

Lost Heart

I cannot, sweetest mother,
  My loom I cannot mind;
Delicate Aphrodite
  With longing leaves me blind.

(p. 376.)

The Maid Unwed

As the sweet apple reddens, high up against the sky,
High on the highest branch, where the pickers passed it by,
Forgetting—ah, no, not forgetting—they never could reach so high.

(p. 376.)

Lost Maidenhead

As the hyacinth high on the mountains under the shepherds' tread
Lies trampled, and to earthward bows down its purple head. . . .

(p. 377.)

Evensong

All things thou bringest, Hesper, that the bright Dawn did part—
Sheep and goat to the fold, and the child to the mother's heart.

(p. 378.)

SOLON OF ATHENS

(c. 640–c. 560 B.C.)

Apart from drama (and prose-poetry like some of Plato's) the Athenians seem to have been less gifted poetically—though we are so dazzled by the other brilliance of Athens that no one apparently dares to say so—than many smaller and obscurer Greek cities. Attica produced few non-dramatic poets besides Solon; and even Solon is a rather prosaic poet. His poetry is nearly all politics; as the poetry of that other supposed Athenian, Tyrtaeus, is nearly all military. At that early date Solon had no choice but to write in verse. But it is fair to add that few politicians have written poems even as good as Solon's.

His birth was noble. He is said to have nerved his discouraged countrymen to renew their efforts to drive the Megarians from Salamis, the island at the very gates of Peiraeus, by a poem of which part is given below. He certainly in his archonship of 594 B.C. brought back some political and economic justice to his troubled city. But, like most moderates, he displeased extremists on either wing; and, after vainly warning Athens of the growing threat of despotism, the old statesman who had disdained to make himself dictator died under the dictatorship of Pisistratus.

In temper Solon of Athens remains closer to Hēsiod in the neighbouring Boeotia than to most other poets before him; he shows the same practical morality, the same passion for justice. But the finest of his works was his life.

The Shame of Losing Salamis

Why, then, let Phōlegandros or Síkinos be my city,
    Not Athens! Be my country some other land than this!
For now through all the world our shame shall make men witty—
    'This is an Attic fellow, beaten from Salamis.'

(Diehl, 1, p. 21.)

The Rise of Dictatorship

As on the fiery lightning followeth the thunder,
    As from the cloudrack comes the driving hail and snow,
From men of power comes a city's ruin; so it falls under
    A despot—by their folly its folk to bondage go.
Once a man is exalted, hard he grows to restrain.
Already the time is on ye to see that issue plain.

(p. 28.)

THEOGNIS OF MEGARA
(c. 540 B.C.)

A complete contrast to the enlightened liberal Solon is the embittered conservative Theognis, from the adjacent city of Mégara on the Isthmus of Corinth. But if Theognis was a smaller man, he was a better poet. Like Alcaeus and Sappho, he too was driven out by democrats to taste the bitter bread of exile. He typifies indeed the recurrent tragedy of the aristocratic landowner fighting a lost battle against the new money-makers in trade and industry; of the gentleman outdated by the parvenu. In Chekhov or Galsworthy, after twenty-four centuries, the same conflict is still there; but the political hatred of Theognis has a passion of bitterness such as England, happily, has seldom even conceived.[1]

Nor were his private passions happier. His poems to his loved squire, Cyrnus, show as agonized an alternation of affection and resentment, admiration and scorn, as the Sonnets of Shakespeare.

It is not surprising to find the philosophy of such a man darkening into pessimism—anguish at youth's passing, loathing for the relentless inroads of old age, fury at the lack of loyalty or justice in the world. At moments, he might be Byron (without the humour), or Baudelaire (without the decadence). It is easy to understand why this sombre, yet indomitable aristocrat should have deeply appealed to Nietzsche.

But, after all, whatever such violence of passion may do to a man's happiness, it can be the lifeblood of poetry, when it goes with a sense of beauty—such as Theognis shows in passages like his description of the nativity of Apollo, where he even, for once, forgets himself. Theognis remains a minor poet; but no other Greek poetry, before or after him (except perhaps Palladas), achieves quite the same power of bitterness.[2] Perhaps his nearest counterpart is, at moments, a poet of our own century, A. E. Housman:

> Ay, look: high heaven and earth ail from the prime foundation;
>   All thoughts to rive the heart are here, and all in vain:
> Horror and scorn and hate and fear and indignation—
>   Oh why did I awake? when shall I sleep again?

---

[1] Cf. the comment of a Greek officer on hearing of the 1945 election results—'I suppose Churchill has taken to the hills?'

[2] Criticism is complicated by the intrusion of other poets' work in the collection that bears his name.

The Soldier

See from yon looming summit the beacon, Cyrnus, beckon,
  Like to a tongueless herald, that tells of tearful war.
Get our swift steeds bridled—little the time, I reckon,
  Before the ranks of foemen shall bar the path before.
Soon they will be upon us—they lie not far behind,
Unless the Gods in Heaven have left my judgment blind.

(ll. 549–54.)

The Wanderer

I have travelled to Euboea and her plains with vineyards growing,
  I have travelled, in times past over, to the shores of Sicily,
And to glorious Lacedaemon, and seen Eurōtas flowing
  Amid his reeds; most noble was their hospitality.
And yet, for all their kindness, no gladness filled my breast:
So true it was that all men must love their own land best.

(783–8.)

The Refugee

I heard, O Polypāïdes, I heard the bird's shrill crying,
  That comes to tell the tiller that time has come to plough,
And it stabbed the dark heart in me, to think my lands are lying,
  My flowered fields, in keeping of other masters now;
That no team of mine goes straining against the yoke today,
Since by its cursed pilots our city's cast away.

(1197–1202.)

Against the Demos

Now to my prayer in season, O Zeus of Olympus, hearken!
  After so many evils, give me some good again.
Let me die, if I find no respite, amid my days that darken,
  If I cannot avenge me, and pay back pain for pain.
This were but just. Yet of justice upon these evil-doers,
  What sign, though they keep the riches that from my hands they tore?
The robbers! Poor as a hound I have fled from my pursuers—
  All, in the torrent's fury, I lost ere I came to shore.
Ah, could I drink their dark-red blood! Could some just power
Govern it so, and grant me, at last, to have my hour!

(341–50.)

An Eye for an Eye

Now fall the height of Heaven in headlong ruin above me,
　　Where it hangs its brazen menace above the heads of men,
If I give not love and helping to all the hearts that love me,
　　And to all that hate I give not havoc and hate again!

(869–72.)

Vendetta

Speak fair to him that hates thee, till he falls in thy hand at last,
Then linger not for reasons, but pay him for the past.

(363–4.)

Poverty

Whatever the worth of a man, yet poverty can bring him
　　Lower than burning ague, or grey senility.
Sooner than bear it, Cyrnus, better a man should fling him
　　From crags that no foot can clamber, or down the gulfs of sea.
He dare not do a deed, he cannot utter sound,
Once penury has chained him. His very tongue lies bound.

(173–8.)

Friendlessness

The exile has never a friend of loyal and steadfast will;
Bitter enough is exile; but *this* is bitterer still.

(209–10.)

Plutocracy

In most men's eyes one virtue, alone, is worth endeavour—
　　Riches. It seems that nothing, save this, shall profit us!
Vain to be self-controlled as Rhădamanthys, clever
　　As Sīsyphus aforetime, that son of Aeŏlus
Who came back even from Hades by his wisdom, and persuaded
　　By the cunning of his speeches even Persephone,
That dims men's minds with Lethe, till their memory hath faded—
　　Never another mortal devised such subtlety,

63

Once the dark cloud of Death around his head had risen
  And he reached the land of shadows, that the souls of the perished fill,
Beyond those dark-blue portals which evermore imprison
  The wraiths of the departed, so sore against their will.
Yet Sīsyphus the hero even from thence ascended
  Back to the light of the sun, so much his wise heart knew.
But vain is it now to be gifted with skill in speech as splendid
  As was the godlike Nestor's, that made false things seem true;
Vain, though thy speed in the race leave the Harpies overtaken
  And outrun Boreas' sons, winged feet through the heavens hurled.
This truth let all mankind henceforward trust unshaken—
  Gold it is that holds now dominion through the world.

                                            (699–718.)

Eugenics

A ram or a stallion, Cyrnus, of good stock each man chooses,
  Or an ass for siring—we seek the purest race
For *cattle*! But, in marriage, not our noblest now refuses,
  If gold enough goes with her, the base child of the base.
Now an ignoble lover by never a girl is dreaded,
  So he be rich—the wealthy, and not the good, must speed.
Money it is, men worship. The honourable have wedded
  The mean, and the mean the noble. Wealth has confounded breed.
Wonder no more, my Cyrnus, if the blood of our city still
Degenerates, when good things are thus confused with ill.

                                            (183–92.)

Race

Ne'er yet from the root of a squill did rose or hyacinth wave;
Nor came a son of freedom from out the womb of a slave.

                                            (537–8.)

Critics

Pass with all men's approval through life to Hades' portals
  None can—none ever could, of all that have come to birth.
Not even He that reigns o'er mortals and Immortals,
  Zeus, the son of Crŏnus, can please all men on earth.

                                            (801–4.)

'Hurler avec les Loups'

Among the mad, none madder; and in the company
Of the virtuous, for virtue there is no man like me.

(313–14.)

Protective Colouring

Be like the twisted polyp that coiling round a boulder
    Takes the rock's own colour, whatever hue it be;
So change thine own complexion to humour each beholder.
    Better by far is cunning than steadfast constancy.

(215–18.)

Loyalty

'I loathe a man that's evil. My face in my veil I'll cover
    And pass him by as lightly as a bird flies from the snare.'
'I hate a gadding woman, I hate a wanton lover
    That in another's acre would thrust his own ploughshare.'

(579–82.)

The Beloved

To thee, my love, for ever I have given wings to raise thee
    To fly the wide world over, to cross the infinite sea,
Swift as a thought: laid lightly on the lips of men that praise thee
    At every feast and revel in the midst thou too shalt be.
And youths in the flower of their beauty, to the flute's clear voice replying
    With voices as clear and lovely, in order due shall sing
Of thee; and when thou goest to that place of bitter crying,
    Deep in earth's abysses, where Hades sits as king,
Not even in death shall thy glory fade, thy memory wither,
    Thou shalt not lie forgotten, not even in the grave;
Through Greece, through the Isles, my Cyrnus, thou shalt wander,
        hither, thither,
    Journeying for ever o'er the tireless, teeming wave;
Riding, but not upon horses. Not steeds, but the glorious guerdon
    Of the Muses shall bear thee onward, the Violet-garlanded;
All that love *them* hereafter, shall make *thy* name the burden
    Of a song that sounds for ever, till earth and sun be dead.
And yet for all this, my Cyrnus, I am nothing in thine eyes!
Shameless, thou hast deceived me, like a little child, with lies.

(237–54.)

The False One

Now at his hour Love rises, while all the earth is springing,
   Springing into blossom with all the flowers of May.
Out of lovely Cyprus, Love comes and wanders flinging
   His seed in hearts of menfolk through all the world away.
Alas! Love came and whispered to thee of me, and bade
That thou shouldst turn elsewhither and leave my love betrayed.

                                   (1275–78B.)

The Adder

Thou hast stolen again—I know it—on the path thy feet did follow
   Before this, in thy falsehood, our old love to forsake.
Begone!—by all Gods hated, by all men known for hollow—
   Thou whom I clasped to my bosom, a cold and spotted snake.

                                   (599–602.)

Love's Blindness

When two men hate, my Cyrnus, they find traps hard to lay:
But a lover finds a lover a trifle to betray.

                                   (1219–20.)

The Broken Chain

I love the lad no longer; I have spurned my bitter sadness;
   I am escaped rejoicing from the toils of misery.
The fair-crowned Cytherēa has delivered me from madness;
   Boy, thou art fair no longer, no longer fair to me.

                                   (1337–40.)

'Cherchez Fortune Ailleurs'

I drank at a spring, time was, where dark the water bubbled;
   Sweet it seemed to my lips, and fair to my eye its gleam.
But now some foot has befouled it, with mud it lies all troubled;
   Another fount I must find me, drink from another stream.

                                   (959–62.)

'Vive hodie'

Now is the time to surrender our hearts to merry-making,
  While life's fair things can give us a joy that is not vain.
For the glory of youth goes by us, swift as a thought, o'ertaking
  Even the speed of steeds whose charging hoofs amain
Whirl some king in his car to the press of the spear-fought fray,
Over the young green furrows, exulting on their way.

(983–8.)

Dust to Dust

Make merry, heart within me. Others shall come to birth
So soon, and I be lying but blackened earth in earth.

(877–8.)

The Years

'Alas for grim old age! Alas for youth!' I cry—
The one so swift departing, the other drawing nigh.

(527–8.)

The Problem

Dear Zeus, at Thy ways I wonder. For all that live adore Thee,
  The power to Thee, and the glory, all mankind accord:
There is not a heart, not a thought, but stands revealed before Thee;
  There standeth no dominion to match with Thine, O Lord.
How then can Thy wisdom look in so indifferent fashion
  On those whose deeds are evil, and who deal righteously?—
Whether a man refrain his heart; or sate his passion
  In works of overweening and iniquity?

(373–80.)

Despair

Not to be born at all is the happiest lot for mortal,
  Never to open eyelids on the bright shafts of the sun:
Or, born, as soon as may be to pass beyond Death's portal,
  To pull earth's heavy mantle above him and have done.

(425–8.)

The Stoic

What is my fate to suffer, my Cyrnus, knows no cure:
What is my fate to suffer, I fear not to endure.

(817–18.)

Nativity

Lord Phoebus, when our Lady, the gracious Lēto, bore Thee
    Beside the round mere's margin, when Thou camest from her womb,
While her slim hands clasped the palm-tree, all Dēlos to adore Thee,
    Fairest of the Immortals, grew fragrant with perfume,
Ambrosial, passing measure—then laughed the endless earth
And the deep seas' hoary surges made answer in their mirth.

(5–10.)

IBYCUS OF RHEGIUM
(mid 6th century B.C.)

Íbycus of Rhēgium in southern Italy later removed to the court of Poly-
crates in Samos. Only fragments of his work survive; but his ancient
reputation was based on the grace and fire of his love-lyrics. A legend,
retold in Schiller's poem, related that he was murdered by robbers and
called, as he died, for vengeance to a flight of cranes winging overhead;
the robbers repaired to the theatre at Corinth and one of them, seeing
cranes pass over, whispered to his fellow: 'The cranes of Íbycus!'—an
indiscretion which brought the guilty pair to summary justice.

Passion without Respite

Only in spring do the quince-flowers quiver
Blossoming deep in the garden-close
Sacred to maidenhood, where from the river
Many a quickening channel flows;
Only in spring do the vine-flowers throng
Under the leaves; but all year long
No rest my passion knows.
Sent by the Cyprian (as from the north
Headlong the Thracian tempest breaks,

While from its gloom the lightnings shoot),
Raving it smites me in its wrath,
Shrivelling all—to the very root
My heart it shakes.

(Diehl, II, p. 53.)

HIPPONAX OF EPHESUS
(c. 540 B.C.)

Little remains of one who seems to have been a sort of Villon, consorting with outcasts and criminals, and adapting their slang to his verse. One authority credits him with the invention of parody. He certainly did invent what was called 'the lame iambic' (*scazon*) with a dragging close of three long syllables. Clearly, like Donne, he wished to fit harsh sound to harsh sense.

Misogynist

Two days a woman's best—the day she's wed,
The day she's carried from your doorway—dead.

(Diehl, I, p. 302.)

Economy

Out of the jug we drank; there was no cup
(The boy fell down on that and smashed it up).

(p. 272.)

Pugilist

Take my overcoat and hold it—I 'll hit Būpalus in the eye.
Ambidexterous I am; and so I never aim awry.

(p. 283.)

PHOCYLIDES OF MILETUS
(c. 540 B.C.)

A writer of verse aphorisms, who may perhaps claim to be one of the founders of the epigram in its modern sense—a short poem with a point.

'In Huts where Poor Men Lie'

This said Phocýlides, also; where men live lawfully,
Better a crag-built township, than follies of Nineveh.

(Diehl, 1, p. 49.)

The Exception that proves the Rule

The Lĕrians are evil; all!—and not just a few—
All except only Prŏcles. And Prŏcles is Lĕrian too!

(p. 48.)

ANACREON OF TEOS
(*c.* 570–*c.* 485 B.C.)

Anácreon, though most famous for poems he never wrote—imitations ranging from the Alexandrian to the Byzantine period (see p. 156), has become the prototype of Epicurean poets such as La Fontaine and Herrick. In him the decadence of Ionia, already visible in Mimnermus, has gone further still. Liberty has given place to foreign invader and domestic tyrant; the old energy and daring have died away; rosebuds remain. In the words of Landor:

> But where the land is dim from tyranny,
> There tiny pleasures occupy the place
> Of glories and of duties; as the feet
> Of fabled fairies, when the sun goes down
> Trip o'er the grass where wrestlers strove by day.

At courts like those of Polýcrates in Samos, or Hipparchus in Athens, Anácreon surrendered himself to a graceful frivolity that gaily defied the years. He had fought in youth and, like Archílochus and Alcaeus, had written a poem on losing his shield; but now he turned from Ares to Aphrodite and Dionysus, to become the poet of love, wine, and humorous old age—a character well symbolized in the legend that he died at eighty-five by choking with a grape-pip.

The Coy Mistress

Thracian filly, why so heartless? Why, so shyly sidelong glancing,
  Hold me ever at a distance, like a fool with wit untried?

I could clap a bridle on ye, very well, for all your prancing;
  Down the course I well could rein ye, make ye wheel the way I guide.
Yet a while, across the pastures, go your ways with light feet dancing—
  You have still to find the master that shall curb ye and shall ride.

(Diehl, I, p. 470.)

War's Folly

Timócritus fought well. This is his grave.
For Ares spares the coward; and not the brave.

(Anthologia Palatina, VII, 160.)

XENOPHANES OF COLOPHON
(*c.* 565–470 B.C.)

With Xenóphanes, though himself a poet as well as a philosopher,
begins the long war of philosophy against poetry. Here he is a forerunner
of Plato and Tolstoy. Born at Cólophon in Asia Minor, then driven by
the Persian invader to migrate to South Italy and Sicily, the old sage
speaks of having tossed his thoughts up and down Hellas for seventy
years. A monotheist and doubter of the senses, he was counted the founder
of the Eleatic School continued by Parménides, a profounder thinker
but worse poet.

Wickedness of Poets

Homer and Hēsiod fathered on the Gods' divinity
All deeds most blameful and shameful that here on earth there be—
Yea, thieving and deceiving and adultery.

(Diehl, I, p. 58.)

Anthropomorphism

If oxen, or lions, or horses had hands like men, they too,
If they could fashion pictures, or statues they could hew,
They would shape in their own image each face and form divine—
Horses' gods like horses, like kine the gods of kine.
'Snub-nosed are the Immortals, and black,' the Ethiops say;
But 'No,' the Thracians answer; 'red-haired, with eyes of grey.'

(p. 58.)

The Agnostic

Of the Gods and these other matters none knows the verity—
No man that lived before us, no man that yet shall be.
However full-perfected the system he hath made,
Its maker knoweth nothing. With fancy all's o'erlaid.

(p. 62.)

Rainbow

She, too, whom men call 'Iris' is but a mist in the skies,
That shimmers green, and scarlet, and purple in men's eyes.

(p. 62.)

Athleticism

Now if a man shall show him in speed of foot the faster
  On that ground to Zeus made holy, where the fount of Pisa flows
Through Olympia, or at wrestling shall prove himself the master,
  Or at the pentathlon, or the boxer's bitter blows,
Or from the grim pancration shall rise a winner,
  He seems in the eyes of his city more splendid than before;
His to eat henceforward at the public cost his dinner
  And a gift from the public treasure shall go to increase his store;
His the seat of honour at every celebration—
  And as richly is *he* rewarded whose coursers take the prize,
Though less in worth than *I* am! For of nobler estimation
  Than the strength of men or horses is the wisdom of the wise. . . .
Nay, though a man shall conquer beside the banks of Pisa,
  Small cause to be glad his city shall gain from such as he;
From the curses of disorder no such triumph frees her,
  That cannot fill the coffers of her treasury.

(p. 55.)

HYBRIAS THE CRETAN
(6th or early 5th century B.C.?)

The Freelance

My golden hoard is spear and sword
And the bull's-hide shield I bear before me;

72

With these I plough and reap my bread,
And sweet wine from the grape I tread;
These make my slaves as lord adore me.

But they that fear good sword and spear
And bear no bull's-hide shield before them—
Louting low on bended knee,
These must salute my majesty—
As King of Kings I lord it o'er them.

(Diehl, II, p. 128.)

HYMN TO PAN
(5th century B.C.?)

Though included among the 'Homeric Hymns', this piece is generally
believed not earlier than the fifth century B.C., when the worship of Pan,
originally a local Arcadian God, became more widely spread—witness
the legend that during the Persian invasion of 490 the famous runner
Pheidippides, sent by Athens to hasten Spartan aid, was met returning
across Mount Parthénius, near Tégea, by Pan himself, who asked why
the Athenians did not worship him, and promised his help in the coming
fight. This promise Pan kept at Marathon by casting on the Persians that
'panic' terror with which he can fill the lonely wanderer in the silence
of the hills; as Wordsworth knew:

> I heard among the solitary hills
> Low breathings coming after me and sounds
> Of indistinguishable motions, steps
> Almost as silent as the turf they trod.

Hymn to Pan

Of the dear son of Hermes, O Muse, sing now to me,
That goat-foot, hornéd lover of ringing revelry,
Who wanders the woodland valleys, while his lightfoot Nymphs dance
    round;
Where never a goat can clamber, along the crags they bound,
Calling to Pan, the shepherd-god, with shout and song—
Pan of the glorious locks unkempt, to whom belong

73

All peaks, all snowy summits, all stony mountain-ways.
Through the tangled brakes of the forest, now here, now there, he
    strays—
Sometimes the rivers lure him down to their gentle flow,
Sometimes he turns to scramble, by rocks where none may go,
Up to a towering hilltop, to see where his sheep may lie;
Often the long white ridges behold him hurrying by,
Often with keen, wild glances he scours the upland glen,
Tracking his prey; and returning from his chase in the twilight then
On the reeden pipe of a shepherd he plays his music lone—
No nightingale can utter a strain of lovelier tone,
When in the flowery springtime, perched amid many a leaf,
With notes as sweet as honey she trills her song of grief.
Then round him the lilting voices of the Nymphs of the mountain
    ring,
As by the dark-black water, bubbling from a spring,
Their light feet trip, and the echoes, high from the hilltop, call.
But the God, with his twinkling steps, through their dances leads them
    all,
Now through the midst of them whirling, now this, now the other
    side,
Rapt by the music, and wearing a reddish lynx's hide;
Soft round them lies the forest-lawn and, perfumed sweet,
The hyacinth blends, and the crocus, with the grass beneath their feet.
But the song of the Oreads tells of the blessed Gods on high
And of the long-ridged Olympus; and, above the rest, they cry
The praise of the Gods' fleet herald, of Hermes swift to aid,
And how of old to Cyllēne, to his sacred woodland's shade,
In Arcadia, mother of flocks, land of fair springs, he sped
And there that son of Heaven the sheep of a mortal fed;
For now a tender longing in his heart had come to flower
For Dryops' fair-tressed daughter. The lover found his hour;
And so in her home for Hermes she brought a dear son to birth,
Twy-hornèd and goat-footed, a lover of noisy mirth—
So monstrous, that his mother, dropping him, fled afeared
From the sight of those grim features, that bristled with a beard.
But quickly Hermes the Helper lifted him where he lay
And owned his son; and within him the heart of the God grew gay.
Then Heavenward in haste he turned, wrapping the child
Warm in the furry skin of a hare of the mountain-wild,
And took his seat in Olympus and showed his little lad
To Zeus and the other Immortals—and all of them grew glad,

But most of all Dionysus delighted in the boy.
So 'Pan' was the name they gave him, since he filled 'ALL' Heaven with
    joy.

Farewell, O Lord, I have brought Thee prayer alike and praise;
And I will sing thy glories, anew, in coming days.

SIMONIDES OF CEOS
(c. 556–467 B.C.)

During his long career Simōnides of Ceos (in the Cýclades, off Attica)
wrote both elegiac and lyric poetry. He was patronized by various ruling
personages—Hipparchus at Athens, the Scópadae in Thessaly (until
their banquet-hall fell on their impious heads), and Híero at Syracuse;
but he was also a friend of the democrat Themistŏcles. Ancient tradition
accused him of avarice—which probably means merely that, like Shakespeare, he was a business-like poet. On the other hand he was especially
famous for his power of pathos, so that for Catullus the extremity of
sorrow is something 'sadder than the tears of Simōnides'. That quality
is illustrated by his song of Dánaë; but even here, and still more in his
epigrams, the restraint is not less intense than the sorrow. With Aeschylus
(whom he is said to have defeated in a contest for the best epigram on the
dead of Marathon), Simōnides remains the most representative Greek
poet of the great period of the Persian Wars.

Dánaë Adrift

*Acrisius, king of Argos, was warned by the Delphic oracle that if his daughter
Dánaë had a son, that son would kill him. He therefore shut her up in a tower of
brass; but Zeus loved her, and descended into her room in a shower of gold.
Acrisius then set his daughter and the infant Perseus adrift in a coffer: but they
were cast ashore on the isle of Seríphos. Perseus grew up, killed the Gorgon
Medusa, saved Andrómeda from the sea-monster, and at the funeral-games for
Polydectes, king of Seríphos, accidentally killed his grandfather with a discus
that he threw.*

When she was set in her carven chest,
Whirled by the wind from crest to crest
    Of heaving sea,
On Dánaë's heart fell horror—her tears began to run
And babe to breast the mother pressed, crying 'O little son,
    For me is misery,

75

But thou, my innocent one—
Calmly thou sleepest; and nought to thee
This brass-nailed chest of woe;
Nought is the starless midnight, nought is the dark-blue gloom
Of the wave that welters by us and flings its driving spume
Upon thy curls below;
Nought is the sea-wind's wailing—so soft thy face is laid
On mine, within the purple of my mantle fast asleep.
Nay, terror has no terror, for *thee*—else how dismayed
Thy little ears would listen, to hear thy mother weep!
Sleep on, my babe; sleep, restless sea; sleep, boundless ill
That breaks my heart! O Father, O Zeus, be it thy will
To save us and to spare.
Yet, if too bold my prayer,
If I transgress Thy justice, forgive, forgive me still!'

(Diehl, II, p. 69.)

Life's Best

Health is the best that Heaven sends;
Next, to be comely to look upon;
Third is riches, justly won;
Fourth, to be young among one's friends.

(p. 183.)

The Backbiter's Epitaph

Much I guzzled, much I tippled, and of slander many loads
I vented—now I rest here, Timócreon of Rhodes.

(p. 97.)

The Unlooked-for Bargain

Here Brótachus of Gortȳna, a Cretan born, is laid;
Who came on no such errand, with thought of nought but trade.

(p. 112.)

Lost at Sea

Thou hast but foreign earth, O Cleisthenes, to hide thee,
For Death found thee, a rover, far in the Euxine foam.
The sweetness of returning to thy country was denied thee;
Never again thou camest to sea-girt Ceos home.

(p. 111.)

76

Lost at Sea

Ah, misty Géraneia, ill crag, thou shouldst stand facing
  Where Ister, where endless Tánaïs far off through Scythia flow!—
Not here where the Sea of Scīron is white with rollers racing
  And where along the gorges of Mŏlouris swirls the snow.
Cold, cold upon thy waters he drifts; and emptily
His tomb cries here of the sorrow he found upon the sea.

(p. 89.)

The Hound's Grave

Although beneath this grave-mound thy white bones now are lying,
  Methinks, my huntress Lўcas, the wild things dread thee still.
The memory of thy deeds tall Pēlion keeps undying,
  And the looming peak of Ossa, and Cĭthaeron's lonely hill.

(p. 113.)

The Dead of Athens at Chalcis (506 B.C.)

We died in the glen of Dirphys; here by our country's giving
  This tomb was heaped above us, high on Eurīpus' shore.
'Twas earned. For young we lost the loveliness of living,
  We took instead upon us the bursting storm of war.

(p. 92.)

The Dead of Sparta at Thermópylae (480 B.C.)

Take word to Lacedaemon, passer-by,
That here obedient to their laws we lie.

(p. 94.)

The Dead of Sparta at Plataea (479 B.C.)

These men, to set a crown of ever quenchless glory
  On their dear land, cast round them Death's cloak of cloudy gloom.
Yet even in death they die not. For still their valiant story
  Lifts them again to honour, from out the House of Doom.

(p. 107.)

PINDAR OF THEBES

(c. 518–c. 438 B.C.)

Pindar was born just outside Thebes, and a charming legend tells how one day bees dropped their honey on the infant's lips (compare p. 155). Little is known of his life; but his fame covered the Greek world, from northern Macedon to southern Cyrēne. He was welcomed at the courts of Syracuse and Ácragas in the west: in the east the Rhodians are said to have inscribed one of his odes on the wall of Athena's temple in letters of gold. Even after his death, each night at Delphi, as the shrine of Apollo was closed, the spirit of the poet was summoned to dine with the god. Even a century later, in Alexander's sack of Thebes,

> The great Emathian conqueror bid spare
> The house of Pindarus, when temple and tower
> Went to the ground.

And even today he can intoxicate staid scholars into hyperboles of praise that do not always observe his own doctrine of moderation.

Of his seventeen volumes of lyrics, apart from fragments, about a quarter survives—his poems on athletic victors. This is not the section of his poetry most of us might have chosen; but, actually, it seems to have contained his best work. After all, it was the side of that life he seems most passionately to have loved.

For the translator Pindar remains one of the most impossible poets in the world. To render him literally, as Cowley says, can only give the impression that one madman has translated another. It is not merely that his music is lost; even these surviving libretti are in metres complicated beyond the resources of an accentual prosody like ours. Similarly with the style; it is enough to look at a literal prose version to see how remote from English is this strange blend of gorgeous phrases with shattering banalities, of excessive artifice with extreme simplicity of mind, of naïve personal comments with elaborate mythical allusions; which meant as much to him, no doubt, as Scripture to Milton, but mean little to us—especially as what he finds edifying often strikes us as the reverse. He tumbles intertwisted metaphors over one another like a Metaphysical poet; yet he would have loathed our Metaphysical poets, as he loathed all 'clever devils' with less in them of lion than fox. Indeed Pindar, like Spenser, shows how moderately intelligent even distinguished poets can be. At times, like Lully, 'il n'a pas le sens commun; il n'a que le génie'.

Pindar's power does not lie in the pedigrees of totally unimportant

78

athletes, or the victories of mules that lived twenty-four centuries ago, or the misbehaviour of minor deities who never lived at all. It lies in a splendour of phrase and imagery that suggests the gold and purple of a sunset sky. I can do little more than try to convey by a few brief extracts some faint reflections of that splendour.[1] The physical prowess that so inspired Pindar was a good deal more shrewdly appraised by Xenóphanes and by Euripides (compare pp. 72, 106); but in beauty of form (as in lack of profundity) he recalls, at his best, the radiant Hermes of Praxíteles, found in the ruins of that Olympia which the poet loved so well. This praiser of athletes was, curiously enough, one of the most purely aesthetic artists there have ever been. We cannot hear his music; we cannot see his dancers; but his pure poetry still lives.

The Coming of Jason to Iolcus

Pélias, after usurping the throne from his brother Aeson, was warned by the Delphic oracle to beware of a one-sandalled man. One day Aeson's son Jason, reared to manhood by the centaur Chíron in his cave on Mount Pélion above Iolcus, came down to the city to claim his father's birthright; crossing the torrent Anaurus he lost one of his sandals; and Pélias recognized in him the man of fate. That fate he delayed by persuading Jason first to seek the Golden Fleece from Colchis in the Black Sea. So from all Greece gathered the Argonauts to help him in his quest.

What was it first began their voyaging?
What adamantine nails of peril held them fast?
It was foretold to Pélias the king
He should find death at last
By the hands, or the plans unfailing, of the proud Aeólidae.
For from the navel of Earth, fair mother of many a tree,
Chill on his subtle spirit there struck the word of God—
'To far-seen, famed Iolcus shall come—then heed thy danger,
Whatever it may cost thee—from the huts of the hills a stranger
With a single sandal shod.

'Native or foreign, of him shalt thou beware!'
Years passed. And a wondrous stranger *came*, two spears in hand;
On his bright limbs he wore the garb men wear
In the Magnesian land;

---

[1] There are complete translations by, amongst others, E. Myers (1874), C. J. Billson (1928–30). L. R. Farnell (1930–2), J. E. Sandys (1937), R. Lattimore (1947). See also C. M. Bowta, *Pindar* (1964).

But over it—strange mingling—a leopard's hide was flung,
To ward the hurtling rainstorms, and on his shoulders hung,
Unshorn, his rippling tresses in their young and glorious grace.
Then he put to proof his manhood, as he strode forth, swift, untrembling,
Into the midst of the people, as there they thronged assembling
Within the market-place.

Known to no man he stood there. Yet they whispered in their awe:
'Who *is* he? Not, surely, Apollo? Nor the brazen-charioted
Lover of Aphrodite? And now, 'tis said, no more
Are the sons of Īphimĕdeia—in gleaming Naxos dead
They lie, the lordly Ōtus and Ephialtes the brave;
And Tītyus, too, the resistless shafts of Artemis have slain,
Those shafts whence nought can save,
To warn all men from longing for loves too high to gain.'

(*Pyth.*, IV, 70–92.)

The Mercenary Muse

Freely, with glorious harp in hand, of old men rode away
In the car of the gold-crowned Muses, Thrasybūlus, and let play
Their singing shafts in praise of some young face,
Upon whose comeliness the witching grace
Of fair-throned Aphrodite lay.

For then no miser was the Muse, no hireling yet was she;
Not yet were the honeyed songs of sweet Terpsíchorē
Sold in the mart, their cheeks with silver spread;
But *now* she cites that word the Argive said,
That word too full of verity—
When wealth and friends, together, from him ran,
''Tis money,' quoth he, 'money maketh man.'

(*Isthm.*, II, 1–12.)

The Magic of Melody

O golden lyre, by Apollo and the Muses violet-crowned
Alike beloved; so soon as thy quivering prelude rings,
The feet of dancers bound
In the glory of their motion, and their voices heed thy strings.
Even the warrior lightning, with his spears of quenchless flame,
Thou stillest—even the eagle of Zeus thou makest tame;
There on God's sceptre he sleeps with folded wings.

The king of birds sits drooping his crook-beaked head, his eyes
Locked in enchanted darkness, and soft the feathers o'er
His shoulders fall and rise,
To the throbbing of thy music. The very God of War
Forgets his savage spearthrusts and dreams in peace an hour—
In the Muses deep of bosom, and Apollo, lies such power
Even o'er hearts that live for evermore.

But all things that Zeus loves not, they tremble as they hearken—
On land, on the raging surges—when sing the Piérides;
Yea, Typhōs the hundred-headed, o'er whom Hell's shadows darken,
That foe of Gods, yet fears the voice of these.
Bred in the famed Cilician cave, his shaggy chest
'Neath Cyme's sea-beat headlands, now, and Sicily lies low,
And o'er him columned Etna lifts heavenward her snow,
That biting snow she nurses, year-long, on her breast.

But from her inmost caves rise vomited
Pure streams of fire approachless; like a river, all the day
Their flame-lit smoke goes swirling, all night they glare blood-red,
While on their seaward way
They roll great stones in thunder. And ever—things of dread
To see—to hear of, even—flame-fountains skyward soar
From that fell monster, fettered there outspread
Betwixt earth's floor and Etna with her dark-leaved forest-head,
While rock-jags goad his great back evermore.

(Pyth., 1, 1–28.)

Dēlos

Child of the sea, marvel of earth, made firm for aye,
That art to men
'Dēlos'—but to Olympus' Gods a star,
In earth's blue distance glittering afar.

(Prosodion; J. E. Sandys, Pindar, p. 560.)

Athens

O city of light and song, town of the violet crown,
Bulwark of Hellas, glorious Athens, walls of divine renown.

(Dithyramb, p. 556.)

Spring

When the Seasons clothed with purple have flung their chamber wide,
And fragrant Spring leads back her flowers, as nectar sweet,
Then on the earth divine beneath men's feet
Are violets strewn; then rose-wreathed locks blow free,
And flute and song resound on every side,
And dancers praise the diademed Sémele.

(*Dithyramb*, p. 554.)

The Poet's Praise

No sculptor I of forms whose feet stand clinging
Idly for ever to a pedestal;
From every ship and boat, my song, go winging
With thy sweet call,
Forth from Aegina's harbour—everywhere
Name the stout Pytheas, Lampon's son,
Crowned now in Némea's pancration,
Though not yet blooms on his young cheek the down
Life's summer shall mother there.

(*Nem.*, V, 1–5.)

The Poet's Power

Yet Homer has told of Ajax' worth, and sent his glory ringing
Wide through the world, as he chanted to the beat of his staff of bay,
With godlike words for after-poets' singing.
For noble verse to all eternity
Goes forth clear-voiced; and, with it, upon its endless way
O'er fruitful earth and sea,
The light of splendid deeds shines out unquenched for aye.

(*Isthm.*, IV, 37–42.)

Mortality

Yet, though a man have riches, and none so fair as he,
And his in the games a victor's strength, let him bear in mind alway,
Those limbs he garbs are fashioned of mortality—
He too, when all is over, must don a cloak of clay.

(*Nem.*, XI, 13–16.)

Moderation

Not in *every* generation do virtues long-descended
Breed men of might. Not *always* do the black fields bounteously
Give harvest; not with *every* summer ended
A like wealth loads the fragrant-blossomed tree;
But with changeful alternation. So too for humanity

Fate stands. What God's disposal shall ordain us,
No token tells. And yet we launch out evermore
On perilous quests—our wanton hopes enchain us—
The tides of foresight lie beyond our lore.
Keep measure in ambition. Sharp the pain
Of mad hearts craving what no hand shall gain.

(Nem., xi, 38–48.)

Content at Home

'Shall I, then, covet riches? The lot that the Blest have made
Mine, here in Ceos, shall I cast away
For foreign greatness? Nay!
I should be, always, afraid.
Crave not, my heart, the land of the cypress-tree,
Crave not the pastures under Ida.
My little land of oaks—I seek nought wider;
Here strife nor sorrow vexeth me.'

(Paean iv, 46–53; J. E. Sandys, Pindar, p. 530.)

Courage in Exile

'When some great oak-tree, glorious in men's gaze,
Falls humbled by the trenchant axe, and its boughs in the dust lie broken,
Though now but a barren stock, it still gives token
Of its true worth, as it ends in the wintry blaze;
Or when, above towering columns, it holds aloft the weight
Of the palace of some alien lord—hard though its burden weighs,
And its old home lies desolate.'

(Pyth., iv, 263–9.)

God and Man

One is the race of Gods and men; and yet, though Earth,
One common Mother, brought them both to birth,
Man is a thing of nothing, and Theirs the eternal sky,
In brazen strength for ever. But in us too can lie
Some godlike touch of heart or soul,
Though day and night we wander, powerless to descry
Where Fate hath drawn our goal.

(Nem., VI, 1–7.)

Elysium

While we in night lie hidden, there in the world below
Bright shines the sun; in the meadows about their city's wall
The fruits of gold hang heavy, crimson the roses blow,
From fragrance-breathing boughs the shadows fall. . . .
With steeds, and games of strength, and games of skill,
And music they make merry; perfect peace
Wreaths all their days with flowers;
While perfumes fill
That lovely land, where without cease
From the Gods' far-flaming altars the mingled incense towers.
But, opposite, the livid streams of night
Belch blackness infinite. . . .

(Dirge; J. E. Sandys, Pindar, p. 586.)

BACCHYLIDES OF CEOS
(*c.* 510–*c.* 430 B.C.)

Bacchýlides was the son of Simōnides' sister and, like his uncle, a lyric poet who found favour at the court of Syracuse. Till 1896 he remained little more than a name; but in that year the British Museum acquired a papyrus in some two hundred fragments, containing about a thousand lines of his poetry. It had been written, probably, in the first century B.C.; was found by natives in Egypt; and was published in 1897.

Beside the passionate inspiration of Pindar, Bacchýlides is a much quieter and more even poet—like Marvell beside Milton. Indeed the Greek treatise *On the Grand Style* falsely attributed to 'Longīnus', which probably dates from the first century A.D., when it argues (very reasonably) that faulty genius stands above faultless talent, takes Pindar as an example of genius, Bacchýlides of faultlessness. All the same Bacchýlides will seem to many a far better poet than is implied by Pindar's contemptuous comparison of him and his uncle Simōnides to 'jackdaws chattering against the eagle'. Certainly he is far less impossible to translate.

The Eagle (to Híero of Syracuse)

As towering through the height
Of Heaven with swift brown wing
The eagle cleaves his flight,
That messenger of Zeus the Lord of Thunder,
King of All—
Proud in his strength whereunder
All lesser birds shrill-twittering
Cower and fall
(For through the boundless earth no peaks can stay him,
No foam that flies
From the steep surge of sleepless seas dismay him,
As through the wild waste skies
Before the western gale
Those great soft pinions sail,
A marvel in all men's eyes)—

So, free as he, I have infinite flights before me
Whereon my song may soar
To praise ye, whom dark-haired Nīke crowns with glory,
And the bronze-breasted God of War.

(*Odes*, v, 16–34.)

Croesus

In 564 B.C. Croesus, the rich king of Lydia—encouraged (says the story) by an ambiguous Delphic oracle that if he crossed the River Hălys he would destroy a mighty empire—attacked Cyrus king of Persia. After an indecisive battle he retired; and his capital, Sardis, was stormed by the Persians. Cyrus, however, spared his fallen enemy.[1] The version given here, which makes Apollo save the pious Lydian king by a miracle, in return for his many offerings to Delphi, may well have been of Delphic origin.

---

[1] See the enchanting narrative of Herodotus, I, 76 ff.

Thronged now the shrines with revel and sacrifice,
  The streets, with festival and dances;
  Before the fane of Phoebus glances
The gold of tall, rich tripods, past all price;

And there beside the banks of Castaly,
  Through the wide precinct of Apollo,
  To prayer the files of Delphians follow—
Praise Him, with gifts!—the best of Saviours He!

Witness that day when Sardis
  Was sacked of the Persian horde,
As the doom of Zeus appointed;
  Yet the Lydian horsemen's lord,
King Croesus, was delivered by Apollo,
  God of the Golden Sword.

For when on Lydia's Lord so sudden fell
  That day of weeping and disaster,
  Scorning to bow before a master
He built outside his bronze-walled citadel

A mighty pyre, and mounting there on high
  With his true Queen, his young Princesses,
  That sobbed and tore their radiant tresses,
He lifted hands to Heaven with the cry—

'Is this, O haughty God,
  Thy gratitude divine?
Where lingers Lēto's son,
  While falls Alyattes' line?
Thus are my gifts and offerings, past all telling,
  Repaid by Pytho's shrine?

'My city falls to Persian sword and flame;
  With blood Pactōlus' golden waters
  Run crimson; and our wives and daughters
Are dragged from their rich palaces in shame.

'Then welcome horror!—Death is kindliest.'
  He called—and a soft-paced Lydian lighted
  That tower of timber. But crying, affrighted,
The maidens clung about their mother's breast.

For ever man's heart finds grimmest
   Death when it rises nigh.
Yet, as a glittering tongue
   Of fierce flame quivered high,
To quench its yellow glare, a cloud black-looming
   Zeus drew athwart the sky.

Nought is too hard for Heaven's ordering hand;
   So then did the God of Dēlos bring
   Slim-ankled maidens and ancient king
Far, far away to the Hyperborean land:

Because, of all men, honouring things divine,
He gave the most to Pytho's hallowed shrine.

(III, 15-62.)

Hēracles and the Wraith of Meleāger

*Hēracles, descending to Hades to fetch the three-headed hound Cerberus, there
saw the phantom of Meleāger, whose sister Dējanīra he was destined to wed on
his return to earth—but to his own undoing. (For she sent her husband a tunic
smeared with the poisoned blood of the centaur Nessus, believing it a love-philtre;
and in his agony Hēracles had himself burnt on Mount Oeta.)*

Once the sacker of towns, men say,
Matchless son of the lightning's Lord,
Down from the sunlight took his way,
To where lightfoot Persephone
Dwells in Hell's obscurity,
To catch that hound with jaggéd teeth
Whelped by Echidna the abhorred.
And there in Hades' House beneath
He saw, beside Cōcȳtus' flow,
The hapless shades drift dense and deep,
As wind-tossed leaves amid the sheep
Up Ida's sunlit headlands blow;
And glorious in the midst of these
He marked one mighty spearman go,
The wraith of Porthaónides.

Soon as Alcmēna's hero-son
Saw that armed ghost glittering,
Swift on his bow he stretched the string,
Twanging shrilly, and thereon
From his opened quiver slipped,
In haste, an arrow brazen-tipped.
But Meleāger's shade descried
That face well-known and, standing forth,
'Son of mighty Zeus,' he cried,
'Stay!—and lay aside thy wrath.

'Shoot not bitter shafts in vain
At the spectres of the slain.
Nay, fear not *me*!' Then wondering said
The royal son of Amphítryon,
'What God—or who of mortal birth
Begot the like of thee on earth?
Say, in what country wast thou bred?
Who slew thee? *Such* a champion
The Queen of Heaven girdled fair
Would gladly use, to lay me low;
Yet Pallas of the golden hair
Shall be my succour, well I know.'
But Meleāger answered him
(While with tears his eyes grew dim),
'What Heaven's will has ordered so,

'For men to alter hard it is.
Else my own horse-taming sire,
Oeneus, had appeased the ire
Of mighty, white-armed Artemis.
But vain his prayers. In vain to slay
Before the flower-crowned Virgin's shrine
Herds of goats and red-backed kine—
Nought could turn her wrath away.
A boar of boundless strength she sent,
A brute most pitiless, to vent
The full tide of his fury, where
Danced once the maids of Cálydon.
Our vineyards with his tusks he rent,
Our sheep, and every mother's son
That crossed his rage, he slaughtered there.

'Against him gathered all the flower
Of Hellas. Six days savagely
We fought the beast, till came the hour
God gave the Aetōlians mastery.
Then we laid our dead to rest,
Whom his wild-shrieking onset tore—
Ancaeus—Agelāus, best
Of my brave brothers; ay, of all
Whom once in Oeneus' glorious hall
My mother, Queen Althaea, bore.

'And others, too, doom's bitter lot
Destroyed. For She that loves the chase,
Lētō's fierce daughter, quieted not
Her anger; no less savagely
Against the stout Cūrētes we
Clashed in battle, face to face,
For the sake of that monster's tawny hide.
By me, with many more beside,
Iphiclus and brave Áphares,
My mother's gallant brothers, died.
For nought of kin stark Ares knows;
And nought the hurtling javelin sees,
Thirsty for the blood of foes,
To this or that breast bringing death,
Just as God's will ordereth.

'But no such thought could make less hard
My mother's anger—Thestius' child;
Fierce, fearless woman, evil-starred,
She turned to compass death for me.
From its chest carved curiously,
Forth with lamentations wild
She brought, and lit, the magic brand
Of sudden death, that destiny
As limit of my life had planned.
It chanced I stood in act to slay
Brave Clýmenus, Daípylus' son,
Whose fair form I had overrun
Before their city's towers (for they
Were fleeing routed, one and all,
Back to Pleuron's ancient wall).

'Then did my sweet life fail from me—
I felt my strength go ebbing fast,
And wept—alas, how bitterly!—
To leave behind youth's radiant years!'
Then, for the first time and the last,
Amphítryon's fearless son, they say,
Felt his own eyes fill with tears,
Pitying him that passed away
So haplessly. He answered then:
'Not to be born is best for men,

'Nor ever to behold the sun;
Yet, since it profits not at all,
To weep for sorrows that are done,
Best speak of what may still be won.
Say then if still in Oeneus' hall
Any maiden daughter be,
In breed and beauty like to thee?
For gladly, if I had my will,
Her beauty would I take for bride.'
Then gallant Meleăger's shade
Answered: 'On the day I died,
A single lovely-throated maid,
Dējanīra, dwelt there still,
A girl as yet—nought knoweth she
Of golden Love's sweet witchery.'

(v, 56–175.)

The Coming of Theseus towards Athens

Aegeus, king of Athens, had a child by Aethra, princess of Troezēn. Growing up, the young Theseus set out to find his lost father in Athens; slaying on his way many robbers and evil-doers—Periphētes, Sinis, Scīron, Kerkyon, and Procrustes.

CHORUS

Lord of Athene's holy hill,
  The grace-loving Ionians' king,
Why is the bronze-mouthed trumpet loud
  With calls to war and mustering?

Are hostile armies near?
　Do enemies invade
Our realm's frontier?
　Or evil robbers raid
From out our shepherds' hands
The flocks that graze our lands?
　What makes thy soul dismayed?
Speak, lord. For, sure, if ever king there were
　Could call to arms a host
　Of valiant youth, that boast
Is thine, Pandīon and Creūsa's heir!

AEGEUS

A messenger is come with speed
　By the long road from the Isthmus here,
With word of many a marvellous deed
　Wrought by a mighty stranger's spear.
He hath slain Sīnis in fight,
　The great Earth-shaker's son,
Unmatched in might.
　Foul Scīron he hath done
To death, and in Crommyon's glen
The swine that ravened men;
　And outwrestled Kerkyon;
And faced at last by a mightier than he,
　Procoptes cast from him
　Polypēmon's hammer grim.
I dread what the end of all these things may be.

CHORUS

Who is this stranger? Do they say
　From whence he hails? What garb he bore?
Comes he marching on his way
　With a mighty host of war?
Or leading but a few
　Followers of his own,
As travellers do
　That visit lands unknown?
What valour and strength were his
To quell such men as this!
　Surely by God alone

F

To scourge all evil-doers he is sent?
  How else should he prevail
  O'er foe on foe, nor fail?
But Time shall bring these things accomplishment.

AEGEUS

Of but two servants he is lord,
  'Tis said; and, slung from his shoulder white,
He bears an ivory-hilted sword;
  A spear in each hand, burnished bright;
A thick Thessalian wrap,
  A tunic of purple fair,
And a Spartan cap
  To crown his golden hair;
But deep within his eyes
  A flame—such flames as rise
  Where the fires of Lemnos glare.
In years a lad; yet his heart is set on fight
  And the clash of swords at play;
  And his journey's goal, they say,
Is Athens—land that glories in the light!

(XVII, 1–60.)

PRAXILLA OF SICYON
(c. 455 B.C.)

A lyric poetess, of whom little is known.

' Neither Maid nor Wife '

O fair face at the window, looking down alone—
Face of a maid, and yet—loosed now thy maiden zone.

(Diehl, II, p. 130.)

EMPEDOCLES OF ACRAGAS
(c. 494–c. 434 B.C.)

Empédocles seems to have been a Greek Paracelsus—part scientist, part quack. In his poem *Of Nature* the scientist describes how the universe

92

is built of air, earth, fire, and water, now mingled by love, now severed by strife or repulsion; in his *Purifications*, the miracle-worker claims to be himself divine, and preaches reincarnation, purification, and vegetarianism. The real Empédocles appears to have died in the Peloponnesus, not (as in the legend followed by Matthew Arnold) to have leapt down the crater of Etna.

Karma

There stands a decree of Destiny, from the immemorial past,
A law of the Gods, that fails not, with weighty oaths sealed fast:
That if ever a blessed spirit, born to eternal life,
Shall stain his guilty hands with blood, or swayed by strife
Shall falsely swear, and burden his soul with perjury,
For thrice ten thousand years his banishment shall be.
From the seat of the Blest he shall wander in ceaseless shapes of change,
Through the bitter paths of Being, doomed without rest to range.
For the might of the aether flings him to seaward, and the main
Spews him upon earth's threshold, and earth to the sun again,
And again to the eddying aether by the bright sun he is hurled,
From one to another driven, abhorred through all the world.

(H. Diels, *Fragmenta der Vorsokratiker* (1922), I, p. 267.)

Pre-Existence

A lad, and a lass, aforetime it was my lot to be,
And a bush I was, and a bird, and a dumb fish in the sea.

(p. 268.)

PLATO
(*c*. 428–*c*. 348 B.C.)

This is no place for a detailed account of the most famous of philosophers, who in his too austere maturity banned poets from his ideal state, except under the bleakest of censorships. In his more gracious youth, however, he had himself been a poet; and some of the epigrams attributed to him may be genuine, though the last two selected here are generally thought spurious.

Love Lies Sleeping

We came to a wood and within it, where dark its shadows run,
Fair as a rosy apple, lay Cytherēa's son.
He had not his quivered arrows, he had not his curving bow,
Under the leafy branches we spied them hanging low;
But there lay Love himself among the roses red,
Smiling, locked in the toils of sleep, and overhead
On those sweet lips, from a honeycomb, brown bees their honey shed.

(*Anthologia Palatina,* XVI, 210.)

Love's Apple

I throw my apple towards you. If you will love me, take it
    And give me in repayment your own maidenhead:
If your will is what I would not, yet keep it still; and make it
    Your lesson of how swiftly all loveliness is fled.

(V, 79.)

Ecstasy

As I kissed Ágathon, my soul
    All but passed away:
To my very lips, poor wretch, she stole—
    So close her Heaven lay.

(V, 78.)

The Young Astronomer

At the stars thou gazest, Aster. Ah, would that I could be
That sky with its myriad eyes, to fix them all on thee!

(VII, 669.)

The Young Astronomer Dead

Awhile, O Dawn-star of the living,
    On life thy light was shed.
Now death hath made thee Hesper, giving
    New radiance to the dead.

(VII, 670.)

'Passing the Love of Women'

For Hecuba, for Troy's daughters, a doom of tears and sorrow
  The Destinies appointed, from the hour that they were born.
Your triumph was won, my Dïon; but lo, upon the morrow,
  Your spacious visions likewise the high gods flung to scorn.
Yet in your wide∕wayed city, honoured at last, you rest,
O Dïon, whose love once maddened the heart within this breast.

(VII, 99.)

'Quand Vous serez bien Vieille'

I Laïs, whose proud laughter mocked Hellas; whose alluring
  Thronged thick my gates with lovers, to the Paphian give my glass:
Since now to see my likeness, as it is, grows past enduring;
  Since I no more may see it, as in old days it was.

(VI, I.)

Pan's Piping

Hush now, O wooded hill of the Dryads! Hush your leaping
  Down from the rocks, ye fountains! Hush, myriad∕bleating ewes!
For along his reeden pipe now Pan Himself is sweeping
  His supple lip to waken the sweet cry of the Muse;
And with feet untired for dancing, about him gathered gleam
The Dryads from the forest, the Naiads from the stream.

(IX, 823.)

TIMOTHEÜS OF MILETUS
(c. 450–360 B.C.)

Timótheüs may have been better as a musician—we have no evidence
(his vast popularity at the time is none). But as a poet, since the discovery
of part of his *Persians* in 1905, he is remarkable among Greek writers as
being, for once, really detestable—crude, vulgar, blatant, and ridiculous.
It is this which adds a very modern irony to the boast that follows.

'Contemporaneity'

I sing no out-of-date matter,
For our new songs are better.
Crŏnus was master aforetime,
But Zeus is the monarch of *our* time.
The old Muse—hence let her get her.

(Diehl, II, p. 150.)

PARRHASIUS OF EPHESUS
(*c.* 400 B.C.)

Parrhasius, one of the most famous painters of antiquity, was no less
famous for his pride and dandyism. 'No one', says Pliny, 'ever enjoyed
reputation more insolently.' He claimed divine descent from Apollo and
pretended, with Blake-like assurance, to have painted his Hēracles from
visions of the hero in person.

The Artist's Last Word

I say it, though none believe me. I say that clear for ever
  Henceforth the furthest limits of the painter's art stand set
By this my hand. Beyond it shall pass no man's endeavour;
  Though the beauty that men blamed not, was never fashioned yet.

(Athenaeus, XII, 543E.)

ERINNA
(mid 4th century B.C. or later?)

A poetess said to have died at nineteen, but ranked with Sappho by
some ancient judgments, though little of her work survives. Her chief
poem was a lament, *The Distaff*, for her dead girl-friend Baucis.

The Eternal Silence

Nought to the far-off Hades but an empty echo cries.
There, mid the dead, is silence. My voice in the darkness dies.

(Diehl, I, p. 486.)

CLEANTHES OF ASSOS (IN MYSIA)
(c. 331–232 B.C.)

Cleanthes, disciple of Zēno and second of the great Stoic philosophers, is said to have begun life as a boxer. He composed philosophical works in prose and a *Hymn to Zeus*. The Stoic creed, not very intelligent, but with a bleak nobility of its own, pictured the world as governed by 'unalterable law', '$\dot{\eta}$ $\epsilon i\mu\alpha\rho\mu\acute{e}\nu\eta$'; and happiness was to be found by the sage only in complete and passive acceptance of this law—all other seeming goods and ills are illusory.

The Stoic's Resignation

Lead ye me on, O God and Destiny,
To the end ye have appointed. Without flinching,
Still I will follow. For, though I turned craven
And cried ye nay, yet I must follow still.

(J. U. Powell, *Collectanea Alexandrina*, p. 229.)

PERSES
(late 4th century B.C.)

The God of the Lowly

Little am I among lesser gods; but call in season
Even on me, and I hearken. Yet ask me for nothing grand.
Things that a god of the people may look to give in reason,
When a poor labourer prays him—these lie in Tÿchon's hand.

(*Anthologia Palatina*, IX, 334.)

ADDAEUS OF MACEDONIA
(late 4th century B.C.?)

Probably a contemporary of Alexander the Great, for whom he wrote an epitaph.

The Pensioned Ox

His yoke-ox, growing feeble with age and years of ploughing,
Alcon its master pitied, and saved from the blood-stained knife,
Honouring its true service; mid the meadow-grasses' soughing
Knee-deep it lows, contented and furrow-free for life.

(VI, 228.)

97

From ARCHILOCHUS to ALEXANDER

ARCHILOCHUS

[p. 46] *The Freelance.* Cf. Hybrias, p. 72.

[p. 46] *Wine from the Thracian land.* Wine of Ismărus, the same as Odysseus used to fuddle Polyphemus.

[p. 46] *Some Thracian.* More precisely 'Saïan', a tribe near Abdēra. Evidently the incident occurred in some clash between the Greek colonists of Thăsos and the natives on the mainland. Archílochus' laughter at his own discomfiture was imitated by Alcaeus, Anacreon, and Horace (who fled at Philippi in 42 B.C.).

[p. 46] *When thou winnest . . . When thou losest. . . .* Cf. that noble praise of the Elizabethan soldier Sir Francis Vere—that none seeing him return from a victory could have known that he had not lost, none seeing him ride back from defeat have guessed that he had not won.

ALCMAN

[p. 48] *The halcyon's lot.* It was believed that the male halcyon, grow-ing old, was borne through the air by the female birds. Here the old poet, too frail to dance, wishes half sadly, half laughingly, that he were a sea-bird and his chorus of Spartan girls could bear him soaring on his way.

[p. 48] *Vesper.* Bowra (*Greek Lyric Poetry*, p. 73) suggests that the scene of this is the Vale of Sparta (which lies in such smiling, un-Spartan fruitfulness under the snowy mountain-wall of Taÿgetus). But I feel that the poem's landscape needs the sea: at Sparta this lies 20 miles away, hidden beyond the southward hills.

In Sept. 1780, on the wall of a forest-hut on the Gickelhahn near Ilmenau, Goethe wrote his *Wandrers Nachtlied*:

> Über allen Gipfeln
> Ist Ruh,
> In allen Wipfeln
> Spürest du

Kaum einen Hauch;
Die Vögelein schweigen im Walde.
Warte nur, balde
Ruhest du auch.

(He is said to have come on the poem again in August 1831, at 82, and to have sadly repeated its last two lines.)

MIMNERMUS

[p. 49] *Ugly at once and base.* Or, with a different reading, 'that brings to one level ugly and comely alike'.

[p. 49] *At the end of sixty years.* Solon wrote a poem in reply, suggesting *eighty* years as better.

HYMN TO DIONYSUS

Dionysus' adventure with the pirates is depicted in relief on the choragic monument of Lysícrates at Athens (334 B.C.).

[p. 50] *Tyrsēnian.* Here probably 'Pelasgian' (pre-Greek race in Aegean area), though later applied to the Etruscans (who may have been of the same stock).

[p. 51] *Hyperborean land.* A legendary country 'beyond the North Wind' (though it is doubtful if this ancient etymology is right). Cf. p. 112.

CLEOBULUS?

[p. 54] *Midas.* The name of several Phrygian kings, the most famous being that legendary monarch who got into trouble (like some modern governments) by turning everything to gold; and was credited (like many critics of all ages) with ass's ears, bestowed on him by the angry Apollo for tastelessly preferring the flutings of the Satyr Marsyas (p. 225) to the God's own lyre.

ALCAEUS

[p. 55] *To his Brother.* Antiménidas, driven from Lesbos like Alcaeus by the popular party, took service with Nebuchadnezzar (605–562 B.C.) and must have fought this duel against some Syrian, Jewish, or Egyptian champion.

[p. 55] *Five royal cubits.* $5 \times 20\frac{1}{2}$ ins. = 8 ft. $6\frac{1}{2}$ ins. A span = 3 ins. or a little over. The giant therefore stood 8 ft. $3\frac{1}{2}$ ins.

A great city is that which has the greatest men and women,
If it be a few ragged huts, it is still the greatest city in the whole world.

And Cobbett: 'It is *men*, and not *machines*, that constitute a nation.'

SAPPHO

[p. 57] *The Beloved*. The girl seems to be imagined sitting next her bridegroom at the wedding feast in her father's house. Catullus addressed a rendering of the poem to his mistress Clodia, whom he called 'Lesbia'.

[p. 58] *And madness*. Adopting Bergk's conjecture ἄλλα—'distraught'.

[p. 58] *Atthis*. One of Sappho's pupils. At first sight, Sappho had thought her a child lacking in grace; but the feeling deepened, until Atthis forsook the poetess for a rival—Andrómeda. A fragmentary line still recalls the deserted Sappho's grief:

'I loved thee, Atthis, once, in days long past.'

[p. 58] *Anactória*. Another of the girls in Sappho's circle (the restoration of her name here is conjectural). Whoever it was, she has here left Lesbos, presumably as a wife, for the Lydian capital, Sardis, 100 miles away.

[p. 58] *Outshines the stars*. Cf. Sir Henry Wotton on Elizabeth of Bohemia:

You meaner beauties of the night
That poorly satisfy our eyes
More by your number than your light
You common people of the skies;
What are you when the moon shall rise?

[p. 58] *Anthrysc*. An umbellifer.

[p. 58] *Melilótus*. Melilot, a clover specially rich in honey.

[p. 59] *To a Rich, Uncultured Woman*. The first clear statement in European poetry of literary immortality (cf. Sappho's fragmentary line: 'I say that some shall remember us, even in years to come'). It becomes much more emphatic in Theognis (p. 65).

[p. 59] *Forsaken*. Possibly folksong, not Sappho's. Adapted by A. E. Housman in the poem beginning:

The weeping Pleiads wester,
And the moon is under seas;
From bourn to bourn of midnight
Far sighs the rainy breeze.

Cf. also Ronsard (ed. Vaganay) iv, 164:

> Ja la lune s'est couchée,
> La poussiniere est cachée,
> Et ja la my-nuit brunette
> Vers l'Aurore s'est panchée,
> Et je dors au lict seulette.

[p. 59] *The Maid Unwed*. This and the next two fragments come from a marriage-song. Cf. Catullus, 62.

[p. 59] *Evensong*. Cf. Byron, *Don Juan*, iii, cvii:

> Oh, Hesperus! thou bringest all good things—
>   Home to the weary, to the hungry cheer,
> To the young bird the parent's brooding wings,
>   The welcome stall to the o'erlabour'd steer;
> Whate'er of peace about our hearthstone clings,
>   Whate'er our household gods protect of dear,
> Are gather'd round us by thy look of rest;
> Thou bring'st the child, too, to the mother's breast.

Also Housman, *Epithalamium*:

> Happy bridegroom, Hesper brings
> All desired and timely things.
> All whom morning sends to roam,
> Hesper loves to lead them home.
> Home return who him behold,
> Child to mother, sheep to fold,
> Bird to nest from wandering wide:
> Happy bridegroom, seek your bride.

But neither, I think, equals the simple brevity of Sappho's fragment.

Certain other fragmentary verses attributed to Alcaeus and Sappho have been sometimes taken as a gallant address from poet to poetess followed by a crushing retort from her to him (Diehl, 1, pp. 386, 416):

> 'Pure and violet-crowned, honey-smiling Sappho,
> Somewhat would I say—but my tongue is shamefast.'
> 'Were good the aim that makes you so passionate,
> Did not your tongue stir something dishonourable,
>   No shame would bow your eyes to earthward;
>   Frank would your speech be of things more honest.'

But (1) it is not certain that the first line belongs to this context at all; (2) the other five lines *may* be part of a dialogue-poem of Sappho's (like Horace's quarrel with Lydia, *Odes*, III, 9); but Sappho's poem may also present fictitious persons in a fictitious situation.

SOLON

[p. 60] *The Shame of Losing Salamis.* The story is that, weary of war with Mégara for the island of Salamis, the Athenians made it a capital offence even to propose renewing the struggle; Solon evaded this by feigning madness and reciting in the market-place a patriotic poem (from which these lines are taken), with such success that the law was rescinded and he led his countrymen to a new and victorious campaign. He is said, when he died, to have had his ashes scattered over the island he had won for Athens.

[p. 60] *Phólegandros, Síkinos.* Obscure islands SW. of Naxos, NW. of Thera (Santorin).

THEOGNIS

[p. 62] *Polypáïdes.* The young Cyrnus, son of Polypas.

[p. 62] *The bird's shrill crying.* The migrant crane (p. 10).

[p. 63] *An Eye for an Eye.* Not very Christian; but very forcible.

[p. 63] *Rhădamanthys.* A Cretan king, son of Zeus and Europa, and brother of Minos. So just was his reign on earth that he was made ruler of the blessed in Elysium, or one of the judges of the dead in Hades.

[p. 63] *Sísyphus*, King of Corinth, was a byword for cunning. He outwitted even the thievish Autólycus (who used to steal his cattle) by fastening under their hoofs lead plates with the legend 'Stolen by Autólycus', so that he could track them down. He enchained even Death, until rescued by Ares; then, coming himself to die, Sísyphus bade his wife not bury his body. Thereby he was enabled to get leave of absence from Hades, in order to punish this impious woman; and, once returned to earth, gaily overstayed his leave. Finally Hermes dragged him back to the Netherworld, where he was punished by having to push a rock up a mountain through eternity.

[p. 64] *Harpies.* Personified storm-winds.

[p. 64] *Boreas' sons.* Zētes and Cálaïs, the wing-footed sons of the North Wind by the Athenian princess Oreithyia, whom he carried off. They sailed in Argo and fought the Harpies.

[p. 64] *Eugenics.* Plato (*Republic*, 459A) elaborates the same view into his genial scheme for nationalizing love and the family.

[p. 64] *A ram.* Theognis' own city, Mégara, was noted for its sheep and its boors (also, curiously enough, for its philosophers); so that Diogenes could jest that it was better to be a Megarian's ram than his son. (Cf. Shaw's proposal that children be periodically shot like partridges, in the hope that they might then be as carefully preserved.)

[p. 64] *Critics.* Cf. the Bulgarian proverb: 'Not even God can please everybody.'

[p. 65] *Loyalty.* Apparently a lovers' quarrel, the woman speaking first.

[p. 65] *The Beloved.* Perhaps the most eloquent of all Theognis' poems. Cf. Shakespeare, *Sonnets*, 55:

> Not marble, nor the gilded monuments
> Of princes, shall outlive this powerful rhyme. . . .

For the sudden sting in the tail of the poem (which has needlessly bothered some commentators) cf. the next piece and the endings of *Sonnets* 84 and 92:

> You to your beauteous blessings add a curse,
> Being fond on praise, which makes your praises worse.

> But what's so blessed-fair that fears no blot?
> Thou mayst be false, and yet I know it not.

[p. 66] *The Broken Chain.* Cf. Sir Thomas Wyat, *He Rejoiceth that he had broken the Snares of Love*:

> Was never birde tangled in lyme
> That brake awaye yn better tyme,
> Then I that rotten bowes ded clyme,
> And had no hurte, but scaped fre.
> Now ha! ha! ha! full well is me,
> For I am nowe at libertye.

[p. 66] *I drank at a spring.* Cf. Shakespeare, *Sonnets*, 35:

> No more be griev'd at that which thou hast done:
> Roses have thorns, and silver fountains mud.

And *Othello*, IV, ii, 60 (of Desdemona): 'The fountain from the which my current runs.'

[p. 67] *The Problem.* Cf. G. M. Hopkins, in his bewildered *Justus quidem tu es, Domine*:

> Thou art indeed just, Lord, if I contend
> With thee; but, Sir, so what I plead is just.
> Why do sinners' ways prosper? and why must
> Disappointment all I endeavour end?

[p. 67] *Despair.* This clear-eyed melancholy, which yet, for centuries, did not sap Greek vitality, already appears in Homer and in legends like that which tells how King Midas, having captured a Silēnus, hoped to learn precious wisdom from its lips: but was only told that the best thing for man was not to be born; the next best, to die as soon as possible. Or again there is the tale of Cléobis and Biton (Herodotus, I, 31), whose mother, priestess of Argive Hēra, prayed the Gods to reward her sons' piety with the best gift Heaven could give—that same night they died in their sleep. (Their sixth-century statues have been found at Delphi.) The same theme is the burden of the most famous chorus of the *Oedipus at Colonus*, written by the fortunate and popular Sophocles at the close of his long life:

> He that craves in life a span
> Past the common lot of man
> Sets his heart, past questioning,
> On a vain and empty thing;
> Whoso lives beyond his share,
> Slowly sees the creeping years
> Leave no trace of gladness there,
> Turning all his joys that were
> Into things more close to tears;
> Till One alone is left to heed his call—
> One no bridesong gladdeneth,
> Nor yet dance, nor music—Death,
> That brings an end of all.
>
> Never to be born is best;
> Next to that, far happiest
> He that hastens from his birth,
> Fast as may be, back to earth.
> Soon as, with its follies light,
> On its way our Youth is past,
> Then, of sorrows infinite,
> What is spared us?—tongues that bite,
> Faction, battle, slaughter—last,

There comes Old Age, the strengthless, the accurst,
Age that knows no love, no friend,
On whose solitude attend
Griefs of *all* griefs the worst.

(*Oedipus at Colonus*, 1211–38.)

Similarly in a fragment of Euripides, *Cresphontes* (Fr. 449):

Wiser it were to gather and lament
For every babe that enters this sad world;
But when man dies and all his trouble's over,
Bear him with joy and blessings from his home.

Cf. Tennyson, *Tithonus*:

the homes
Of happy men that have the power to *die*,
And grassy barrows of the happier dead.

Note, however, that this later Greek pessimism goes beyond Homer's. Zeus in Homer may call man the unhappiest of created things; but he does *not* say it is better never to be born or else to die as soon as possible. The difference suggests a certain decline in Greek vitality.

[p. 68] *The Stoic*. No ill motto for the twentieth century.

[p. 68] *Nativity*. Cf. the *Hymn to Apollo* (p. 20).

[p. 68] *The round mere*. A round pool near the shore of Dēlos, where in historic times swam the sacred swans of Apollo. The *Hymn* had located the birth at the foot of Cynthus, a quarter of a mile away from the pool.

IBYCUS

[p. 68] *Quince-flowers*. Our word 'quince' is really the plural of 'quine', 'coyn', from Latin (*malum*) *Cydonium*, 'apple of Cydonia' (now Canea), in Crete. Like apples, quinces were love-symbols (cf. pp. 59, 94).

HIPPONAX

[p. 69] *Misogynist*. The authorship is not certain. Cf. Prior:

Women 'twixt sheets are best, 'tis said,
Be they of holland or of lead.

[p. 69] *Būpalus*. A Chian sculptor detested by Hippōnax.

PHOCYLIDES

[p. 70] *The Exception.* Adapted by Porson in his satire on Gottfried Hermann:

> The Germans in Greek
> Are sadly to seek;
> Not five in five score,
> But ninety-five more:
> All; save only Herman—
> And Herman's a German.

ANACREON

[p. 70] *The Coy Mistress.* Anácreon may have met his Thracian girl when he fled in 545 B.C. with his fellow-citizens of Teos (SW. of Smyrna) before the invading Persians to Abdēra on the coast of Thrace. The poem is imitated by Ronsard (ed. Vaganay), III, 270: 'Pourquoy comme une jeune poutre De travers guignes tu vers moy?'

XENOPHANES

[p. 71] *Wickedness of Poets.* Similar criticisms of the morality of traditional theology recur in Pindar and, above all, Euripides. Cf. *Hēracles Mad*, 1341–6:

> I cannot think Gods do adultery,
> Nay, I have ever scorned, and ever shall,
> To dream a God can bind a God with chains,
> Or one be born by Fate another's master.
> For God if God indeed, has need of nothing.
> These are but poets' old unhappy tales.

[p. 71] *Anthropomorphism.* Still more neatly in Montesquieu: 'Si les triangles avaient un dieu, il aurait trois côtés.'

[p. 72] *Rainbow.*

> There was an awful rainbow once in Heaven:
> We know her woof, her texture; she is given
> In the dull catalogue of common things.
> Philosophy will clip an Angel's wings.—Keats, *Lamia*.

[p. 72] *Athleticism.* In the Greek world, as in ours, professionalism in sport and the consequent idolatry of athletes became a curse. Euripides is said himself to have trained in youth as one; but in a fragment of his *Autólycus* he attacks them more bitterly even than Xenóphanes.

> Now of ten thousand curses that plague Hellas
> None is more pestilent than this breed of athletes,
> Who never yet discovered how to live,
> And could not, though they would. . . .
> Oh, they go brave in youth, the strutting ornament
> Each of his city. But once grim age has clutched them,
> *Then* see them slinking threadbare, out at elbows.
> It gets no praise of me, our Grecian way
> Of gathering in multitudes for *their* sakes,
> Making a festival for such idle toys.
> For what stout wrestler, or what nimble runner,
> Or discus-thrower, or brave jawbone-breaker,
> Profits his country by the crown he wins?
> Will they go grappling in the grip of war,
> Quoits in their hands? Or in the clash of shields
> Will wrestlers' trips o'erthrow the enemy?
> None meddles with such fooleries, when he faces
> Steel! Keep your wreaths to honour wiser heads—
> For good men, temperate leaders of their land,
> Whose words can put a curb on reckless doings,
> And calm strife and sedition. *These* are gifts
> To bless alike our country and all Hellas.

See also Norman Gardiner, *Olympia*; and, for stories of typical Greek athletes, the chapter on Olympia in my *From Olympus to the Styx*.

[p. 72] *Pentathlon.* 'Five contests'—running, long jump, discus-throwing, javelin-throwing, and wrestling.

[p. 72] *Grim pancration.* The epithet was deserved. The pancration was a kind of all-in wrestling and boxing where everything was allowed —arm-twisting, kicking in the stomach, and so forth—except only biting and gouging. It went on till the vanquished held up his hand—or, sometimes, died.

[p. 72] *Less in worth than* I *am.* An almost Shavian freedom from false modesty!

HYBRIAS THE CRETAN

A drinking-song (cf. Archílochus, p. 46) or perhaps a song for a war-dance (see Bowra, *Gk. Lyric Poetry*, pp. 437–43). It was translated by T. Campbell and may recall Peacock's equally spirited *War-Song of Dinas Vawr*:

The mountain sheep are sweeter,
But the valley sheep are fatter;
We therefore thought it meeter
To carry off the latter.

[p. 72] *Bull's-hide shield*. It is disputed whether the Greek *laiseion* means shield of hide, or hide in place of a shield (which seems rather poor for such a fire-eater as Hybrias), or some kind of body-armour.

[p. 73] *My slaves*. Greek *mnoïai*, the name given to public serfs in Crete (cf. Sparta's Helots). Possibly connected with 'Minos', Greek invaders having enslaved a pre-Greek Minoan race.

[p. 73] *King of Kings*. The Greek *megan basilea*, 'Great King', suggests an allusion to the Great King of Persia.

HYMN TO PAN

[p. 74] *Long white ridges, i.e.* of the whitish limestone common in Greek lands.

[p. 74] *On the reeden pipe of a shepherd*. Cf. p. 95.

[p. 74] *Cyllēne*. A mountain in NE. Arcadia (7,800 feet), where Hermes was born.

[p. 74] *Drÿops*. Son of Apollo by Dia, daughter of Lycāon, King of Arcadia. She hid her babe in an oak (*drys*), whence his name Drÿops— appropriate enough to the grandfather of a woodland god.

[p. 75] *Pan*. The Greeks derived the name from *pan*, 'all' (it is more probably connected with a root *pa*, found also in 'pasture', 'pastoral'; so that Pan would mean 'the Feeder', 'the Shepherd').

SIMONIDES

[p. 76] *Life's Best*. Authorship doubtful.

[p. 76] *Timócreon* of Iálysus in Rhodes, a famous athlete and eater, became after the Persian conquest of his country a buffoon of the Great King at Susa. When the Persians were defeated in 480, he hoped Themistŏcles might secure him an amnesty to return home. Disappointed, he lampooned the Athenian as having taken his money, then broken the bargain. The flight of Themistŏcles himself to Persia naturally delighted Timócreon, who sang: 'I am not the only fox to lose his tail.' Here Simōnides, who had been a friend of Themistŏcles, retaliates. (In the Palatine MS. some scribe has made on this epigram the engaging comment: 'Just like my uncle.')

[p. 76] *Gortÿna*. In S. Crete, SSW. of Cnossus.

[p. 77] *Géraneia*. A mountain-mass (4,500 feet) barring the Isthmus W. of Mégara.

[p. 77] *Ister . . . Tánaïs.* Danube . . . Don.

[p. 77] *Scīron.* This famous robber used to make travellers wash his feet on the Scironian Cliffs (at the SE. end of Géraneia), then kicked them over into the sea for a tortoise to eat; until Theseus served him to his own tortoise.

[p. 77] *Mŏlouris.* A neighbouring crag over which Ĭno leapt with her child Melicertes into the sea, after her husband, King Áthamas, had run mad and killed her other son.

[p. 77] *The Dead of Athens at Chalcis.* After her expulsion of the despot Hippias in 510, Athens was attacked by Sparta, the Boeotians, and the Chalcidians. In 506 the Athenians defeated the Boeotians near the Eurīpus, then crossing into Euboea won a second victory over the Chalcidians on the same day.

[p 77] *Dirphys.* A peak in mid Euboea (5,725 feet), whose lovely pyramid of snow haunts everywhere the walker in NE. Attica.

[p. 77] *Eurīpus.* The narrow strait at Chalcis (now bridged) between Euboea and the mainland.

[p. 77] *Thermópylae.* The famous pass between Mt Oeta and the sea, opposite the NW. tip of Euboea, where Leōnidas fell with 300 Spartans and 700 Thespians. Since translating this, I see that W. L. Bowles (1762–1850) anticipated my second line:

> Go tell the Spartans, thou that passest by,
> That here obedient to their laws we lie.

In 1833 'Christopher North' gave preference to Bowles's version, out of five by other writers and forty-eight by himself. (See *Oxford Book of Greek Verse in Translation*, p. lxv.)

Whether the couplet is really by Simōnides has been disputed.

[p. 77] *Plataea.* Under Mt Cĭthaeron in Boeotia, where in 479 the Greeks finally defeated Mardonius and the Persian army left by Xerxes.

PINDAR

[p. 79] *The Coming of Jason.* From an ode written for the victory of King Arcésilas of Cyrēne in the four-horse chariot-race at the Pythian Games of 462.

[p. 79] *Aeólidae.* Jason was son of Aeson, son of Crētheus, son of Aeŏlus.

[p. 79] *Navel of Earth.* Delphi, at earth's centre; as Zeus found by releasing from the earth's opposite extremities two eagles which met there.

[p. 79] *Far-seen.* Or perhaps 'sunlit'.

[p. 79] *Single sandal.* Jason lost the other while fording the Anaurus.

[p. 79] *Magnesian land.* Coastal Thessaly from Ossa to Pēlion. Perhaps Pindar means here a close-fitting dress suited to its wooded mountains.

[p. 80] *Lover of Aphrodite.* Ares.

[p. 80] *Sons of Iphimĕdeia.* Iphimĕdeia, wife of Alōeus, claimed that their father was Poseidon. At nine years old, they already stood nine fathoms high; and they planned to overthrow the Gods by piling Ossa on Olympus, Pēlion on Ossa; but were slain, while yet ungrown, by Apollo.

[p. 80] *Tityus.* Another giant, slain for trying to ravish Lēto or Artemis. Near Pánopeus was shown his gigantic grave; and the *Odyssey* describes him in Hades, sprawling over nine acres, while two vultures tore his liver. It seems doubtful, however, if the brilliant picture of Jason's beauty is really enhanced by adding these vast figures.

[p. 80] *The Mercenary Muse.* Written for Thrasybūlus, nephew of Thēron despot of Ácragas; probably after the despot's death, perhaps after the fall of the dynasty. Pindar himself, like Simōnides, took rewards for his odes; but here he seems regretting that general necessity, in this poem freely offered to a friend whose family has now fallen. There may be also a hit at the supposed avarice of Simōnides.

[p. 80] *Terpsíchore.* Muse of choral lyric.

[p. 80] *Cheeks with silver spread.* Perhaps with allusion to dancers sticking silver coins on their cheeks. But it may be merely one of Pindar's audacious metaphors.

[p. 80] *The Argive.* A certain Aristodāmus.

[p. 80] *The Magic of Melody.* For a chariot-victory of Híero, despot of Syracuse, at the Pythian Games of 470. The poem opens with this famous passage on the civilizing power of music.

[p. 80] *The eagle of Zeus.* Cf. Gray, *Progress of Poesy*:

> On Thracia's hills the Lord of War
> Has curb'd the fury of his car,
> And dropt his thirsty lance at thy command.
> Perching on the sceptred hand
> Of Jove, thy magic lulls the feather'd king
> With ruffled plumes and flagging wing:
> Quench'd in dark clouds of slumber lie
> The terror of his beak, and lightnings of his eye.

[p. 81] *Typhōs.* A monster who battled against the Gods and was whelmed by Zeus beneath Etna.

[p. 81] *Cyme.* Cumae, 10 miles W. of Naples, in another volcanic area. Here in 474 Híero's navy had defeated the Etruscans.

[p. 81] *Etna.* At the mountain's foot, about 474, Híero founded the city of Aitna. Possibly this ode was sung at the installation of his son Deinómenes as its king. There had been a violent eruption of Etna in 479, lasting perhaps till 476.

[p. 81] *Dēlos* means 'clear' (though the derivation of the island's name is uncertain). Pindar here alludes also to its other ancient name, Astérie (from *aster*, 'star').

[p. 81] *Made firm.* Previously a floating island, Dēlos was made fast for Apollo's birth.

[p. 81] *Athens.* From a dithyramb in praise of Athens (474 B.C.). The gratified Athenians repaid the poet with 10,000 drachmas; and Aristo-phanes mocks his countrymen for their persistent vanity about this description of their city. 'Violet-crowned' has been explained (too fancifully) as referring to the purple of sunset on Hymettus, or of the neighbouring sea. But violet wreaths were presented to the Gods or worn by men at the vernal Dionysia; and perhaps Athens herself is here conceived as a festal deity, crowned with violets like Aphrodite, the Muses, or the Graces (see A. B. Cook in *Journal of Hellenic Studies*, 1900).

[p. 82] *The Poet's Praise.* For an Aeginetan lad, victor at Némea in the pancration (see p. 107).

[p. 82] *From every ship and boat.* Pindar's verse seems rather difficult for sailors and fishermen. But cf. W. Whitman: 'In vessels that sail my words sail, I go with fishermen and seamen and love them'; and the singing of Tasso by Venetian fishermen.

[p. 82] *Though not yet blooms. . . .* Lit. 'though he does not yet show on his cheek the summer-ripeness which is the tender mother of vine-like down'. No poet ever recked less of mixing metaphors; whether always with success, remains a matter of taste.

[p. 83] *Content at Home.* From a papyrus giving part of a Paean (to the Delian Apollo) composed to be sung in Ceos. Pindar, praising contentment at home, quotes King Euxantius of Ceos, son of Minos by a Cean mother (perhaps a far-off memory of Minoan supremacy in S. Greece). For, though offered a seventh share, beside the sons of Minos and Pasíphaë, in the hundred cities of Crete, he preferred to remain in his own quiet isle.

[p. 83] *Cypress-tree . . . oaks.* Crete was famous for its cypresses; Ceos for its oaks (*Quercus aegilops*). Bent describes it as still covered by a million and a half of them, their acorn-cups producing the valonia used in tanning.

[p. 83] *Courage in Exile.* Towards the close of *Pythian* IV, Pindar tactfully appeals to Arcésilas King of Cyrēne to amnesty the exiled noble

Damóphilus, quoting this utterance which he ascribes to the exiled Oedipus.

[p. 84] *From the Gods' far-flaming altars.* . . . Adapted by Tennyson for the close of his *Tiresias*:

> And every way the vales
> Wind, clouded with the grateful incense-fume
> Of those who mix all odours to the Gods
> On one far height in one far-shining fire.

BACCHYLIDES

[p. 85] *The Eagle.* A fine companion-piece to the sleeping eagle of Pindar (p. 80). The ode celebrates the victory of Híero of Syracuse in the horse-race at Olympia (476).

[p. 85] *To praise ye.* Híero and his brothers.

[p. 85] *God of War.* Probably refers to the Syracusan defeat of Carthage at Himera (480).

[p. 86] *Thronged now the shrines.* . . . These two lines are usually referred to rejoicings at Syracuse for Híero's victory at the Olympiad of 468 B.C. in the four-horse chariot-race (the previous stanza had described the acclamations at Olympia itself). But it seems simpler to pass direct from Olympia to Delphi (where the 'rich tripods' are offerings from the rulers of Syracuse).

[p. 86] *Castaly.* The spring of Apollo, gushing into a square rock-hewn basin from the Phaedriad crags which tower sheer above Delphi.

[p. 86] *Bronze-walled.* Adorned with bronze plates.

[p. 86] *Alyattes.* The founder of Lydian power (*c.* 617–560). Croesus was son of Alyattes, son of Sadyattes, son of Ardys, son of Gyges.

[p. 86] *Pactōlus.* A small stream flowing W. of Sardis to join the Hermus. Gold was anciently found in its reddish mud.

[p. 87] *Hyperborean land.* Here in the far north Apollo was sometimes imagined to pass the winter. Its inhabitants, pious vegetarians, lived without war or sickness for a thousand years; till, wearying of this tranquil existence, they leapt, garland-crowned, from a rock into the sea.

[p. 87] *Hēracles and the Wraith of Meleāger.* Earlier in this poem Bacchýlides has warned his patron Híero to remember in his good fortune that none can prosper always—witness the fates of Hēracles and Meleāger.

[p. 87] *Sacker of towns.* Hēracles, son of Zeus by Alcmēna (wife of Amphítryon King of Thebes) sacked Troy, Pylos, and Oechalia. As one of his Twelve Labours, he was sent by his cousin Eurystheus to fetch Cerberus, the three-headed Hound of Hell.

[p. 87] *Echidna*, a primitive monster, half woman, half snake, some-times located in Scythia, was credited with a large, miscellaneous, and unpleasant progeny—Cerberus, the Hydra, the Chimera slain by Bellerophon, the Dragon of the Hesperides, the Dragon of the Golden Fleece, the Sphinx, Scylla, the Gorgons, the Nemean lion, and the eagle that ate Prometheus' liver.

[p. 87] *Cōcȳtus,* 'Wailing', one of the streams of Hell.

[p. 87] *As wind-tossed leaves*. . . . A sudden flash of sunlight across the gloom of Hell.

[p. 87] *Porthaónides*. Meleāger, son of Oeneus, son of Porthāon.

[p. 88] *Queen of Heaven*. Hēra, who persecuted Hēracles in her jealousy of his mother Alcmēna.

[p. 88] *Meleāger answered*. . . . He says nothing of Atalanta; though Euripides in a lost play made Meleāger's passion for her the root of the tragedy. Compare Swinburne's *Atalanta in Calydon*.

[p. 89] *Magic brand*. For similar folklore in which a man's life is bound up with fire or other external objects, see Frazer, *Golden Bough*, II, 265; XI, 103.

[p. 90] *Not to be born is best*. See p. 67 and note.

[p. 90] *Ionians*. Here Athenians. Athens regarded herself as mother-city of Ionia.

[p. 91] *Sinis*, son of Poseidon, waylaying travellers at the Isthmus, tied them to two pine-trees bent earthward, so as to be torn in half when the stems were released; till Theseus did the like to him.

[p. 91] *Scīron*. See p. 109.

[p. 91] *Crommyon*, 12 miles E. of Corinth.

[p. 91] *Kerkyon*, another son of Poseidon, at Eleusis, wrestled with all comers and killed them.

[p. 91] *Procoptes* (or Procrustes), apparently son of Polypēmon, fitted his victims to his famous bed, stretching them if too short, lopping them if too long.

[p. 92] *Lemnos*. Though no longer volcanic, Lemnos seems formerly to have been so; and was associated, like Etna, with Hephaestus.

PRAXILLA

[p. 92] *'Neither Maid nor Wife.'* Cf. Sir Henry Taylor, *Elena's Song*:

> Quoth tongue of neither maid nor wife
> To heart of neither wife nor maid—
> Lead we not here a jolly life
> Between the shine and shade?

> Quoth heart of neither maid nor wife
> To tongue of neither wife nor maid—
> Thou wagg'st, but I am worn with strife
> And feel like flowers that fade.

PLATO

[p. 94] *Ágathon* (*c.* 445–401). A brilliant but decadent tragic dramatist, friend of Euripides and butt of Aristophanes. He appears also as a speaker in Plato's *Symposium*, whose setting is the celebration at Ágathon's house of his first victory, in 416.

[p. 94] *Aster*. Supposedly a youth with whom Plato studied astronomy.

[p. 95] *Dīon*, a wealthy Syracusan, soninlaw of the elder Dionysius, despot of Syracuse, became an ardent disciple of Plato. Banished by his brotherinlaw, the younger Dionysius, he lived at Athens (366–57); then, returning with troops, mastered Syracuse. But he made himself unpopular and was murdered by a fellowPlatonist, Callippus, in 353. Platonist ventures into practical politics were, indeed, singularly unsuccessful.

[p. 95] *Laïs*. There were at least two famous courtesans of the name. This is perhaps the elder or eldest, who lived at Corinth in the later 5th century and counted among her lovers the hedonist philosopher Aristippus (who philosophically commented: 'She is mine, I am *not* hers'). On her grave there stood a lioness (often associated with Aphrodite), tearing a ram. Prior has adapted this epigram:

> Venus, take my votive glass,
> Since I am not what I was;
> What from this day I shall be,
> Venus, let me never see.

TIMOTHEÜS

[p. 96] '*Contemporaneity*'. It is said that in conservative Sparta, at the musicfestival of the Carneia, one of the Ephors snatched from Timótheüs the elevenstringed lyre he had introduced in place of the old sevenstringed instrument, and hacked four of its strings away.

CLEANTHES

[p. 97] *The Stoic's Resignation*. An adaptation of these lines by J. A. Symonds was put on his tomb.

PERSES

[p. 97] *Tўchon*. God of luck; perhaps connected with Priāpus.

PART THREE

ALEXANDRIAN PERIOD

3rd–2nd centuries B.C.

PHILETAS OF COS

(*c.* 300 B.C.)

AN elegiac poet and grammarian, who was tutor to the children of
Ptolemy I of Egypt and one of the poetic masters of Theócritus.

' Nothing is here to wail'

I mourn you not, best friend. Much good and fair
You knew. Of evil, too, God sent your share.

(Stobaeus, *Florilegium*, CXXIV, p. 616.).

ARATUS OF SOLI

(*c.* 315–*c.* 240 B.C.)

J'ai l'esprit tout ennuyé,
D'avoir trop étudié
Les Phénomènes *d'Arate;*
Il est temps que je m'ébatte
Et que j'aille aux champs jouer.
Bons Dieux! qui voudrait louer
Ceux qui collés sur un livre
N'ont jamais souci de vivre.

Ronsard.

Wordsworth looked forward to a poetry of science. But it has hardly
arrived, though the idea of it was already known to the ancients. With
his versified astronomy, the *Phaenomena*, Arātus attained a reputation
hard now to understand; he was imitated by Virgil, quoted by St Paul,
translated by Cicero, Germanicus Caesar, and the fourth-century
Avienus. In a sense Arātus revives the didactic epic of Hēsiod, as
Apollonius Rhodins the heroic epic of Homer. But where Hēsiod's work
smells of rain-wet earth, that of Arātus reeks of the lamp. He has none
of the passion of Lucretius' *De Rerum Natura*, none of the charm of

Fontenelle's prose in his *Sur la Pluralité des Mondes*. Alexandria, indeed, produced too much *Professorenpoesie*. Arātus wrote also a poem on medicines, shorter pieces, an edition of the *Odyssey*, and a critical work on Homer; but these are lost.

Signs of Rain

Often the birds of mere or main, with ceaseless dives,
Plunge headlong into the waters; or the swallow drives,
With belly that skims the ripples, about the lake for hours;
Or that race not so happy, whom the watersnake devours,
The fathers of the tadpole, within their shallows croak;
Or the lonely tree-frog murmurs, as soon as dawn hath woke.
Oft, when a storm is coming, along some jutting strand
The chattering crow betakes him towards the shelter of the land;
Or, from his head to where his shoulders first begin,
Splashes himself by a riverside, or dives full in,
Or with loud caws by the water stalks round and round again
And oxen, too, give warning of the coming of the rain,
Lifting their heads towards Heaven and snuffing at the air;
And from their hollow homes in haste the ants will bear
The eggs that are their treasure; and quickly up the wall
The centipede goes swarming; and widely wandering crawl
Those worms that men have named 'the sable earth's entrails';
While all the race of Chanticleer, through wings and tails,
Peck eagerly for vermin, or loudly gurgling go,
With a sound as when dripping water on water drops below.

(*Phaenomena*, 942–62.)

CALLIMACHUS OF CYRENE
(*c.* 310–*c.* 240 B.C.)

Un petit ruisselet a toujours l'onde nette;
Aussi le papillon et la gentille avette
Y vont puiser de l'eau, et non en ces torrents,
Qui tonnent d'un grand bruit par les roches courants.
Petits sonnets bien faits, belles chansons petites,
Petits discours gentils, sont les fleurs des Charites.

Ronsard.

Callímachus is a typical Alexandrian poet. For the Alexandrians laboured under the difficulties that beset creative writers in an age when literature has passed one of its great periods, and they grow painfully conscious of living in the lengthening shadow cast by giant predecessors. They are heirs to great wealth, yet they feel impoverished; they are more cultured than their fathers, yet more sterile; their shelves teem with books, their heads with knowledge, yet they lack the old passion, energy, and life. For when the past becomes more than the future, memories than hopes, then a man—or a race—is growing old. And so, in this autumnal atmosphere, some of the Alexandrians turned to science; some to scholarship; some to a sort of literary Parnassianism, despising the popular, avoiding the trite, striving by elaboration of technique and depth of learning to find and gather laurels yet uncut. Poets like Callímachus took the view of Théophile Gautier that the artist must work, like a gem-engraver, in a hard medium; the view of Edgar Allan Poe that poems must essentially be brief—or at least that they must *now* be brief. 'A big book', said Callímachus, 'is a big curse.' Other poets, like Apollonius of Rhodes, still hoped by more curious erudition and subtler psychology to revive the spacious glories of the epic. Others still, like Theócritus— the most successful, turned back from the hot and hustling streets of giant Alexandria to nature and the piping of simple shepherds among the eternal silence of the hills. Unfortunately writers are often not content to leave their theories of art for practice to prove and for time to judge; between Callímachus and Apollonius there broke out a wordy warfare of barbed epigram and bitter allusion—dust of a day now covered in the dust of years.

Callímachus, born in Cyrēne, became a schoolmaster at Alexandria, then an official of its library (where he played a chief part in compiling the catalogue), antiquarian, critic, and literary historian, as well as poet. Of the 800 volumes attributed to him, our chief remains are six *Hymns*, parts of his *Aitia* (*Origins*) and of his *Hécale*, and some epigrams, which include his finest work. His *Hymns* cannot challenge their 'Homeric' predecessors; what they gain in erudition they lose in poetry; the pages that follow include the best part of the best among them, *The Bathing of Pallas*. The *Aitia* seems to have been on similar lines to Ovid's *Fasti*—a form giving scope in its antiquarian framework for anecdotes like the romance of Acontius and Cydippe, retold by Morris in his *Earthly Paradise*. The *Hécale* is about an old woman who entertains Theseus on his way to fight the Marathonian Bull, and rambles on about a miscellany of matters to her guest—a typical attempt to treat an old theme from a novel angle. But, for the artist, novelty proved a will-o'-the-wisp; then as now. His essential aim, I believe, should be not 'progress'—that he can leave to scientists—but perfection; not to be new, but to be true. If he has personality, novelty can take care of itself—it will come unsought. Work that chases the new seldom lives to grow old.

Callímachus' *Lock of Berenice* (subsequently embodied in the *Aitia*) is likewise lost, though we have a Latin version by Catullus. Its theme—that a newly discovered constellation was really one of the queen's tresses—takes us into the frigid world of court-poetry, as dull under the Ptolemies as under the Bourbons. Yet fate is a grim ironist; no astronomical flatteries were to save Queen Berenice from being murdered by her own son.

Callímachus was a dominant figure in his day. He deeply influenced Roman poets like Catullus, Propertius, and Ovid. But, like many neo-classic poets of the eighteenth century in France and England, he seems often to have let his heart be cramped by his head, his creation be inhibited by his self-criticism. He remains a somewhat cold writer, who can strike out fine flashes, but kindle no enduring fire. Hence the superiority of his epigrams. For himself, he *was* right to prefer short poems; and there was wisdom in the advice he attributed to Apollo—that a poet should offer fat beasts but slender verses. It is when Callímachus mourns for the dead schoolgirl whose stories will never again delight her playmates, for the dead friend with whom he will never again talk down the sun to setting, that his voice after all these centuries once more becomes alive.

The Bathing of Pallas

Maidens, in Thebes Athene loved once a nymph past measure,
    One nymph of her chosen comrades she cherished best of all—
The mother of Teirésias. She took no pleasure
    Save with her friend; and whenever to Thespiae's ancient wall
Or to Corōnēa, beside Courálius' river,
    Where, fragrant with their incense, her grove and altars are,
The Maiden Goddess drove her team—ay, or whenever
    She sped to Háliartus, through the fields of Boeotia,
Often she took Charīclo in her chariot beside her;
    And unless, when the Nymphs were gathered for talk or dance, her
        friend
Was foremost there, Athene felt all her joy denied her:
    Yet bitter grief for Charīclo lay waiting in the end.
It helped not that Athene had loved her once so dearly;
    For it chanced that one day, unclasping their raiment on the Hill
Of Helicon, where the Horse's Spring runs sparkling clearly,
    They bathed—as the hush of noon o'er the mountainside lay still.

Ay, 'twas the hour of noontide, as they bathed there, those two only,
  While deep the silence brooded upon the mountain-peak;
But into that holy place with his hound came, wandering lonely,
  Teirésias (there darkened the first beard on his cheek),
And athirst past all endurance, he turned where that stream rose springing:
  Alas! For there he discovered the beauty none may see.
No ill he meant. But, in anger, Athene's voice rose ringing:
  'What evil spirit hath led thee this road of calamity?
Henceforward, Euēreides, no light shall ever quicken
  Thine eyes again.' As she said it, upon him closed the dark.
Speechless he stood—his tongue with sudden horror stricken,
  And fast in the grip of anguish his knees grew stiff and stark.
But loud screamed the Nymph, his mother: 'My queen, to the son I
    cherish
  What hast thou done? Is it *thus*, that ye Gods show loving care?
Thou hast robbed my child of his vision! O son born but to perish,
  Thine eyes have beheld Athene with breast and body bare—
But never again the sunlight! O heart with sorrow shaken!
  O peaks I shall shun for ever—hillsides of Helicon!
To exact so much for so little! For a few deer he had taken,
  For a few fawns, ye have stolen the eyesight of my son!'
So cried that weeping mother; then, in her arms enfolding
  Her dear son, with such wailings as nightingales awake,
Led him away. But Athene grew pitiful, beholding
  The sorrow of her comrade; and thus in turn she spake:
'Take back, dear deart and honoured, those words of fierce misprision.
  Not by *my* doing was it, that thy son hath lost his eyes.
No joy it is to Athene to rob youth of its vision;
  But thus the solemn edict of the Son of Crŏnus lies—
Who sees an Immortal's beauty (save the God himself reveal it)
  For that moment's revelation a bitter price must pay.
And what is done, honoured lady, no power can now repeal it;
  Such was the thread Fate spun him, upon his life's first day,
When he came from the womb of his mother. But thou, take what is
    given,
  And bear, O Euēreides, the doom of destiny.
How many sacrifices shall be burnt one day to Heaven
  By Aristaeus, and Cadmus' child, could they but see
Their only son, Actaeon—even with eyes that fail him!
  Yet, though he shares the hunting of the mighty Artemis,
The shafts they shot together on the hills shall not avail him,
  Nor all their days of hunting, against the doom that's his,

When he shall see, unwilling, bare in the pool before him
    The beauty of his Goddess; for then his hounds shall run
To banquet on their master, and everywhere she that bore him
    Shall search the woods to gather the bones of her own son.
Yea, *that* day she shall call thee "most blest"—"a happy mother"—
    Since safe to thy arms, though blinded, he came from the mountain-
        brake.
Dear friend, grieve not too sorely; I promise many another
    Honour to this thy son, henceforward, for thy sake.
A prophet I will make him, and bards unborn shall utter
    His name, as far the greatest of any earthly seer.
He shall know which birds betoken good—and which birds flutter
    Idly—and which come winging with signs for men to fear.
Boeotia shall hearken to the words of God he showeth,
    And Cadmus and, thereafter, the great Labdácidae.
I will give him a mighty staff, to guide him where he goeth;
    A long life I will give him, and many his years shall be.
And even in death his wisdom, alone, shall keep its worth,
Honoured of Him that gathers the peoples of the earth.'

                                                    (*Hymns*, V, 57–130.)

The Parnassian

Once in the ear of Apollo said Envy, privily:
'I honour only a poet with songs wide as the sea.'
But, spurning Envy from Him, Apollo thus replied:
'Full flows Assyria's river; yet thickly down its tide
The sweepings and the scourings of the earth wash weltering:
But her servants bear to Demeter—not draughts from *any* spring—
Nought but the flower of waters, that from some fount divine
Rills in a slender streamlet, unsullied, crystalline.'

                                                    (*Hymns*, II, 105–11.)

The Aesthete

I loathe bards' commonplaces. No beaten track delights me,
    Where the feet of multitudes go thronging soon and late.
I hate light loves and easy. No public fount invites me.
    Everything that is common do I abominate.

                                                    (*Epigrams*, XXX, 1–4.)

The Dead Playmate

For Crēthis the teller of stories, for that sweet head so clever
  At common task or playtime, the maids of Samos call
Oft and in vain. But that gay tongue sleeps here for ever
    The sleep that waits them all.

(XVIII.)

Don Juan

The huntsman, Epicȳdes, across the mountains follows
  The track of every hare, the slot of every hind,
In the teeth of frost and blizzard. But if a comrade hollows—
  'See, one is down!—before you!'—to that he has no mind.
Such is my love: so eager to follow all that flies,
Onward it sweeps disdaining what at its mercy lies.

(XXXIII.)

The Dead Poet

One told me, Heraclítus, you were dead; and left me weeping,
  As once more I remembered how often down the west
We talked the sun to setting. And now—dust in earth's keeping—
  Old friend from Halicarnassus, long since, it seems, you rest.
Yet still the songs you sang us, your Nightingales, abide:
Not Death's own hand can seize them, that clutches all beside.

(II.)

' Pulvis et Umbra '

'Sleeps Cháridas beneath you?' 'If you would ask concerning
  The dead son of Arimmas, from Cyrēne, here he lies.'
'What of the grave, friend?' 'Darkness.' 'What of the dead's returning?'
  'False.' 'What of Pluto?' 'A fable. What dies for ever dies.
This is the truth. Would you rather some pleasant fairy tale?
Why then, in Hell for a penny fat oxen stand on sale.'

(XV.)

The Misanthrope

'Now you are buried, Timon, is the darkness worse, or the light?'
'The dark. For ye swarm yet thicker, here in the House of Night.'

(V.)

THEOCRITUS OF SYRACUSE

(*c.* 310 B.C.–?)

Ah! leave the smoke, the wealth, the roar
Of London, and the bustling street,
For still, by the Sicilian shore,
The murmur of the Muse is sweet.
Still, still the suns of summer greet
The mountain-grave of Helikê
And shepherds still their songs repeat
Where breaks the blue Sicilian sea.

Andrew Lang.

Theócritus serves as an example of what a real poet *can* do even if he has the misfortune to be born in an age of decadence, when everything seems already said. Probably a Syracusan by birth, he spent part of his life in the green and pleasant island of Cos, off south-west Asia Minor, and in the vast new city of Alexandria. Hence he is a poet of both town and country, loving the country as only those can who have stifled in great towns.

Like Callímachus, he felt that long poems risked tedium; his *Idylls* (that is, 'Short Pieces') are sketches of town and country life, of heroic legends, of happy or unhappy love. The first of regular pastoral poets, he remains the finest. For though his countryside is already somewhat idealized (it is enough to contrast the harsher realism of Hësiod), he did at least know his shepherds, while some of his successors give the impression of never having talked to a real rustic in their lives. Hence Theócritus contrives to keep an admirable balance between realism and romance. Even with the most vivid figures of Attic drama one seems to hear and feel the tread of the tragic buskin: but those of Theócritus still go springing with bare brown feet across the grass and rock of Cos or Sicily. More actual than Virgil or Spenser, he does not on the other hand, like Wordsworth, sometimes give his countrymen too much an air of oaf or boor. Theócritus, indeed, could not have written *Michael*; but then neither could Wordsworth have created the passionate young sorceress of Theócritus. Here is none of the grey brooding mystery of the cloud-raked crags of Westmorland; but no Greek poet since Homer has painted so vividly the sunlit beauty, yet sadness, of Mediterranean hillside and Sicilian sea.

124

Daphnis

THYRSIS

Sweet is the whisper, goatherd, of yonder pine that sings
There by the running water—and sweet your piping rings.
Next to Pan's self, in music, yours is the mastery—
If He were to win the horned he-goat, yours would the milch-goat be;
Or, if Pan chose the she-goat, then yours the kid to win—
And a kid is delicate eating, till her milking days begin.

GOATHERD

Sweeter your song flows, shepherd, than the murmuring tone
Of the streamlet plashing yonder, down from its lofty stone.
If, matched with you, the Muses for *their* prize chose the sheep,
Then yours the lamb, as second. Or if they chose to keep
The yeanling, then its mother were yours as next in skill.

THYRSIS

By the Nymphs, I beg you, goatherd, I beg you, on this hill
Sit you down for a little, where the tamarisks grow, and play
Your pipe. And I will be watching that none of your goats shall stray.

GOATHERD

Ah, shepherd, pipe we may not. Not in the hushed noontide.
For fear of Pan we may not. For then on the mountainside,
Tired with the chase, He slumbers. And savage of heart is He,
And the snarling anger hovers at His nostrils, perilously.
But come—the sorrows of Daphnis, O Thyrsis, you can sing,
So sweetly that never a herdsman can match your carolling.
Then hither beneath the elm-tree—come hither now and sit,
Here, with the carved Priäpus and the Spring-nymphs opposite,
Where the shepherd's seat and the oak-trees are. And if for me
You sing as well as once you sang, in rivalry
With Libyan Chrŏmis, you shall have—to milk her thrice—
My goat that, though twin her kidlings, yet brims the milkpail twice;
And my deep dish of ivy-wood, with sweet wax polished well,
Twin-handled, fresh from the chisel, still full of the clean wood-smell.
Round its lip, at the top, there twists an ivy-spray—
Ivy-leaves dotted, between, with berries golden-gay;
And there within—as a God might carve—is a woman in the pride
Of splendid robe and headband; and by her, on each side,

A fair and long-tressed lover. Passionately that pair
Of rivals bandy insults; but she—she does not care.
At one she glances smiling—and then she turns again,
Inclining more to the other. But *they*—from love's long pain
Their eyes are ringed with blackness. Yet all their labour's nought.
Next these, an aged fisher on a rugged rock is wrought—
There, with the look of one that is toiling hard and fast,
The old man stands and gathers his great net for a cast.
He is straining the strength of his body to the utmost, you can tell,
All round his neck, so tensely, the corded muscles swell;
For though his hair is grizzled, hale as a youth is he.
Next, a little aside from that ancient of the sea,
Is a vineyard purple-clustered, growing fair and tall;
Close by, there sits to guard it, upon a loose stone-wall,
A little lad; and, near him, two foxes—one that goes
Along the vines, devouring; with all the guile she knows,
The other stalks his wallet, determinedly intent
On a more solid breakfast. But he—he is wholly bent
On plaiting a lovely locust-trap, with asphodel and reeds,
And lost in that loving labour nor food, nor vines, he heeds.
Lastly, a lithe acanthus goes twining about the bowl.
It is a thing of rapture, a sight to witch your soul.
I bought it from a sailor of a Calydnian ship,
For a goat and a great, white, cream-made cheese. But never lip
Of mine has touched its virgin wood—'tis yours this day,
And welcome, friend!—if only you'll sing your lovely lay.
Come, I speak true! Your song now! For take it you cannot
Down to the House of Hades, that makes all things forgot.

THYRSIS (*sings*)

Lift up the song, dear Muses, lift up the herdsman's song.
Thyrsis from Etna calls you—Thyrsis the sweet of tongue.
While Daphnis' heart was breaking, ah Nymphs, where were ye then,
Where were ye? In vales of Pindus? In Tempe's lovely glen?
For, sure, by broad Anāpus ye were not wandering,
Nor high on the peak of Etna, nor by Ācis' holy spring.
  Lift up the song, dear Muses, lift up the herdsman's song.

For him the very jackals, the wild wolves howled and cried;
Even the lion from the thicket sorrowed when Daphnis died.
  Lift up the song, dear Muses, lift up the herdsman's song.

Round his feet, as he lay there, mourning with heavy cheer
Stood many a calf and heifer, many a mighty steer.
  Lift up the song, dear Muses, lift up the herdsman's song.

First, Hermes came from the mountain, and said—'Who makes thee
    weep,
Dear son? Who is it, Daphnis, that stirs thy heart so deep?'
  Lift up the song, dear Muses, lift up the herdsman's song.

The neatherds came—the shepherds—the goatherds—to his side,
And asked what evil ailed him. Priāpus came, and cried,
'Why grieving, wretched Daphnis?—while now by every rill
For thee the girl goes wandering, by every woodland, still—'
  Lift up the song, dear Muses, lift up the herdsman's song.

'Searching for thee!—oh feeble, feckless in love, art thou.
"The neatherd" once men called thee—no better than goatherd now!'
  Lift up the song, dear Muses, lift up the herdsman's song.

'The goatherd, craven creature, watching his he-goat cover
The bleating flock, cries weeping—"Had I but been their lover!"'
  Lift up the song, dear Muses, lift up the herdsman's song.

'So thou, as girls go gaily laughing in thy sight,
Weepest—"Ah, to join them in their dances, what delight!"'
But the herdsman answered nothing; he bore his bitter doom
Of passion, uncomplaining; he bore it to the tomb.
  Lift up again, dear Muses, lift up the herdsman's song.

Last, with her lovely laughter, came Cypris—secretly
Laughing, yet nursing anger still—'Daphnis,' said she,
'Once thou didst boast, in wrestling thou couldst o'ermaster Love:
Is Love not a grimmer wrestler?—thou under, he above?'
  Lift up again, dear Muses, lift up the herdsman's song.

Then Daphnis groaned in answer: 'Ah, Love, thou thing of pain,
Love abhorred and accursèd; Love, thou mortal bane,
Now indeed thou deemest that my last sun is set;
But Daphnis, even in Hades, shall make Love suffer yet.'
  Lift up again, dear Muses, lift up the herdsman's song.

'To Ida—go!—to Anchises! Runs there not a tale,
Of herdsman and Cyprian there, mid oak and galingale?'
   Lift up again, dear Muses, lift up the herdsman's song.

'And ripe, too, is Adonis—one herdsman more for thee!—
Who hunts the cowering hare and all the beasts that flee.'
   Lift up again, dear Muses, lift up the herdsman's song.

'Nay, turn thee back to the battle, face Diomēdes now,
And say: "I have conquered Daphnis, the herdsman—meet me *thou*!"'
   Lift up again, dear Muses, lift up the hersdman's song.

'Farewell, ye wolves, and jackals, and bears in your mountain caves,
Ye shall meet the herdsman Daphnis no more where woodland waves,
No more in brake or coppice. Arethusa, evermore
Farewell!—and ye, fair rivers whose floods down Thymbris pour.'
   Lift up again, dear Muses, lift up the herdsman's song.

'It is Daphnis calls upon ye, whose herds once roamed your hills;
Daphnis, whose steers and heifers were watered at your rills.'
   Lift up again, dear Muses, lift up the herdsman's song.

'O Pan, O Pan, where art thou? Wherever thou treadst this while—
Tall Maenălus, long Lycaeon—to this Sicilian isle
Come!—from the grave of Hélice, come to me here—
From that high mound of Arcas, that even the Gods revere.'
   Now cease your song, dear Muses, now cease your herdsman's song.

'Come hither, take my panpipe—the honeyed scent is cast
Still, from the wax, O Master, that binds its fair lip fast:
Down to the House of Hades I am dragged by love at last.'
   Now cease your song, dear Muses, now cease your herdsman's song.

'Now let the briar and bramble bear violets, if they will;
On the juniper let blossom the dainty daffodil.
Since Daphnis dies, come chaos! Let pears on the pine be found;
Let the hind turn now on the hunter, and worry the hunting-hound;
Let the music of nightingales by owls from the hills be drowned.'
   Now cease your song, dear Muses, now cease your herdsman's song.

So saying, his voice fell silent. To lift that fallen head
In vain strove Aphrodite. The Fates had spun his thread.

128

The Stream of Death took Daphnis—and down its flood was borne
The singer loved of the Muses, the youth no Nymph could scorn.
  Now cease your song, dear Muses, now cease your herdsman's song.

Now bring your bowl and the goat, for me to milk and do
Libation to the Muses. Muses, farewell to you!
Farewell! I will bring ye hereafter a song that is sweeter still.

GOATHERD

  Ah Thyrsis, I wish you honey, yes, honeycombs, to fill
Your tuneful mouth, and figs from Aegïlus to eat,
Sweet figs—for never cicada was heard to sing so sweet.
Here is the bowl. Now try, friend!—smells not its fragrance good?
You would think the fruitful Seasons in their fount had steeped its wood.
Hither, Kissaitha! Milk her! And you, ye goats, take care!
Have done with your wanton gambols, lest the he-goat catch ye there.
                                                    (*Idylls*, I.)

The Sorceress

Where are my leaves of laurel? Quick!—lay them in my hand,
Thestÿlis. And my philtres! And twist a crimson strand
Of finest wool on the vessel's lip. I mean to cast
A spell on my heartless lover. Wretch, that for twelve days past
Has left me!—although he knows not, am I living yet or dead?
No more on my door he batters. Ah, shameless! Has Love led—
Love and the Queen of Desire—that fickle heart astray?
To Tīmāgētus' wrestling-school, at morn, I will take my way—
Find him and curse his unkindness; but spells of fire this night
Shall bind him first. O Selēne, fair shine thy lovely light!—
While low to Thee, and Hecatē, I sing, who fills with dread
The very dogs as She comes, through the blood, through the graves, of
    the dead.
Hail Hecatē, Queen of Terror—be near me Thou to the end!
Such power as once to Circe, or Mēdēa, Thou didst lend,
Or to fair-haired Perimēde—such may my magic be!
  My wheel, draw that man hither, oh draw him home to me!

Now wastes in the flame the barley—come now, more quickly!—throw,
Thestÿlis! Wretched girl, what leaves you dreaming so?
Am I grown so vile in your eyes—a jest to you too at last!
Scatter the barley, saying: 'It is Delphis' bones I cast.'
  My wheel, draw that man hither, oh draw him home to me!

Delphis has done me wrong—I burn these leaves of bay
For Delphis. And as this laurel crackles and burns away,
Bursting to flame in an instant, leaving no ash behind,
Let a fire as fierce, as wasting, round the limbs of Delphis wind.
My wheel, draw that man hither, oh draw him home to me!

Now will I burn the corn-husks. O Artemis, Thy spell
Can shatter all that's hardest—ay, the adamant of Hell.
The dogs howl, up through the city! They hear the Goddess pass,
Thestȳlis, by the crossways! Beat—quickly!—on the brass!
My wheel, draw that man hither, oh draw him home to me!

Listen! The winds lie silent, and silent lies the sea,
But nothing can quiet the anguish that fills the heart in me.
For all my soul lies flaming for him that has betrayed
My love to its undoing—left me no more a maid.
My wheel, draw that man hither, oh draw him home to me!

Now as this wax is melted, so by the Goddess' power,
May he melt, Myndian Delphis, with passion at this hour.
As my brazen roarer circles, by Aphrodite's will
Let him circle, mad with passion, about my doorway still.
My wheel, draw that man hither, oh draw him home to me!

Thrice now I pour libation—and thrice, O Queen, I cry—
Whether this night beside him woman or lad may lie,
Let them fade from his mind forgotten, as once from Theseus' mind
The fair-tressed Ariadne, in Dīa left behind.
My wheel, draw that man hither, oh draw him home to me!

Arcadia breeds the horsewort, the herb whose longing thrills
Mare and filly to madness, galloping through the hills;
So might these eyes see Delphis race from the wrestling-school
To dash against my doorway, mad as a raving fool.
My wheel, draw that man hither, oh draw him home to me!

I take this stolen tassel, that from Delphis' mantle came,
I tear it and toss its fragments in the fiercest of the flame.
O Love, why wilt thou cling so, bleeding me white, to slake
Thy thirst, O Love devouring, like horseleech from the lake?
My wheel, draw that man hither, oh draw him home to me!

I will pound a poisonous lizard and bear the brew to him
Tomorrow. But take these simples, now while the night hangs dim,
And over his threshold knead them, Thestŷlis, and say,
With muttering mouth, 'I am kneading Delphis' bones away.'
   My wheel, draw that man hither, oh draw him home to me!

She is gone. How shall I mourn, now, my love's memory?
Ah, where begin? Who was it, first brought this curse on me?
Eubūlus' daughter, Anaxo, was chosen out to bear
A basket to Artemis' temple; and in procession there
Many a beast should follow—a lioness as well.
   Listen, O Queen Selēne, how first in love I fell.

Theumáridas' nurse, the Thracian, poor soul that now is dead,
Came from her house close by us, and begged me hard, and said,
We *must* go see that pageant. And I (oh, unhappiness!),
I let her tongue cajole me—o'er a fair, long linen dress
I cast Cleärista's mantle, and then we went our way.
But with half our path behind us, where Lŷcon's gardens lay—
   Listen, O Queen Selēne, how first in love I fell—

I noticed Eudamippus, walking together there
With Delphis—but more golden than helichryse the hair
Gleamed on their cheeks, and brighter, O Moon, their breasts than Thou,
(For the athletes had been trying their glorious strength but now).
   Listen, O Queen Selēne, how first in love I fell.

I saw him—and madness seized me—and my poor heart took flame.
Blanched was all my beauty. I gave no heed what came
In all that day's long pageant. Home how I found my way,
I know not. Ague shook me. Shivering I lay
On my bed ten days together, ten nights—till all my hue
As sallow and as yellow as the dye of Thapsus grew.
   Listen, O Queen Selēne, how first in love I fell.

I pined to a thing of skin and bone; my long hair fell—
Ah, what old beldame's cottage, that dealt in charm or spell,
Did I not haunt? Yet it helped not. And ever the days slipped past—
Till to my maid I uttered all of the truth at last.
   Listen, O Queen Selēne, how first in love I fell.

'Thestÿlis, for this madness find me a remedy.
I am sick for Delphis, body and soul. Go now for me
To the school of Tīmāgētus, and watch—there oftenest
He comes; and *there* is the seat that of all he loves the best.'
 Listen, O Queen Selēne, how first in love I fell.

'When alone there you have found him, nod quickly with your head
And whisper "Sīmaetha calls you"—and bring him.' So I said,
And away she went and, returning, hither home she brought
The youth in his glorious beauty. At sight of that face long sought—
 Listen, O Queen Selēne, how first in love I fell—

As there he came through my doorway, so lightly, I grew cold
As ice through all my body. Down from my forehead rolled
Sweat like the pelting raindrops—I could not utter sound
As faint as the moan for its mother, of child in slumber drowned.
I lay with every limb, like a puppet, stiffened fast.
My loveless lover scanned me; and then, with eyes downcast—
 Listen, O Queen Selēne, how first in love I fell—

Taking his seat, 'Sīmaetha,' he said, 'as narrowly
As *I* beat fair Philīnus once, now *you* have outrun *me*,
In calling me to your bedside, before uncalled I came.
Else, by the joys of Eros, I *had* come, all the same—'
 Listen, O Queen Selēne, how first in love I fell—

'Two or three comrades with me, before this eve was old,
With apples of Dionysus wrapped in my mantle's fold,
My head enwreathed with the poplar beloved of Hēracles,
And twined with purple ribbons. And then—if you should please—'
 Listen, O Queen Selēne, how first in love I fell—

'To give us ready welcome, then all would have been well;
For gay am I and gallant, as all our youth can tell.
With a kiss from your lovely lips, I could have slept once more.
But, had you barred me out, and bolted fast your door,
We had axe and torches ready, at need, to break our way.
So, as it is, to Cypris my thanks in full I pay—
To Cypris first and, next, to you—that from the fire
Have snatched me by your summons, when already my desire
Had left me half in ashes. In truth Love's hotter far
Than the blaze Hephaestus kindles in his forge of Lípara.

He can hound with his bitter madness the young lass from her room,
And the bride but a moment risen from the warm bed of her groom.'
  Listen, O Queen Selēne, how first in love I fell.

Such were the words he uttered—and I, poor fool, gave ear,
And took his hand, and beside me on the soft bed drew him near.
Then flesh against flesh grew melted, and now our faces flushed
With a new warmth and, between us, passed whispers softly hushed.
Alas, O Queen Selēne, not long the tale to tell—
All I could give was given—to love's embrace we fell.
And yet till now there was nothing that he found in me to blame,
Nothing I found in *him*; but now, today, there came
Our flute-girl Philista's mother, and Melixo's, just as Morn
Climbed rosy from the Ocean, by her swift steeds upward borne;
And said, among her gossip, that Delphis certainly
Was fallen in love with another—if woman or lad it be,
She could not tell me surely—only he sat all day
And drank wine, neat, to Eros; then suddenly rushed away
To wreathe, he said, with garlands the door of that love of his.
So the old woman tattled. But very truth it is.
For thrice a day, or four times, he used to haunt my door,
And he left his Dorian oilflask, here in my care, before;
But now, since last I saw him—twelve days! Ah, doubt it not,
He has turned to another pleasure, and *my* love lies forgot.
So now I will try upon him, if the flame can work its spell;
Then—if he still torments me—against the Gate of Hell
He shall knock—by the Fates I swear it! Such salves in my chest I save,
Which that Assyrian stranger once taught to me, and gave.
But Thou, farewell, O Mistress. Turn to the Western Sea
Thy horses—I will bear it, this grief I took on me.
Farewell, O Moon, I bid Thee, throned in Thy lovely light;
Farewell, ye stars that follow on the noiseless wheels of Night.

                                                    (*Idylls*, II.)

The Festival

So, as we lay there resting, thick rustled overhead
Many an elm and poplar, while babbling down its bed
Out of the Nymphs' own cavern a sacred water sprang,
And deep in the woodland shadows the dusky crickets sang,
Making a busy music. And where the brambles lay,
Thick with their thorns, the tree-frog sat crooning far away.

There trilled the lark, and the linnet piped, to the wood-dove's coo,
And over the bubbling wellhead ever the brown bees flew.
There all smelt sweet of summer, all smelt of autumn sweet,
There at our sides the apples, the pears fell at our feet,
Tumbling in headlong bounty; while earthward, overcome
By the riot of fruit upon them, bent the branches of the plum.

    Then from the mouths of the wine-jars was the four-years' seal torn free.
Ah, Nymphs of high Parnassus, ye Nymphs of Castaly,
Was it ever such wine as yonder, that in Phŏlus' craggy cave
To Hēracles aforetime the Centaur Chīron gave?
Was it ever such peerless nectar that by Anāpus' stream
Sent reeling round his sheep-fold the giant Polypheme,
Who hurled at ships whole mountains?—as we mingled with your spring,
O Nymphs, by Demeter's altar? Be it mine, *again*, to bring
A mighty fan for setting in Her corn-heap, while She stands
Smiling, with gathered corn-ears and poppies in Her hands!

                            (*Idylls*, VII, 135-57.)

Hylas

    Not, Nīcias, as we dreamed once, for us alone was Love
Begotten—whoever his parent, among the powers above;
To feel how fair life's fair things are, not first are we
Who look not on the morrow, in our mortality.
Long since that iron heart of the son of Amphítryon,
That braved the lion of the mountain, by the love of a lad was won—
By the young beauty of Hylas and the grace of his tossing hair.
He taught the boy those lessons, with a loving father's care,
That had made himself a hero, sung in the mouths of men;
Never an hour could part them—not the high noon, nor when
The white-maned steeds of Morning charged up the Heaven's steep,
Nor when the piping chickens were looking up to sleep
Where aloft on the sooty rafter their mother flapped her wings—
That the boy might grow to a manhood perfect in all things,
A yokefellow true and trusted, after the hero's heart.

    Then fell the days when Jason made ready to depart
In quest of the Golden Fleece; and now on every hand
Each warrior of valour, the flower of every land,
Flocked to the muster—among them, to rich Iolcus' shore,
That man of many labours, whom once Alcmēna bore,
The heroine of Mīdeia; and in his company

Came Hylas, where fair-benched Argo lay beached beside the sea—
Argo, that like an eagle, soaring the watery waste,
Passed untouched through the Clashing Rocks, and onward raced
Towards the deep mouth of Phāsis—while rooted crags grew *they*.
But, at the Pleiads' rising, when Spring has gone her way,
And on the upland borders the young lambs flock to feed,
Then to the quest before them the heroes gave their heed;
The thwarts of hollow Argo they manned, and spreading sail
On the third day reached the Hellespont, before the south-west gale;
And moored her within Propontis, where the Kiānians' kine
Drive broad through the loam their furrow, till bright their ploughshares
    shine.
Then springing ashore her rowers made ready at evenfall,
Pair by pair, their supper—but a common couch for all;
For many bladed rushes, much galingale grew deep
There in the mead; and they mowed them, to make soft beds to sleep.
    But now for water Hylas, the golden-haired, was gone,
To cook the supper of Hēracles and dauntless Télamon
(For ever they ate as comrades beside the selfsame board).
Brazen pitcher in hand, quickly he came where poured
A spring from a lowly hollow—thick grew the rushes there,
Thick the dark celandine and pale-green maidenhair,
And parsley lush, and reed-grass that loves the marsh's cool.
But there the Nymphs had gathered, to dance in the midmost pool,
Those sleepless Nymphs, from whose dread power the peasant flies—
Euneica; Mālis; Nycheia, with springtime in her eyes.
So, as the boy bent o'er the brink, in haste to dip
The wide mouth of his pitcher, all at once their grip
Closed on his wrist—for passion had thrilled their hearts to see
The Argive lad—and his body went shooting suddenly
Down the dark depths; as when, from Heaven, a star ablaze
Shoots on a sudden seaward, and sailor to sailor says:
'Quick, lads, and lighten sail aloft—'tis coming on to blow!'
On their knees the Nymphs took Hylas, there in the depths below,
With gentle words of comfort to charm away his tears;
But now Amphítryon's son, tormented with his fears,
Strode forth to seek his squire, with trusty club in hand
And curving bow, such as Scythians wield, beside Maeōtis' strand.
Thrice he thundered 'Hylas!' with the strength of his stalwart frame,
And thrice the boy cried answer; but his voice so faintly came
From the pool's depth, that far he seemed, although so near.
Then, as a lion devouring, when falls upon his ear

In his lair high up the mountains the cry of some young fawn,
Rushes to seize his quarry; so through the pathless thorn
Hēracles went searching, in anguish, far and wide.
Stubborn indeed are lovers—far o'er the countryside
He tramped, forgetting Jason, by thicket, hill, and dale,
While Argo, with all aboard her and ready-hoisted sail,
Waited. At last, near midnight, the heroes lowered once more
Her yard, to bide his coming. But onward still he tore,
Blindly and madly searching, by raging Love possest.
    So was the lovely Hylas numbered with the Blest;
But bitterly the heroes called curses on the name
Of Hēracles, 'the deserter', that quitted, to his shame,
The thirty thwarts of Argo; and so afoot came he
Unto the Colchian kingdom's inhospitality.

(Idylls, XIII.)

The Hunter Hunted

In the leaf-strewn cavern, Daphnis, thy wearied limbs lie sleeping,
    While for the beasts on the mountain thy hunting-nets are spread;
But see, to hunt the hunter, into thy cave comes creeping
    Pan, and Priāpus with him, that wreathes his lovely head
With the yellow-blooming ivy. Quick, Daphnis, quickly! Flee—
Up, and shake off the slumber that softly steals on thee!

(Epigrams, III.)

' And Thou beside me Singing in the Wilderness '

Not all the Isle of Pĕlops, nor King's treasures past appraising,
    Nor feet more fleet than wind are anything to me.
I will sing beneath this boulder, with my arms about you, gazing
    At our flocks together grazing and the sea of Sicily.

(Idylls, VIII, 53-6.)

Lovers' Meeting

Have you come then, O my darling!—with the third night's end, at last!
Have you come! Ah, love-sick lovers grow old ere a day be past.

(Idylls, XII, 1-2.)

Transience

Lovely the rose; and yet—its beauty Time deflowers:
Lovely in spring the violet—but brief its hours:
White is the lily—but fast it falls, and fades away:
White is the snow—but it melts from earth's face where it lay:
Lovely the loveliness of youth—yet lives but for a day.

(Idylls, XXIII, 28–32.)

AUTOMEDON OF AETOLIA or THEOCRITUS
(3rd century B.C.?)

Ill Merchandise

O man, on thyself have mercy. What madness bids ye follow
  The sea, when the year grows stormy. Too fast, at best, life flies.
In haste for shining Thăsos, from Syria the Hollow,
  Unhappy Cleonĭcus, you sailed with merchandise.
Ill merchandise, Cleonĭcus! You that sailed recklessly
As the Pleiad set, with the Pleiad yourself yourself sank under sea.

(Anth. Pal., VII, 534.)

NICIAS OF MILETUS
(early 3rd century B.C.)

This poet-physician was a friend of Theócritus, who addressed two
of his *Idylls* to him, and another to his wife, with the gift of an ivory
distaff.

The Wayside Fount

Traveller the long way wearies, under my poplars seat thee;
  Draw near and to my waters bow down thy thirsty head.
And far away, hereafter, still may my memory greet thee.
  Me Simus made for Gillus, his son, that here lies dead.

(Anth. Pal., IX. 215.)

DIOTIMUS or LEONIDAS OF TARENTUM
(4th–3rd century B.C.)

Lightning

Unherded came the cattle from the hills with falling even,
 Home to the byre, and about them the snow-drifts gathered deep.
But under an oak their herdsman lay. For fire from Heaven,
 In the night that knows no waking, had stretched him there asleep.

(Anth. Pal., VII, 173.)

LEONIDAS OF TARENTUM
(early 3rd century B.C.)

Leōnidas celebrates in one of his epigrams a victory won in 274 B.C. by that Pyrrhus of Epīrus who had vainly tried to save the poet's native Tarentum from Rome. He seems also to have wandered to the Eastern Mediterranean and may possibly be portrayed in the 'Lycidas' of Theó-critus' seventh *Idyll*. Poor himself, he wrote many of his poems on the poor. 'Love had he found in huts where poor men lie.'

The Cricket's Grave

Though little be the tombstone, O passer-by, above me,
 Though it lies thus lowly in the dust before your feet,
Give honour to Phīlaenis, good friend, that she did love me,
 Her once wild thistle-climber, her clamberer in the wheat,
Her cricket, her sweet songster, whom for two years she cherished,
 Loving the sleepy music of my whirring wing.
She has not forgot me: she gave me, when I perished,
 This tiny tomb in honour of so versatile a thing.

(Anth. Pal., VII, 198.)

The Goatherds' Thank-offering

Athwart the whirling hailstones, through the darkness of December,
 Fleeing from the headlong blizzard and the bitter cold that kills,
A lonely lion and ancient, way-worn in every member,
 Came down on a fold of the goatherds that haunt high up the hills.

They cowered, their goats forgotten, with the fear of death before them,
  And unto Zeus the Saviour wildly they turned to pray;
But that great beast of the darkness sat out the storm, nor tore them,
  Nor fell upon their cattle, but stalked from the fold away.
And so for Zeus of the Hilltops, they raised in memory
That marvel fairly painted upon this stout oak-tree.

(VI, 221.)

The Shepherd's Last Sleep

Shepherds all, that wander this ridge of the mountains, feeding
  Your flocks of goats and fleecy sheep, grant now to me,
Cleitágoras, a little boon yet kindly, heeding
  My prayer in the name of Earth and Queen Persephone.
Let your sheep bleat still beside me, and sitting on a boulder
  Softly let pipe a shepherd to his flock that feeds beneath;
And let the countryman gather, ere each spring grows older,
  Rathe meadow-flowers and twine them to make my tomb a wreath;
And bring from the flock the mother of some fair lamb, and setting
  Her udder full of milk above my gravestone's base,
Let the white stream spirt upon it. Deem not the grave forgetting;
  Even the dead can render a grace for a kindly grace.

(VII, 657.)

The Farmer's Rest

Spare to this humble hillock, this stone that stands so lowly,
  Where poor Alcímenes slumbers, one word in passing, friend,
Though beneath briar and bramble it now lies hidden wholly—
  Those same old foes that, living, I fought with to the end.

(VII, 656.)

POSEIDIPPUS
(3rd century B.C. ?)

The Courtesan to Aphrodite

O thou that hauntest Cyprus, and Milētus, and Cythera,
  And that proud Syrian plain where the hammering horsehoofs roar,
Let Callistion, O Goddess, of Thy grace to Thee be dearer;
  Never she turned a lover, disdainful, from her door.

(Anth. Pal., XII, 131.)

Sappho

Long since your bones have mouldered; long, Dōricha, the binding
   Of your curls, long all the fragrance from your robe has passed away,
That you flung round fair Chăraxus and caught him in its winding
   And breast to breast lay drinking, at the dawning of the day.
But the white page of Sappho lives on and lives for ever,
   Breathing in its sweetness your name thrice-blest the while,
That Naucrătis shall remember while ships shall breast her river,
   Standing in from seaward to the long lagoons of Nile.

                      (Athenaeus, XIII, 596C.)

ASCLEPIADES OF SAMOS
(early 3rd century B.C.)

Asclēpĭădes is praised by Theócritus as a master-poet, together with
Philētas; and his work compared by Meleāger, in his garland of poets,
to 'wind-flowers'.

The Coy Mistress

Your maidenhead—you grudge it?—for what? Beyond Death's river
   You will find no lover waiting, lass, the day you die.
Love's joys are for the living. In Hades' house for ever,
   Ashes and bone, proud maiden, we shall slumber, you and I.

                      (*Anth. Pal.,* v, 85.)

Joy's Crown of Joy

O sweet is snow to June-parched lips; when winter's over,
   Sweet the west wind of springtime to sailors o'er the sea;
Yet sweeter beneath one mantle when lover lies by lover
   And both, O Love, breathe blessings upon the name of Thee.

                      (v, 169.)

Light Love

With Hermíone the witching as I played once, she was wearing
   A girdle of many colours, O Love, about her waist,
Broidered in golden letters—'Love me! Yet no despairing,
   If you behold my beauty by a new love's arms enlaced!'

                      (v, 158.)

Bitter-Sweet

Ah me, once Archĕădes pressed near and ever nearer;
  Today, not even in play our glances meet again.
Not even Love, the honeyed, is always sweet; yet dearer
  Often he grows to lovers, when his joy has turned to pain.

(XII, 153.)

'Fill the Can and Fill the Cup'

Drink, drink, Asclēpiădes. What use to wail your sorrows?
  Are you the first that Cypris beneath her heel hath thrust?
Your heart the first that felt how grim Love whets his arrows
  And bends his bow for smiting? You live. Why gnaw the dust?
Come, pour the wine!—no water! Look, in the east, Dawn's finger!
  Must we wait for the laggard lantern that bids men bedward creep?
Then here's a health, wan lover. Brief, brief our time to linger,
  Poor fool, ere we are lying, night without end, asleep.

(XII, 50.)

NOSSIS
(c. 300 B.C.)

A poetess of Locri in South Italy.

The Rose of Love

Than love there's nothing sweeter. No joys are worth the weighing
  Beside it. Even honey I spit from off my tongue.
Whom Love's Queen never kissed—I, Nossis, leave this saying—
  She knows not what the rose is the summer's flowers among.

(Anth. Pal., V, 170.)

ANYTE OF TEGEA
(early 3rd century B.C.?)

A poetess of whom little remains; but some of it gifted with an effortless simplicity worthy of her native Arcadia.

The Spring of Hermes

Beside the grey sea-shingle, here at the cross-roads' meeting,
  I, Hermes, stand and wait, where the windswept orchard grows.
I give, to wanderers weary, rest from the road and greeting:
  Cool and unpolluted from my spring the water flows.

                           (*Anth. Pal.,* IX. 314.)

The Dolphin's Tomb

Never again rejoicing in the surges that I sunder
  Shall I toss my neck aloft, as I leap from gulfs of sea;
Nor, circling round a galley, at its fair prow snort with wonder,
  Proud to find it fashioned in the shape of me.
For the dark-blue rollers hurled me high on the land's dry breast,
And in this narrow shingle I am laid to rest.

                           (VII, 215.)

Death the Leveller

In life, Mānēs the slave; but, since he died,
As great as King Darius in his pride.

                           (VII, 538.)

APOLLONIUS RHODIUS
(*c.* 280–*c.* 200 B.C.)

Apollonius, poet, scholar, and finally librarian of Alexandria, was a
native of that city, and appears to have withdrawn for a time to Rhodes
in consequence of his famous quarrel with Callímachus as to whether
poems should be long or short. His attempt to revive the glories of the
epic with his *Argonautica* (5,835 lines) hardly proved his case; for that
poem lives today, not as a whole, but by episodes like Mēdēa's love for
Jason. With all his learning, Apollonius lacked the art to give his story
a unity like Homer's; it seems too long; yet even so he omits some of the
most moving incidents of the original legend—the coming of the young
Jason to Iolcus, so magnificently told by Pindar (p. 79); the final quarrel
with Mēdēa, on which Euripides wrote his tragedy; and the death of the
hero, struck by the falling sternpost of Argo, which forms the fitting close
of Morris's *Jason*. These human touches are ill replaced by deserts of
fabulous geography and antiquarianism. The strength of Apollonius

lies in his power of romantic description, above all in his picture of Mēdēa's passion, which was one day to help Virgil in creating Dido. When this bookish poet turns to analyse the growth of love in a girl's heart, her hesitations, her conflicts, his own heart strangely quickens, and he becomes a forerunner not only of Virgil, but of medieval romance and the modern novel. Only one character of his epic lives; to her it owes what life it still retains.

The Sailing of Argo

Pélias usurped the kingdom of Iolcus from his brother Aeson; but Aeson's infant son, Jason, was brought up by the centaur Chīron on Mount Pēlion. Growing to manhood, the young hero descended to Iolcus to reclaim the throne; but his uncle impelled him first to sail to Colchis in the Black Sea and bring back the Golden Fleece of the winged ram which had once borne their cousin Phrixus to the Colchian land. For this quest Jason gathered the greatest heroes of all Greece; and for them was built the ship Argo, whence their name of Argonauts.

But far astern of Argo her whitening wake was seen,
As when a footpath glimmers amid the meadows' green;
And the Gods gazed down from Heaven on the vessel and her crew
Of race divine, the noblest that then the sea-ways knew;
From highest peaks of Pēlion the Nymphs that lurk
Within its glens, looked wondering on Athene's handiwork
And all the heroes in her, heaving at the oar;
But down from the mountain's summit came Chīron to the shore
And stood there up to the fetlocks, where frothed the grey sea's foam,
To wish them, with great hand waving, a glad returning home;
While the Centaur's wife beside him held high above the swell
In her arms the babe Achilles, for his father's last farewell. . . .
   Then over the watery pathways, up from the gulfs of sea,
Little and great, the fishes came gambolling merrily.
As when behind their shepherd, filled with sweet grass, his sheep
Troop in their countless thousands home to the fold to sleep—
Gaily he goes before them, playing a shepherd's song
Sweet and shrill on the pipe of Pan; so dense a throng
Of fishes followed Argo, as the fresh breeze filled her sail.
   Soon there sank from sight behind them, misty-pale,
The rich Pelasgian corn-lands; racing down the bay,
They watched the mountain-walls of Pēlion pass away.
Cape Sēpias sank. Before them Peirésiae rose afar,

143

And, clear in the summer sunlight, the coasts of Magnesia,
And Scíathus' isle, and the barrow where Dŏlops lies beneath—
That evening, there they landed, for the wind turned in their teeth.

(Argonautica, I, 545-58, 572-86.)

When they reached Colchis its king, Aeētes, would only give up the Fleece if Jason could first yoke two fire-breathing bulls, plough with them the Field of Ares, sow it with dragon's teeth, and slay the earth-born warriors who sprang up from that seed. That task would have been impossible, even for Jason, had not Mēdēa, the king's daughter, fallen in love with the young stranger.

The Heart-searchings of Mēdēa

Now night drew darkness over earth; far out at sea
Sailors aboard their ships were watching Hélice
And the stars that shape Orion—the traveller on his way,
And by his gate the porter, felt drowsy—slumber lay
On the eyes of the mother, even, whose little ones had died.
Hushed was the city's echoing roar; no watchdog cried,
Now, through the streets; the gloom, fast thickening, grew dumb.
And yet to the eyes of Mēdēa no such sweet sleep would come.
For still her love of Jason, and sorrow for his sake,
And fear of the bulls in their giant strength, held her awake—
Sure, in that field of Ares, miserably lost,
The youth would die! With torment, the heart in her was tossed.
As round a room the sunlight flickers from the face
Of water in pail or cauldron poured—in endless chase
Headlong hither and thither its sparkles wheel and whirl;
So leapt her heart, and quivered, in the bosom of the girl.
With pitying tears her eyes grew wet; and all her frame
Shuddered with inward anguish as with a smouldering flame.
Through each fine nerve, through the meeting of head and nape, it pressed
(For there the ache is keenest, when the Loves that know not rest,
Let loose upon men's hearts the arrows of their pain).
Now she resolved to reveal him her magic—now again
Resolved she would not give it; but die herself as well—
Then vowed she would neither perish nor yet bestow the spell,
But still endure to the end, dumb though infatuate.
So down she sat and said, her soul torn with debate:
'Ah, wretch! To what choice of evils must I turn me in my grief?
Whatever I do, my spirit fails, nor finds relief.

Nothing can quench its fever. Ah, would that Artemis
With the swiftness of her arrows had struck me down ere this!—
Or ever I looked on Jason, or the sons of Chalcíope
Set foot on the coasts of Achaea! To bring us misery
Some God, or some Erīnys, has sent them here again.
Nay then, let Jason perish, if destiny ordain
His death in the field of Ares! If I fashion him the spell,
How hide it from my parents? What story can I tell?
What stratagem can save him from being overthrown?
Can I meet him without his comrades?—can I go to him alone?
Ah bitter, although he perish, e'en then what hope have I
Of respite from unhappiness?—though he should die,
His memory will haunt me still. Nay now, have done
With shame, have done with honour! Once that my hand has won
His life, let him sail in safety—wherever he would be!
And then, his quest accomplished, let *that* day bring to me
Death!—no matter whether from a beam of the roof I sway,
Throat in a noose; or swallow some poison swift to slay.
And yet, although I perish so, they will heap my name
With insults—ay, every city shall shout aloud my shame,
Through many a land! And here, from tongue to taunting tongue
Of all the Colchian women, shall my ill fame be flung—
"A girl that in her passion for a stranger's foreign face
Died covering her parents and her home with black disgrace,
A lewd and blinded wanton!" What scorn must I not bear!
Ay me for this infatuate heart! Better it were
This night in my maiden chamber should make an end of me,
Dead none knows how, delivered from all their calumny,
Rather than such dishonour—too foul for lips to say.'
With that she sought, arising, a casket wherein lay
Her many drugs—some healing, and some of deadly bane,
And on her knees she set it down, while in her pain
For the fate now come upon her, her tears streamed on unstayed,
Till wet grew all her bosom. Now her resolve was made
To choose some deadly venom there—to taste and die;
Unhappy lass, already she was turning to untie
With feverish hands the coffer—yet suddenly there fell
Upon her heart a horror of the hateful gloom of Hell.
Long dazed and speechless there she sat—now rose up clear
Before her eyes, in vision, the joys that make life dear.
She thought again of the pleasures that gladden the living still,
She thought of her gay companions—as a maiden will;

145

And as she recalled all these, with longing, one by one,
Sweeter it seemed, once more, to look upon the sun;
She put aside the casket from off her knees again,
Swayed by the will of Hēra. And now her plan grew plain.

(III, 744–819.)

Accordingly Mēdēa met Jason in the temple of Hecate

So without voice, without murmur, they stood there face to face,
As oaks or towering pine-trees stand rooted in their place,
Side by side, unmoving, high up among the hills,
When winds are hushed—but, sudden, a gust through their branches
    thrills
And they whisper with infinite voices. So now before Love's gale
Those two were doomed, in a moment, to tell their whole hearts' tale.

(III, 967–72.)

*Then Jason begged her to help him; as Ariadne, daughter of Minos king of
Crete and Queen Pasíphaë, once helped Theseus in his danger, and reconciled
her father to him and sailed away aboard his ship, to find undying glory and a
place among the stars.*

She tells him now to win the Fleece

So he spoke in her honour. Downward she cast her gaze,
With a smile like the Gods' own nectar; and, kindled by his praise,
Her heart was melted in her. Once more his eyes she met,
Not knowing, of all she must tell him now, what word to set
First—for all together they crowded to her tongue.
Irresolute no longer, she drew from where it hung
By her fragrant waist, the magic charm; and swift and glad
He grasped it. She would have taken the very life she had
Within her breast, to give him; happy in his desire—
So dazzling, from Jason's golden head, Love flashed his own sweet fire.
For indeed the youth had stolen her own bright eyes away
And the heart within her wasted, as wastes in morning's ray
The dewdrop on a roseleaf. Now on the ground they cast
Their eyes, ashamed—now, between them, looks swift and sudden passed,
With lovelight in their glances and radiance in their smile;
Then, faltering, spoke the maiden, when mute she had stood a while:

146

'Listen now, while I tell thee the help that I have planned.
When thou hast gone to my father and taken at his hand
Those deadly teeth from the Dragon's jaw, that thou must sow,
Wait, until half the night is gone, and half is still to go;
Then wash thee in the waters of the river's tireless speed
And alone, far from thy comrades, clad in a sable weed,
Thou shalt dig a hole of rounded shape, and in the pit
A new-grown ewe thou shalt slaughter—hew not the flesh of it,
But burn it whole on a pyre, by the pit's edge mounded high.
On Hecate, only-begotten of Perses, thou shalt cry
And pour from a cup the sweetness wrought by the hiving bee;
But when thou hast duly prayed Her to look with grace on thee,
Then from the blazing pyre draw back—and let no sound
Of steps, or of dogs baying, tempt thee to turn around,
Or look behind, lest the rites that thou hast wrought be vain
And in evil case to thy comrades thou go thy ways again.
But steep this charm in water, as breaks the morning light,
And smear it, like oil, on thy naked limbs—then infinite
Thy strength shall wax, till thou feelest in battle thou art peer
Not merely of men, but of deathless Gods. And on thy spear
Spread it, on sword and buckler—no lance of earth-born men
Shall pierce thee, no flame resistless have power upon thee, then,
Breathed from those grim bulls' nostrils. Only a little while
Thou shalt be thus—for a single day; but from thy trial
Flinch not! And this I tell thee, to help thee in thy need:
When thou hast yoked yon raging bulls, and ploughed with speed,
By thy valour and thy manhood, the length of that stubborn field,
And sown are the teeth of the Dragon, and thou seest rise revealed
The Giants from the dusky furrows, thick as the corn in spring,
Then cast a great stone among them, by stealth!—and, as ravening
Hounds for their meat do battle, they too shall turn to smite
Each other. Then plunge, thyself, headlong into the fight.
So, far away from Aea, thou shalt bear the Fleece with thee
To Hellas home—wherever thou wilt—wherever thy heart would be.'
   So she spoke, and in silence her eyes on the earth she cast,
And down her perfect cheeks the hot tears hurried fast,
In grief to think in a little he must launch across the main,
Far from her side. Then, anguished, she spoke to him again,
Searching his face, and seizing his hand in her distress—
For now no more her glances were bowed in bashfulness:
'And yet, if thou comest, ever, safe to thy home one day,
Remember the name of Mēdēa. And when thou art far away,

I will remember also. But I beg thee, tell me where
Thy home is? Across the waters whither wilt thou fare?
To Orchómenus the wealthy shall thy journey bring thee near?
Or the island of Aeaea? And who then—tell me clear—
Who was this famous maiden—the child of Pasíphaë?
For unto the king, my father, sister by blood was *she*.'

 Such were her words; but, in Jason, the maiden's tears awoke
The pitiless power of passion; and thus in turn he spoke:
'Surely I cannot think it, that either by night or day
Ever I shall forget thee, if home I find my way,
From death escaped unscathed, back to Achaea's shore,
And Aeëtes does not set us some worse trial than before.
But if, indeed, thou askest where my own country is,
Listen—for no less happy am I to tell thee this.
There lies a land—and, around it, rise up the mountains wild—
Rich in fair flocks and pastures, where once Iápetus' child,
Prometheus, had for offspring the noble Deucálion,
Who was the first of menfolk to sit on a kingly throne.
Shrines to the Gods, and cities, he too was first to found.
"Haemónia", that land is called, by all the dwellers round.
There my own home, Iolcus, stands; and there as well
Many another township. Their peoples ne'er heard tell
Of the name of Aeaea's island; but Mínyas, 'tis told,
Mínyas, sprung of Aeölus' line, went thence of old
And built Orchómenus once, nigh the Cadmēan wall.
And yet why talk of things that matter not at all?—
Of my home?—of Ariadne, King Minos' child far-famed?
(For so indeed that maiden of high renown was named,
Of whom thou bad'st me tell thee.) As Minos, for his child,
Loved Theseus, I would thy father with *us* were reconciled.'

 So Jason spoke to soothe her, with words of gentleness;
But bitterly she answered, angry and comfortless,
While within her spirit all pain and passion stirred:
'In Greece, maybe, it is honour to keep a plighted word.
But not such is Aeëtes, as the lord of Pasíphaë,
King Minos, by thy telling was. Nor liken me
To Theseus' love. Nay, talk not of hospitality!
I say but this—when thou comest at last to Iolcus, still
Remember me! And I—despite my parents' will—
I shall remember, always. May there come from far away
Some word, some bird of message, to tell me, on the day
Thou shalt forget!—or a tempest upon its stormwings sweep

My body hence to Iolcus, far out across the deep—
There to reproach thee, face to face, that from this land
'Twas I alone that saved thee once! Ay, let me stand,
A sudden guest, undreamed-of, that day by thy fireside!'
    With that the tears burst from her, and miserably she cried;
But quickly Jason answered: 'Ah, lady, let thy birds,
Thy storm-winds wander where thy will. All idle words!
If ever thou comest thither, to Hellas, thou shalt then
Be honoured among women, and reverenced of men.
Like to a God they shall worship thee; because for some,
Thanks to thy wit, safe homeward once more their sons are come;
Loved husbands some shall owe thee, or their brothers, or their kin,
Delivered from destruction. Then shalt thou make within
My bedchamber thy bridal-bed; the love we plight,
Nothing shall break, till round us Death draws the last long night.'

(III, 1008—1130.)

THEODORIDAS OF SYRACUSE
(later 3rd century B.C.)

On a Shipwrecked Sailor

Here lies one that made shipwreck. But thou, sail on. The day
We foundered, other vessels still kept their onward way.

(Anth. Pal., VII, 282.)

DAMAGETUS
(3rd–2nd century B.C.)

The Last Word

O famed Phocaean city, with this last cry despairing
    Theāno passed to the darkness wherein no man may reap:
'Apellichus my husband—ah bitterness past bearing!—
    Where *are* you, in your galley far off across the deep?
So close stands Death beside me—would but to God that I
Could feel your hand, to hold it, dear heart, before I die.'

(Anth. Pal., VII, 735.)

THYMOCLES
(3rd–2nd century B.C.?)

'And Left the Thorn'

Maybe now you remember my solemn warning given:
  'Sweet is the hour of blooming, the hour of bloom is fleet—
So fleet it can outsoar the swiftest bird in Heaven.'
  Lo, on the earth, already, your flower lies at your feet.

(Anth. Pal., XII, 32.)

PHAEDIMUS OF BISANTHE
(3rd–2nd century B.C.?)

Lost at Sea

I mourn for Polyanthus, who died new-wed, O stranger;
  Here his young wife laid him, Aristágore;
The Aegean surges sank him by Scíathus in their anger,
  And nought but bone and dust came home to her from sea.
For that ill-fated body, as dawn was breaking through,
Into Torōne's haven, O friend, the fishers drew.

(Anth. Pal., VII, 739.)

ANON
(late 3rd century B.C.?)

The Humbling of Sparta

Lacedaemon, land unconquered, that no foeman's foot molested,
  Lo now the destroyers' campfires by Eurōtas smoking high!
Felled lie thy trees; on shadeless fields thy birds have nested,
  Crying; but the wolves that listen hear now no sheepfolds cry.

(Anth. Pal., VII, 723.)

DIONYSIUS THE SOPHIST
(2nd century B.C.?)

The Rose-girl

Rose-girl, fair as a rose is, what do you come to sell?
Is it yourself, or your roses? Or them and yourself as well?

(Anth. Pal., v., 81.)

ANTIPATER OF SIDON
(later 2nd century B.C.)

A Greek poet who moved in Roman society and is mentioned by
Cicero.

The Vengeance of the Nymphs

The hunting-hound of Midas, Lampon, perished thirsting,
    Though in the face of death fiercely and hard he fought.
With his paws he dug where the earth lay damp; but no stream came
      bursting,
    So deep, in its sluggard darkness, slept that blind spring he sought.
Too late, as he sank down lifeless, it flowed. Ah, surely you
Were angered, O Nymphs, with Lampon for all the deer he slew.

(Anth. Pal., IX, 417.)

Himself He could not Save

Dāmis the Nysaean of a little bark was master,
    Bound from Ionian waters south to Pĕlops' shore.
Out of her course and reckoning wild seas and storm-winds cast her,
    But safe with all aboard her he brought her in once more.
Yet, as their anchor gripped the rocks, escaped from danger,
    The old man's head sank forward, chilled by that snow-swept gloom:
To the haven where they would be, he brought those others, stranger,
    But himself made fast for ever within the Port of Doom.

(VII, 498.)

The Poetess Erinna

Terse-tongued and sparely worded was the singing of Erinna,
    And yet on those brief pages the Muses' blessing came;
Therefore the memory fails not, that her words had power to win her,
    No shadowy wing of darkness casts night upon her name;
While we, earth's latter singers, O stranger, are left lying
    To moulder unremembered, in heaps past numbering.
Better the muted music of the swan than all the crying
    Of jackdaws chattering shrilly across the clouds of spring.

(VII, 713.)

The Sea-birds crying above the Ruins of Corinth

Where are the towers that crowned thee, the wealth that filled thy portals,
   Thy beauty, Dorian Corinth, whereon men stood to gaze?
Thy proud dames sprung from Sīsyphus, thy shrined Immortals,
   Thy palaces, the myriads that swarmed along thy ways?
Not a trace, not a trace, unhappy, hast thou left behind in falling—
   All has been seized and ravened by the wild throat of war.
We only, Ocean's children, are still left calling, calling,
   The sea-birds of thy sorrows, along thy lonely shore.

(IX, 151.)

Orpheus

No more shall stones nor oakwoods on thy sweet music follow,
   Nor the beasts that know no shepherd—O Orpheus, never again.
Never again shalt thou lull asleep the storm-wind's hollo,
   Nor the hail, nor the driving blizzard, nor the booming of the main.
Now thou art dead. All the daughters of Memory went wailing
   Loud for thy loss; and loudest, thy mother, Callíope.
Why groan for our children perished, when we see how unavailing
   Even the Gods to hinder their sons' mortality?

(VII, 8.)

BION OF SMYRNA
(later 2nd century B.C.)

Bion, who seems to have moved from Smyrna to Sicily, is one of the
last Greek bucolic poets, writing Idylls (not merely pastorals) in the
tradition of Theócritus. The *Lament for Bion*, translated below, states that
he was poisoned by jealous rivals. His best-known poem (if really his)
is the passionate but florid *Lament for Adonis*; the amusing trifle printed
first here is much closer to the *Anacreontea*, or to the Cupids in the Pom-
peian House of the Vettii.

Love Hunted

A lad that was a fowler, deep in a leafy grove
Was stalking birds, when lo, he spied the wingéd Love,
Sitting high up on a box-tree bough. Then at the sight,
Thinking how fine a bird was here, in wild delight

152

One within another he fixed each jointed rod
And hither stalked, and thither, the flutterings of the God—
Till at last the lad in anger that he could not catch his prey,
Threw down his reeds, and ran to a ploughman old and grey,
Who first had taught him fowling; and when his tale was said,
Pointed where Love was sitting. But the ancient shook his head,
And smiled at the boyish hunter, and answered him—'Beware
Of that same bird—and seek not to hunt him, nor to snare.
It is a savage creature. Shun him; and well for thee,
So long as thou failst to catch him—once thou art man, then he
That flees away so nimbly, shall no more flee at all,
But turn unsought of a sudden and on thy head shall fall.'

(J. M. Edmonds, Greek Bucolic Poets, IV.)

Love's Tryst

Hesper, thou golden light of Love's Queen sprung from the sea,
Hesper beloved, thou glory of Night's black mystery,
Brighter the moon than thou art, yet bright art thou above
All other stars—I greet thee. To the shepherd that I love
As I go serenading, in the moon's stead light the sky;
For all too soon has her crescent set. No thief am I,
I do not seek through the darkness travellers for my prey;
I love. And 'tis to thy honour to help love on its way.

(IX.)

ANON
LAMENT FOR BION
(later 2nd century B.C.)

Homere est mort, Anacreon,
Pindare, Hesiode, et Bion,
Et plus n'ont souci de s'enquerre
Du bien et du mal qu'on dit d'eux.

Ronsard.

This *Lament for Bion* used to be attributed to Moschus of Syracuse, who, however, probably lived (*c.* 150 B.C.) before Bion. Over-long and over-emphatic as it is in places, it remains one of the greatest of elegies, the model for more than one famous poem of after-times. In the words of Andrew Lang:

And dirge to dirge that answers, and the weeping
    For Adonaïs by the summer sea,
The plaints for Lycidas and Thyrsis (sleeping
    Far from 'the forest ground called Thessaly')
These hold thy memory, Bion, in their keeping
    And are but echoes of the moan for thee.

For us, in a sense, these lines seem a dirge not only for a fallen poet, but for a fallen race—for the end of the poetry of a free Hellas. The second century saw both Sicily and Greece itself prostrate beneath the eagles of Rome.

Lament for Bion

Weep, wooded glens; weep, Dorian wave; ye rivers, weep,
Lamenting Bion the lovely, that now is laid asleep.
Grieve, all ye green things growing; mourn now, ye forests all;
Defaced let all your flowers in withered clusters fall.
Grow deeper red with sorrow, rose and anemone;
Wild iris, thou that bearest 'Alas' inscribed on thee,
Grave it yet deeper—cry it !—the lord of song lies low.
    Lift loud, Sicilian Muses, lift loud your chant of woe.

Ye nightingales sad-singing, deep in each leafy tree,
Tell to Arethusa, where she flows through Sicily,
That dead is the herdsman Bion—that, now his race is run,
Poesy's self hath perished and Dorian song is done.
    Lift loud, Sicilian Muses, lift loud your chant of woe.

Wail out, ye swans of Strȳmon, by the waters where ye lie,
Raise the dirge above him with your own mournful cry—
Such notes as your own throats utter, when your years are waxen old.
By you be the Nymphs Bistónian and Oeagrus' daughters told
This bitter news: 'The Orpheus of Dorian song lies cold.'
    Lift loud, Sicilian Muses, lift loud your chant of woe.

No more the cattle listen to hear his sweet voice ring;
No more by the lonely oak-trees he sits him down to sing;
His now is Lethe's music, in realms where Death is king.
In silence lie the mountains; the kine that roamed their ways
So happy, now stand lowing and lose the heart to graze.
    Lift loud, Sicilian Muses, lift loud your chant of woe.

For thy death untimely, Bion, Apollo's self bereaved
Wept; and black‑clad Priāpi, and Satyrs for thee grieved;
The Pans of the wood lamented the ending of thy years;
The forest Naiads wailed thee, and their waters turned to tears.
Amid her rocks mourns Echo, sad that she sings no more,
Lacking thy songs to answer. The day thy life was o'er,
The fruit fell from the orchards, no flowers were left alive,
No fair milk flowed from the udder, no honey from the hive.
There was death and dearth in the honeycomb. Nay, what was left
Of sweet for men to gather, of *thy* honey bereft?
   Lift loud, Sicilian Muses, lift loud your chant of woe. . . .

Thy pipe who shall inherit, O poet past compare?
Who shall lay lip to *thy* sweet reed? Ah, who shall dare?
For there thine own lips' sweetness, thy fragrant breath abides,
And still within its hollows thy long‑lost music hides.
To Pan shall I leave it hallowed? Yet even His lips divine
May fear to wake its pipings, lest He fail to match with thine.
   Lift loud, Sicilian Muses, lift loud your chant of woe. . . .

With thee have perished, herdsman, all of the Muses' joys,
The lovely lips of maidens, the mouths of winsome boys.
The Loves with clouded faces about thy body cry;
Thy memory makes Cypris with a bitterer yearning sigh
Than her last kiss to Adonis, the day he came to die.
   Lift loud, Sicilian Muses, lift loud your chant of woe. . . .

Alas and alas, when the mallow dead in the garden lies,
Or the pale‑green parsley withers, or the lush‑curled anise dies,
Yet they rise anew and quicken when spring returns again.
But we the strong, the mighty, the wise, we sons of men,
When we die and the earth is o'er us, ah then how long, how deep,
Unhearing, unwaking, night without end we sleep!
Thou too, in silence huddled, now liest slumbering,
And yet the Nymphs still suffer the ceaseless frog to sing!
They are welcome! Scant the beauty that *it* has power to bring.
   Lift loud, Sicilian Muses, lift loud your chant of woe.

Poison they gave thee, Bion, yea, poison at the last;
How turned it not to honey, as thy sweet lips it passed?
What heart could be so savage, for the songful lips of thee
To brew and bring his venom—hater of melody!
   Lift loud, Sicilian Muses, lift loud your chant of woe.

On *them*, at least, fell justice. But still for thy darkened day
My tears flow on—ah if only my feet could find the way,
Like Orpheus I would have trodden the track to Hell below—
Like Hēracles, like Odysseus, in years of long ago—
In Hades again to see thee, again thy song to hear,
If yet for Death thou singest. Ah, in Persēphone's ear
Pipe, sweet and shrill, some cowherd's tune from Sicily.
She too was once Sicilian—in Aetna's glens played she,
And knows the Dorian music—thou canst not pipe in vain!
As to Orpheus, for his harping, of old she gave again
Eurydice, so thy pipings, O Bion, yet shall make
The Queen of Death restore thee to thy mountains. Could I wake
Such music, I would go piping to Death's self for thy sake.

ANACREONTEA

*Love and my selfe (beleeve me) on a day
At childish Push-pin (for our sport) did play.*

Herrick.

This collection of Anacreontic imitations was long supposed to be
the genuine work of Anacreon, who thus paradoxically gained his
immortality largely by poems written after he was dead. Internal evidence,
however, makes it clear that the pieces there assembled range in date from
the second or first century B.C. to Byzantine times. Those given here may
be roughly placed between about 150 B.C. and A.D. 350

Decadent of course they are; like the Amoretti on the walls of Pompeii,
they illustrate how beauty degenerates to prettiness. But there is no need
to break butterflies because they are not eagles. Grace is not contemptible
in a world that has none too much of it. If the Renaissance overvalued
these gay trifles, modern critics have surely been too hard on work that
could inspire some of the most charming verse of poets like Ronsard or
Herrick.

The Old Reveller

All the women tell me:
'Anacreon, you're old now.
Just look in your own mirror—

You'll see your hair has fallen
And bald is all your forehead.'
Of my hair I can say nothing,
Whether it's there or vanished;
But this at least I *do* know—
All the better reason
For the old man to be merry,
The closer Fate approaches.

(Anacreontea, 7.)

Vive Hodie

I ask not Gyges' riches,
The mighty Lord of Sardis;
Gold doth not bewitch me;
I have no praise for tyrants.
I only care for perfumes
To drench my beard with fragrance;
I only care for roses
To wreathe around my temples;
Today is all I care for—
Who knows aught of tomorrow? . . .

(8.)

Catalogue

If you can tell the number
Of leaves in all the forests,
Or count how many billows
Through all the seas go surging,
I'll appoint you, and no other,
To be my loves' Recorder.
First, then, write in your reckoning
'Twenty loves from Athens—
With fifteen supplementary.'
And next, put down, 'From Corinth—'
Oh, simply strings of others.
For Corinth's in Achaea,
That swarms with lovely women.
Then my affairs in Lesbos,
And downward to Ionia,

And Caria, and Rhŏdos—
They total some two thousand.
What!—lost your count already?
There's Syria to come yet,
And my passions at Canōpus,
And Crete (in Crete there's nothing
You cannot find—for Love there
Runs riot in every city).
And what of my statistics
Beyond the Straits of Gades,
And the times my heart forsook me
In Bactria and the Indies!

(14.)

'Come, fill the cup'

The black earth's always drinking,
There drink from earth the forests;
The sea drinks up the rivers,
The sun drinks from the ocean,
And the moon, she drinks the sunlight.
Then, why my friends, reproach me
If I share their taste for drinking?

(21.)

Beauty's Power

Nature gave horns to cattle,
And hoofs she gave to horses,
And nimble heels to rabbits;
To lions, mighty grinders,
And fins she gave to fishes;
To birds, their wings for flying,
To men, wise understanding.
Had she forgotten women?
Ah, no!—she gave them beauty,
Instead of shield and buckler,
In place of pikes and lances.
Ay, fire and sword are weaker
Than a pretty woman.

(24.)

Love's Nestlings

You, my dearest swallow,
Spring by spring returning,
Build your house for summer;
Winter comes—you vanish
Back to Nile or Memphis.
But Love in me sits making
His nest through *all* the seasons.
One Passion will be sprouting
His feathers; one, half-hatching;
One, in the egg-shell merely.
And from these greedy nestlings
Goes up a ceaseless babel.
In turn each little Passion
Is reared up by a bigger;
And, soon as grown, they set them,
To lay a clutch of new ones.
What *shall* I do about it?—
For such a buzz of Passions
Begins to leave me speechless!

(25.)

Love's Stratagem

Once in the hours of midnight,
When the Bear was wheeling
Alongside of Boötes,
And all the earthly nations
Lay locked in weary slumber,
To my bolted doorway
Eros came a-knocking.
'Who bangs so loud?' I shouted;
'Who breaks upon my dreaming?'
But Eros answered: 'Open!
I'm only—don't be frightened—
A little boy. I'm lost, though,
And wet through in the darkness,
There's not a glint of moonlight.'
And so, just feeling sorry,

159

I rose at once, and lighted
A lamp, and went to open.
A little boy I saw there,
With bow, and wings, and quiver;
So by the fire I set him,
With my hands I warmed his fingers,
And from his hair all dripping
I wrung out streams of water.
But when he'd ceased to shiver,
'My bow!' he cried, 'let's try it,
To see if all that wetting
Has harmed at all my bowstring.'
He bent his bow—his arrow,
To the very heart it stung me.
Then up he jumped, loud laughing:
'My host, congratulate me!
My bow's all right—it's only
Your heart will give you trouble!'

(33.)

Cicada

Oh lucky you, cicada,
Singing in the tree-tops,
Happy as a monarch,
And tipsy with a dewdrop!
You are lord of all you look on,
Of all that ploughlands furnish,
Of all that woodlands foster.
As friend the farmer sees you—
You never did him damage;
And all men pay you honour,
Sweet harbinger of summer!
Dearly the Muses love you,
And dearly, too, Apollo,
Who gave your piercing music.
The years press not upon you,
O clever, earth-born songster;
No blood is yours, no sorrow—
You are all but an Immortal!

(34.)

Love and the Bee

Once Love among the roses
Touched a bee asleep there,
All unawares—it stung him.
Then loud and high he shouted
For that smarting in his finger;
Half running and half flying,
He fled to fair Cythēra,
And cried: 'I'm dying, mother!—
It's killed me and I'm dying.
A little serpent stung me,
All winged—"a bee" they call it,
The people in the country.'
But she answered: 'If a bee-sting
Can hurt you so, my Eros,
What do you think they suffer
Whom *you* sting with your arrows?'

(35.)

NOTES

III. ALEXANDRIAN PERIOD

ARATUS

[p. 118] *Fathers of the tadpole.* It is curious to see Greek poetry here for a moment attacked in its decline by the pompous periphrases characteristic of French and English neoclassic verse (e.g. 'the whisker'd vermin race').

[p. 118] *Along some jutting strand The chattering crow.* . . . Imitated by Virgil with magnificent alliteration (*Georgics*, I, 388–9):

> Tum cornix plena pluviam vocat improba voce
> Et sola in sicca secum spatiatur harena.

With ringing voice then calls for rain the unconscionable crow
And lonely stalks the sandbanks, with solemn steps and slow.

CALLIMACHUS

[p. 120] *The Bathing of Pallas.* Cf. Tennyson, *Tiresias.*

[p. 120] *Thespiae, Corōnēa, Háliartus.* Cities of Boeotia.

[p. 120] *Charīclo.* Wife of Euēres and mother of Teirésias.

[p. 120] *Horse's Spring.* Hippocrēne (p. 38).

[p. 121] *Aristaeus and Cadmus' child.* The hunter Actaeon, son oı Aristaeus by Cadmus' daughter Autónoë, catching sight of Artemis as she bathed on Cĭthaeron, was changed by the angry Goddess to a stag and rent by his own hounds.

[p. 122] *Labdácidae.* The royal house of Thebes. Labdăcus, grandson of its founder Cadmus, was father of Laïus, the father of Oedipus.

[p. 122] *Him that gathers.* . . . Hades, who calls to him the nations of the dead.

[p. 122] *Envy.* A hit at Callímachus' rival Apollonius, upholder of long poems.

[p. 122] *Assyria's river.* Euphrates.

[p. 123] *The Dead Poet.* W. Cory's beautiful rendering of this ('They told me, Heraclitus, they told me you were dead') is probably the best-known version of any Greek epigram. Certainly it is not easy to equal. It is, however, somewhat free; in the Greek, news of his friend's death is not directly *brought* to Callímachus—it merely transpires in the course of some conversation, as an event already distant: '*long since*, it seems, you rest.'

A poem by this Heraclītus, apparently, is *Anth. Pal.*, VII, 465.

[p. 123] *Cháridas*. Seemingly a philosopher. With epitaphs like this, and many others in the *Greek Anthology*, one may contrast the stupendous dictum of Wordsworth: 'Without the belief in immortality . . . neither monuments nor epitaphs . . . could have existed in the world.'

[p. 123] *Timon*. This half-legendary misanthrope, supposedly of the late fifth century B.C., is mentioned by Aristophanes and figures, nearly six centuries later, in the dialogues of Lucian.

THEOCRITUS

[p. 125] *Pan*. See p. 73 and note.

[p. 125] *Daphnis*, the legendary founder of Sicilian pastoral, was son of Hermes by a nymph who bore, or exposed, him in a grove of laurel (*daphne*), whence his name. He grew up a handsome neatherd, piping on the hills of Sicily and beloved by Apollo, Pan, and Priāpus, by nymphs and womankind. But he died young, either because he loved a nymph and was punished by her for infidelity with blindness; or (as here) because, like Hippolytus, he defied love and incurred the wrath of Aphrodite. She kindled in him a passion for a girl; but he resisted, until, against Aphrodite's wish, his heart broke.

[p. 125] *Sing*. Presumably in a low tone that will not disturb Pan as piping would; unless we suppose Pan's ear specially liable to be irritated by panpipes. For superstitious dread of the hush of noon among the hills cf. p. 73.

[p. 125] *Priāpus*. Rustic God of fertility.

[p. 125] *My deep dish*. Admirably discussed by A. S. F. Gow in *Journ. of Hell. Studies*, 1913, p. 207 ff. and in a note on this passage in his *Theocritus*. The Greek word here is *kissybion*, a type of vessel wide and rather shallow; 'deep', therefore, must only mean 'deep of its kind'. (Odysseus offers wine to Polyphemus in one.) Hence I have used 'dish' —cf. Shakespeare, *Rich. II*, III, iii, 150: 'My figured goblets for a dish of wood.' The *interior* of the bowl seems to have the fisherman occupying a circle at its centre; the concentric ring between this inner circle and the bowl's rim would then be filled on one side by the woman and her two lovers, on the other by the boy and his two foxes. On the *outside*, we may picture the acanthus leaves rising all round from the bowl's base, while the ivy encircles its exterior above. Greek pottery provides instances of a very graceful ivy-pattern with alternating leaves and clusters of berries. The work here seems to be in coloured relief; possibly when waxed this would withstand moisture; but Gow suggests that Theócritus has transferred to wood the kind of work he had seen in metal. The general description recalls the more elaborate Shield of Achilles in Homer (also the Hēsiodic Shield of Hēracles).

[p. 126] *Calydnian.* Calydna or Calymnos is an Aegean island N. of Cos. Another reading gives 'Calydonian' (from Cálydon in Aetōlia).

[p. 126] *Where were ye?* Cf. Milton, *Lycidas*:

> Where were ye, Nymphs, when the remorseless deep
> Closed o'er the head of your loved Lycidas?

Similarly Shelley, *Adonais*:

> Where wert thou, mighty Mother, when he lay,
> When thy son lay, pierced by the shaft which flies
> In darkness?

To which Dr Johnson might have replied by asking what had 'Nymphs' to do with Edward King, or 'mighty Mothers' with John Keats. Here in Theócritus such an invocation seems less artificial; for, after all, Daphnis is the son of a nymph and Hermes, and himself beloved of nymph and Pan.

[p. 126] *Anāpus.* River flowing into Syracuse harbour.

[p. 126] *Ācis.* Now Fiume di Jaci; a river of Etna fabled to have sprung from the blood of the fair Ācis, crushed by Polyphemus, his rival for the love of the sea-nymph Galatēa. The ancient name survives also in the neighbouring town of Aci Reale.

[p. 126] *Lion.* As exotic in Theócritus' Sicily as in Shakespeare's Arden; though Herodotus mentions them even in fifth-century Macedonia as attacking Xerxes' baggage-camels.

[p. 127] *Hermes.* Daphnis' father.

[p. 127] *Priāpus*, as god of fertility, is here the cynic advocate of purely physical passion.

[p. 127] *The girl.* Whom Daphnis, in revolt against Aphrodite, refused to let himself love.

[p. 127] *He bore his bitter doom.* Cf. the stoicism of Sĭmaetha, p. 133.

[p. 128] *Diomēdes.* From whom Aphrodite fled at Troy (*Iliad*, v.).

[p. 128] *Arethusa.* A Nymph beloved by the hunter Alpheius in the Peloponnese. Fleeing to the isle of Ortygia, off Syracuse, she was turned into a spring. Alpheius himself then became the river that flows through Olympia, and plunged to reach her under the western sea. Her head, surrounded by dolphins, appears on some lovely coins of ancient Syracuse.

[p. 128] *Thymbris* (or Thybris). Perhaps a mountain NW. of Syracuse.

[p. 128] *Maenălus* (5,115 feet). In Arcadia, sacred to Pan.

[p. 128] *Lycaeon* (4,660 feet). In Arcadia, with a temple of Pan and also an altar of Zeus, where human sacrifices were offered, perhaps as late as the Christian era.

[p. 128] *Hélice*. The nymph Callisto, mother by Zeus of Arcas, was changed into the Great Bear (Hélice), while her son became Arcturus or Boötes. Gow suggests that Theócritus is here recalling the tradition that Pan himself was son of Hélice and twin-brother of Arcas.

[p. 129] *Down its flood was borne*. Perhaps a reminiscence of the other legend that Daphnis, after being blinded, plunged from a cliff into the sea.

[p. 129] *Aegilus*. On the W. coast of S. Attica, and famous for its figs.

[p. 129] *Cicada*. The male insects have a kind of drum on each side of their abdomen with which they make a shrill noise, much loved by the ancients (as by the Chinese), but less poetically compared by modern observers to a scissors-grinder or a railway-whistle. A number of them can be heard a quarter of a mile away. It may be recalled that Tithōnus, another brother of Priam, was actually turned in old age into one of these garrulous creatures (p. 41).

[p. 129] *The Sorceress*. Sĭmaetha, helped by her maid Thestȳlis, tries witchcraft to win back her lover Delphis.

[p. 129] *Hecate*, Artemis, and Selēne (the Moon), are three aspects—infernal, terrestrial, celestial—of the same divinity.

[p. 129] *Perimēde*. Perhaps the same as Agamēde, a famous sorceress, daughter of that Augeas whose notorious stable was cleansed by Hēracles.

[p. 129] *My wheel*. For the whole magic technique see Gow, *Theocritus*, and his article in *Journ. of Hell. Studies*, 1934, p. 1 ff. The wheel has a string threaded through two holes near its centre, and the ends tied; by holding the end of a loop in each hand, with the wheel in the middle, and alternately pulling and slackening, the wheel is rotated back and forth. This little engine the Greeks called *iynx*, lit. 'wryneck'. The bird of that name, belonging to the woodpecker family, at mating-time curiously writhes its neck, as if to attract its mate; and it was obvious sympathetic-magic to spreadeagle one of these unfortunate fowl on a magic wheel, as a love-charm (Pindar says Aphrodite first invented it to make Mēdēa love Jason); later, the wheel alone was used, without the bird, but still with the bird's name. A. R. Burn (*World of Hesiod*, p. 83) quotes a charm used by N. African Arabs to recover a runaway slave—a beetle tethered by a string to a nail. As the beetle walks round and round, continually shortening his tether, so the fugitive will be drawn home.

The incantation that follows here has the magic number of nine quatrains.

[p. 130] *Beat—quickly!—on the brass.* The conjuror has to be on his guard against the dangerous spirits he conjures up. The howl of dogs betrays Hecate's coming: the brass is to keep her from coming too perilously near.

[p. 130] *Wax.* Cf. D. G. Rossetti, *Sister Helen*: 'Why did you melt your waxen man?' The magic use of puppets is old as Ancient Egypt and a case was reported in the Highlands as recently as 1909 (see also Frazer, *Golden Bough*, I, 66 ff.) But here, of course, the wax is not necessarily shaped into a figure; it may be used simply as a substance, like the barley, laurel, and bran.

[p. 130] *Myndian.* From Myndus on the coast of Caria.

[p. 130] *Roarer. Rhombos,* 'bull-roarer', as used by Australian natives; a long rectangle of wood whirled round on a string (it can also be made diamond-shaped, or of metal). See Index to Frazer, *Golden Bough*, under 'bull-roarer'.

[p. 130] *Dia.* Naxos, where Theseus forsook Minos' daughter Ariadne, who had saved him from the Labyrinth.

[p. 130] *Horsewort.* Greek *hippomanes*, 'horse-maddener'.

[p. 131] *Helichryse.* Our Goldflower or Goldilocks, a plant with yellow flower-clusters, used for garlands.

[p. 131] *Dye of Thapsus.* From a shrub producing a yellow dye, said to be found at Thapsus, near Syracuse.

[p. 132] *I grew cold, etc.* Cf. Sappho, p. 58.

[p. 132] *Philinus.* Probably an allusion to a real athlete, Philinus of Cos, who won the stadium at Olympia in 264 and 260, as well as many other events.

[p. 132] *Apples of Dionysus.* Presumably love-symbols, cf. p. 94. Dionysus was a god of fruitful trees, not only of the vine.

[p. 132] *Poplar beloved of Heracles.* He was supposed to have brought the white poplar to Greece from the banks of Acheron in the NW.

[p. 132] *Torches.* Perhaps not only for light, but also to burn the lintel at the point where the door turned in it.

[p. 132] *Lipara.* The Aeolian (now Lipari) islands are volcanic; two, Hiera and Strongyle (now Vulcano and Stromboli), being active.

[p. 133] *The Festival.* In this poem one Simíchidas (apparently Theocritus himself) describes his walk with a friend to a winnowing festival (July or August) in Cos. On the way he meets the goatherd Lycidas (possibly a disguise for a fellow-poet) and the pair have a friendly singing match. The close, given here, pictures the actual festival at the farm. The piece has been thought a memory of the days when Theócritus, Leónidas of Tarentum, Asclēpiădes, Nīcias, and others formed a school of young poets round Philētas (p. 117). But this is guessing (see Gow, *Theocritus* and his article in *Classical Quarterly*, 1940, p. 47 ff.).

Like Homer's similes, this passage proves that, when they chose, the Greeks could be second to none in appreciating, and describing, the beauties of nature.

[p. 134] *Phólus.* A centaur, son of Silēnus by a nymph. Dionysus, when Phólus adjudged him the isle of Naxos, which was claimed also by Hephaestus, rewarded him with a jar of wine—to be opened only when Hēracles should come. Four generations later Hēracles duly came. But when the jar was broached, the other centaurs crowded to the scent, and a battle followed, in which Hēracles slew many of the intruders and among them, by accident, the wise Chīron, who could only escape from his agony and die, by surrendering his immortality to Prometheus. Phólus too perished by picking up in curiosity one of Hēracles' arrows, poisoned with the Hydra's venom, and dropping it on his own foot.

[p. 134] *Anápus.* See p. 164.

[p. 134] *With your spring.* The Greeks were sensitive to the qualities of water from different sources and its suitability for mixing with wine. I have heard of modern villagers on Pēlion debating the merits of their rival springs.

[p. 134] *Fan.* Winnowing-fan, like a broad-bladed oar.

[p. 134] *While She stands.* Probably some festival-effigy of the Corn-mother (see Frazer, *Golden Bough*, VII, 208, 135, 151, etc.).

[p. 134] *Poppies.* Though it makes the picture less beautiful, truth must add that these were probably poppy-heads, which it was customary to give to Demeter; not poppy-flowers. In Cos the poppy blooms as early as April and would be over in August.

[p. 134] *Nīcias.* Physician, poet, and friend of Theócritus (see p. 137).

[p. 134] *Son of Amphítryon.* Hēracles.

[p. 134] *Mídeia.* The city of Electryon, Alcmēna's father, on a hill of some 800 feet on the E. edge of the Argive plain. In this neighbourhood in 1926 was found an unplundered Mycenaean beehive-tomb, with a buried king, queen, and princess. See A. W. Persson, *The Royal Tombs at Dendra.*

[p. 135] *Clashing Rocks.* The Symplēgades, two moving rocks near the Bosphorus, which crushed ships between them, till Argo slipped through with damage only to her sternpost; after which they became fixed. Similar tales occur in folk-lore. See J. R. Bacon, *Voyage of the Argonauts*, 79–80.

[p. 135] *Phāsis.* The river of Colchis or Aea, the kingdom of Aeētes, at the E. end of the Black Sea, S. of Caucasus (a region one day to produce the no less ruthless Stalin).

[p. 135] *Pleiads' rising.* In May (p. 37).

[p. 135] *Kiānians.* The city of Kios stood on the S. shore of the Sea of Marmora, 40 miles S. of Constantinople.

[p. 135] *Nymphs . . . midmost pool.* Even in twentieth-century Greece this fear of water-nymphs, now called 'Nereids of the river' or 'of the spring', had not died. (For a modern Hylas, see J. C. Lawson, *Modern Greek Folklore and Ancient Greek Religion,* p. 161.) The belief that one's image in water is one's soul, is world-wide and lies also behind the tale of Narcissus (who pined away because his soul had been seized; cf. Frazer, *Golden Bough,* III, 94).

[p. 135] *Maeōtis.* Sea of Azov.

[p. 135] *Thrice he thundered 'Hylas!'* At the local Mysian festival of Hylas sacrifice was offered by the pool and the priest thrice called 'Hylas!', though only echo answered. To cry 'Hylas!' became a proverbial phrase for waste of breath.

After reading these three lines of Theócritus to F. T. Palgrave, about 1857, Tennyson added: 'I should be content to die if I had written anything equal to this.' Apollonius also told the story of Hylas (probably before Theócritus) in his *Argonautica*: but far less brilliantly.

[p. 136] *Daphnis;* p. 163.

[p. 137] *Transience.* The idyll from which this comes is generally thought spurious.

AUTOMEDON

[p. 137] *Syria the Hollow.* 'Hollow Syria' was the depression between the ranges of Lebanon and Anti-lebanon; but sometimes included the coast.

[p. 137] *The Pleiad set.* At dawn, *i.e.* in early November.

LEONIDAS

[p. 139] *The Shepherd's Last Sleep.* Cf. André Chénier, *Mnaïs*:
  Que vos agneaux du moins viennent près de ma cendre
  Me bêler les accents de leur voix douce et tendre,
  Et paître au pied d'un roc, où d'un son enchanteur
  Le flûte parlera sous les doigts du pasteur.

POSEIDIPPUS

[p. 140] *Chăraxus.* Sappho's brother (p. 56).

[p. 140] *Sappho.* The point is: 'Though Sappho wrote against you, she made you immortal.'

[p. 140] *Naucrătis.* Assigned to the Greeks by King Amāsis as a free port, on the Canōpic branch of the Nile, some 50 miles E. of Alexandria; after whose foundation by Alexander Naucrătis decayed.

ASCLEPIADES

[p. 140] *The Coy Mistress.* Rendered by Ronsard (ed. Vaganay), IV, 399, but without his usual grace:

> Dame au gros cœur, pourquoy t'espargnes⁄tu
> Faisant d'un rien l'apuy d'une vertu?

[p. 140] *West wind.* Or with another reading, 'the Crown'—a con⁄stellation rising in spring.

APOLLONIUS RHODIUS

[p. 143] *Cape Sēpias, etc.* Magnesia is the coastland from Ossa to Pēlion; Sēpias, its SE. cape (where Pēleus caught his bride, the sea⁄nymph Thētis, and many of Xerxes' ships were wrecked in 480); and Scíathus an adjacent island. Peirésiae is unknown; apparently a site in Magnesia.

[p. 144] *Dŏlops,* son of Hermes, died and was buried in Magnesia. Argo has here reached the S. outlet of the Gulf of Págasae. As I once neared the same point in a small Greek steamer, the dolphins still danced about us as in this tale of two thousand years ago.

[p. 145] *Chalcíope.* Sister of Mēdēa. Her sons had joined the Argonauts and now shared their peril.

[p. 147] *Perses.* A Titan.

[p. 147] *Aea.* Colchis, the kingdom of Aeētes.

[p. 148] *Aeaea.* The isle of Circe, Aeētes' sister, in the far W.

[p. 148] *Pasíphaë.* Another sister of Aeētes; wife of Minos, mother of Ariadne and (by a bull) of the Minotaur.

[p. 148] *Deucálion.* The Greek Noah. Escaping the deluge with his wife Pyrrha, he became the father of Hellen, the Hellenes' ancestor.

[p. 148] *Haemónia.* Ancient name of Thessaly. The antiquarian in Apollonius now begins, as so often, to run away with the poet.

[p. 148] *Mínyas.* Great⁄grandson of Sīsyphus (p. 102) the son of Aeŏlus.

[p. 148] *Orchómenus.* A Boeotian city W. of the Copaic Lake (the draining of which, as well as trade, may have brought its legendary wealth). The site has a Bronze-Age palace and a beehive-tomb like those at Mycenae.

[p. 148] *Cadmēan.* Theban.

[p. 148] *But bitterly she answered.* . . . When this passionate Oriental girl begins to speak, Apollonius regains his poetry.

DAMAGETUS

[p. 149] *Phocaean city.* Phocaea (30 miles NW. of Smyrna), mother-city of Massilia, the modern Marseilles. Theāno seems buried outside its city-gate.

PHAEDIMUS

[p. 150] *I mourn.* Perhaps the lament is thought of as uttered by the figure of a weeping woman on the tomb.

[p. 150] *Torōne*, 65 miles NNE. of Scíathus, on the middle prong of Chalcídice.

THE HUMBLING OF SPARTA

[p. 150] *Campfires.* It had long been the Spartan boast that their women had never seen the smoke from an enemy's campfires; but in the fourth century this boast ceased to be true: 370–369, Theban invasion under Epaminondas; 222–221, surrender to Antígonus of Macedon after Sellasia; 219–218, invasion by Philip V of Macedon; 207, devastation by Philopoe-men, general of the Achaean League, after his victory at Mantinēa; 195, surrender of Nabis, tyrant of Sparta, to Flamanīnus; 188, capture by Philopoemen. In *Oxyrhyncus Papyri* No. 662 there is a very similar epigram, by Amyntas, which definitely names 'the unconquered Philo-poemen' and suggests that the reference here also is to his invasion of 207 or, less probably, that of 188. The obscure word in the second line rendered 'destroyers' should possibly be a proper name 'Olénian', from Ōlenus, a city in Achaea. But this was a very obscure township, a few years later not even inhabited.

[p. 150] *On shadeless fields thy birds have nested.* All fruit-trees being felled by the invader. Mackail compares Stesíchorus' warning to the Locrians not to grow too proud, 'lest their cicadas chirp on the ground'.

ANTIPATER OF SIDON

[p. 151] *The Vengeance of the Nymphs.* This may be by Antípater of *Thessalonica.*

[p. 151] *Ionian waters . . . Pělops' shore:* i.e. sailing down the Greek W. coast to Peloponnesus. (The Iŏnian Sea, supposed to be called after the nymph Io, is to be distinguished from Iōnia in Asia Minor.)

[p. 151] *Erinna.* See p. 96.

[p. 152] *Ruins of Corinth.* Destroyed by Rome in the same year as Carthage, 146 B.C.

[p. 152] *Sisyphus.* Legendary founder of Corinth (p. 102).

[p. 152] *Sea-birds.* Lit. 'halcyons', whose plaintive cry particularly struck the Greeks. Cf. A. Chénier, *La Jeune Tarentine*:

> Pleurez, doux alcyons! ô vous, oiseaux sacrés,
> Oiseaux chers à Thétis, doux alcyons, pleurez!
> Elle a vécu, Myrto, la jeune Tarentine!
> Un vaisseau la portait aux bords de Camarine.

[p. 152] *Orpheus*, after Eurydice's death from a serpent's bite, was torn in pieces by Bacchanals. Cf. Milton, *Lycidas*:

> What could the Muse herself that *Orpheus* bore,
> The Muse herself, for her inchanting son
> Whom Universal nature did lament,
> When by the rout that made the hideous roar,
> His goary visage down the stream was sent,
> Down the swift *Hebrus* to the *Lesbian* shore?

[p. 152] *Booming of the main.* Cf. Gray, *The Bard*:

> Cold is Cadwallo's tongue
> That hush'd the stormy main.

BION

[p. 152] *Love Hunted.* Imitated by Ronsard (ed. Vaganay), II, 420, *L'Amour Oyseau.*

[p. 153] *Each jointed rod.* Fowlers used a set of jointed sticks (like some fishing-rods), the end one made sticky with birdlime.

LAMENT FOR BION

[p. 154] *Dorian.* Greek pastoral employed a Doricized epic diction. Theócritus was born in Dorian Syracuse and had lived in Dorian Cos.

[p. 154] '*Alas*' *inscribed on thee*. The Greek term 'hyacinthos' includes the iris; and the wild iris familiar to walkers on Greek hills is delicately pencilled with lines that can be read as AIAIAI (AIAI = alas) or, the other way up, as a series of *Y*s (initial of Hyacinthus). Hence the legends that this 'sanguine flower inscrib'd with woe' first sprang from the blood of Hyacinthus, a beautiful youth accidentally killed by Apollo with a discus; or from the blood of Ajax (Aias) when he slew himself in rage at being worsted by Odysseus in the contest for Achilles' arms. (See my *From* (p. 191) *Olympus to the Styx*, 2nd ed., p. 80.)

[p. 154] *Arethusa*. p. 164.

[p. 154] *Strȳmon*, now Struma, flows through Orpheus' native Thrace.

[p. 154] *Waxen old*. Swans being supposed to sing before death.

[p. 154] *Bistónian*. The Bistones were a Thracian tribe.

[p. 154] *Oeagrus*. Father of Orpheus, by the Muse Callíope.

[p. 155] *Priăpi*. Rustic deities of fertility.

[p. 155] *Alas and alas*. . . . Adapted in youth by Wordsworth (*Works*, ed. de Selincourt, I, 286):

> Ah me, the lowliest children of the spring,
> Violets and meekest snowdrops, when they lie
> Nipped in the faded garden, soon again
> Put forth fresh leaves and breathe another year,
> But we, the great, the mighty and the wise,
> Soon as we perish, in the hollow earth,
> Unwakeable, unheard of,[1] undisturbed,
> Slumber a dull interminable sleep.

Later, part of these lines was embodied in the last Duddon sonnet, 'Afterthought':

> Still glides the Stream, and shall for ever glide;
> The Form remains, the Function never dies;
> While we, the brave, the mighty, and the wise,
> We Men, who in our morn of youth defied
> The elements, must vanish.

Cf. too Arnold, *Thyrsis*:

> For there thine earth-forgetting eyelids keep
> The morningless and unawakening sleep.

---

[1] Wordsworth has mistaken the meaning; it should be 'unhearing'.

[p. 155] *The frog* looks like a personal allusion to some detested bard.

[p. 156] *She too was once Sicilian*. It was in the fields of Enna (Castro-giovanni), forty miles WSW. of Etna, that

> *Proserpin* gathring flours,
> Herself a fairer Floure by gloomie Dis
> Was gatherd, which cost *Ceres* all that pain
> To seek her through the world.

Cf. Arnold, *Thyrsis*:

> But when Sicilian shepherds lost a mate,
>   Some good survivor with his flute would go,
> Piping a ditty sad for Bion's fate;
>   And cross the unpermitted ferry's flow,
>   And relax Pluto's brow,
> And make leap up with joy the beauteous head
>   Of Proserpine, among whose crowned hair
>   Are flowers first open'd on Sicilian air,
> And flute his friend, like Orpheus, from the dead.
>
> O easy access to the hearer's grace
>   When Dorian shepherds sang to Proserpine!
>   For she herself had trod Sicilian fields,
> She knew the Dorian water's gush divine,
>   She knew each lily white which Enna yields,
>   Each rose with blushing face;
> She loved the Dorian pipe, the Dorian strain.
>   But ah, of our poor Thames she never heard!
>   Her foot the Cumnor cowslips never stirr'd;
> And we should tease her with our plaint in vain!

This singing to Persephone recalls the story of her appearance in a dream to Pindar, complaining that he had left her, alone of the Immortals, without a song—but when he came to her kingdom he should sing her praises too. Within ten days he died. But afterwards an aged kinswoman of his dreamed that the poet recited to her a poem on Persephone; which, on waking, she wrote down. (Cf. the curious tale of Mozart's *Requiem*.)

[p. 156] *I would go piping to Death's self for thy sake*. So in a fragment of the comic poet Philēmon (*c.* 361–262 B.C.) a character exclaims:

> If, as some say, my friend,
> In very deed the dead had consciousness,
> I had hanged myself to see Euripides.

173

The Greek metre of these little pieces ($3\frac{1}{2}$ iambic feet), here reproduced, is similar to that of Longfellow's *Hiawatha* less the first (stressed) syllable.

[p. 157] *Vive Hodie*. Imitated by Baïf, and by Ronsard (ed. Vaganay), III, 256:

> Du grand Turc je n'ay souci,
> Ni du grand Souldan aussi:
> L'or ne maistrise ma vie,
> Aux Rois je ne porte envie.

[p. 157] *Gyges*, bodyguard of Candaules King of Lydia, conspired with the Queen and killed his master (*c.* 685). He made Lydia powerful and attacked Ionia, but was slain in battle by the Cimmerians about 652.

[p. 157] *Catalogue*. For this 'Leporello-list' cf. Ronsard, III, 268 ('Si tu me peux conter les fleurs'):

> Conte, apres, six cens à la fois
> Dont à Paris je me vy prendre,
> Conte cent millions, qu'à Blois
> Je pris dans les yeux de Cassandre.

[p. 158] *Gades*. Cadiz.

[p. 158] *Bactria*. Between Hindu Kush and Oxus. Its city of Bactra is now Balkh.

[p. 158] '*Come, fill the cup.*' Cf. Ronsard, III, 268 ('La terre les eaux va boyvant').

[p. 158] *Beauty's Power*. Cf. Ronsard, III, 136 ('La Nature a donné des cornes aux toreaux').

[p. 159] *Love's Nestlings*. Cf. Ronsard, III, 339 ('Si tost que tu sens arriver'):

> L'un a des ailerons au flanc,
> L'autre de duvet est tout blanc,
> Et l'autre dans le nic s'essore:
> L'un de sa coque à demy sort,
> Et l'autre en a rompu le bort,
> Et l'autre est dedans l'œuf encore.

And contrast the serious passion of Íbycus on the same theme, p. 68.

[p. 159] *Love's Stratagem*. Cf. Ronsard, III, 121 ('Du malheur de recevoir'):

> Il estoit minuict, et l'Ourse
> De son char tournoit le course
> Entre les mains du Bouvier. . . .

and La Fontaine's *L'Amour Mouillé*; also Herrick, *The Cheat of Cupid*:

> One silent night of late,
>   When every creature rested,
> Came one unto my gate,
>   And knocking, me molested.

Cherubini set the episode to music in his opera *Anacreon* (performed at Paris in 1803).

[p. 159] *A little boy.* The Greek idea of Eros grows younger with the centuries—first a youth, then a boy, then the mischievous urchin of the Hellenistic age.

[p. 160] *Cicada.* Cf. Ronsard, III, 263 ('T'oseroit bien quelque Poëte Nier des vers, douce Alouëte?')—where cicada is replaced by lark.

[p. 161] *Love and the Bee.* Cf. Ronsard, III, 249, beginning:

> Le petit enfant Amour
> Cueilloit des fleurs à l'entour
> D'une ruche, où les avettes
> Font leurs petites logettes.

Also Herrick, *The wounded Cupid*:

> *Cupid* as he lay among
> *Roses*, by a Bee was stung.

Spenser breaks the bee upon a wheel of lumbering prolixity in his Madrigal IV.

[p. 161] *Cythēra.* The island of Aphrodite, S. of Peloponnese.

PART FOUR

ROMAN AND EARLY BYZANTINE PERIOD

1st century B.C.–6th century A.D.

MELEAGER OF GADARA
(*c.* 135–*c.* 65 B.C.)

MELEĀGER of Gadara in Palestine—'the Syrian Athens', he calls it—
migrated to Tyre and, in later life, to Cos, where lived (perhaps his last
love) the girl Phānion. A Cynic philosopher and writer of humorous
essays, he also composed short poems and gathered in his 'Garland'—
a selection of such poems by himself and others—the first of those anthologies from which our *Palatine Anthology* was to grow. (See Appendix II.)

The Baby Hare

A little hare new-littered, from my mother's breast they tore me
  (Long my ears and taper, swift my baby feet),
But in her bosom fair-skinned Phānion took and bore me—
  Lovingly she gave me flowers of spring to eat.
No more I missed my mother. But of surfeit unbeseeming
  And banquets overgenerous I fattened and I died.
Next her cottage then she laid me, that in dreaming
  She might see my grave for ever by her own bedside.
                          (*Anth. Pal.,* VII, 207.)

Love for Sale

Sell him!—just as he lies there in his mother's arms a-sleeping!
  Sell him!—why should I trouble to rear this saucy thing!
With his nails that scratch so sharply, and all amid his weeping
  These sudden shouts of laughter; snub nose and wanton wing!
A brazen, lynx-eyed creature, as babbling as a crier,
  A savage that is brutal to his own mother dear,
An utter monster! Come, we'll sell him. Any buyer,
  Outward bound, that wants an infant? Here now, here!
But look, what tears, what pleading! Ah, never fear I will—
It shan't be sold! Live happy, here with my Zēnophil.
                                (V, 178.)

Hue and Cry after Love

O yes! O yes! O yes! I have lost him, Love the gipsy.
   A moment since he fluttered from my bed, at break of day.
Weeps sweetly; laughter roguish; and the child's tongue runs as tipsy;
   Saucy, and swift, and his shoulders with quiver and wings are gay.
His father's name? God knows it. For Heaven and Earth disown him,
   And Ocean swears this urchin was never child of his;
Through all the world he's hated, by all who've ever known him—
   Take care lest he be setting new traps for hearts ere this.
But ah!—there he is!—do you see him? In his lurking place he lies.
I have caught you, archer, ambushed in Zēnophil's bright eyes.

                                       (v, 177.)

'Lenten ys come with Love to Toune'

Now the white violet's blooming, and that lover of the showers,
   Narcissus, and the lilies that go climbing up the hill,
And now, delight of lovers, spring flower among the flowers,
   Sweet rose of Persuasion, blossoms my Zēnophil.
Ah meadows, vain your laughter, in vain your shining hair:
Than all your fragrant garlands the lass I love's more fair.

                                       (v, 144.)

The Siren

Asclēpias, child of passion, bright eyes like the calm sea's blue,
You lure to sail for Cythēra whoever looks on you.

                                       (v, 156.)

'O lente, lente'

Grey daylight, loathed of lovers, how listless slow your crawling
   Round the earth, now another in the arms of Dēmo lies!
When mine was that slim body, malignantly forestalling
   My happiness how swiftly, each morn, you used to rise!

                                       (v, 173.)

Love's Last Sacrament

If aught, my Cleobūlus, befall (for what shall save me,
   Whom Love's fires have left wasted, as a brand that smouldereth?),
Make drunk with wine, I pray you, my urn before you grave me,
   And write these words upon it: 'The gift of Love to Death.'

                                      (xii, 74.)

The Bride of Death

No bridal, but Death for bridegroom Cleärista found her,
  The night she first unfastened her knot of maidenhood.
That eve by her bridal‑chamber the flutes blew shrilling round her,
  And beating on its doorway the merry‑makers stood—
But lo, they cried in the dawning with a voice of lamentation,
  And Hymen, stricken silent, changed to a funeral strain,
And the selfsame pinewood torches that glittered in their station
  Round her bride‑bed, lit her the road none comes again.

                                  (VII, 182.)

MELEAGER or PHILODEMUS

The Coquette

Well my heart warns me, saying: 'Flee, flee from Heliodora!'
  Too bitterly it remembers past jealousy and pain.
So says my heart. Yet what strength have I to flee before her?
  She warns me too, the wanton!—then kisses me again.

                                    (V, 24.)

PHILODEMUS OF GADARA
(c. 110–c. 40 B.C.)

Philodēmus was an Epicurean philosopher patronized by L. Cal‑
purnius Piso (consul 58 B.C.), the father of Caesar's wife Calpurnia.
Cicero, though detesting Piso, praises Philodēmus; Horace quotes him,
and perhaps owed a good deal to his influence. In a villa at Herculaneum,
probably belonging to Piso, was found a room with busts of philosophers
and papyrus‑rolls of philosophy, largely by Philodēmus himself, which
may have been the poet's library.

Moonlit Love

Lady of Night, twy‑hornéd, lover of nightlong dances,
  Look through the latticed windows, O Moon with thy quivering ray,
On my golden lass, Callistion. Immortal glances
  May linger unforbidden on mortal lovers' play.
Sure on us both, O Moon, there rests thy benison—
Once was thine own heart kindled to love Endymion.

                            (*Anth. Pal.,* V, 123.)

Years of Discretion

I have loved—but then who has not? Frolicked—who has not tasted
  Such frolics once? Done follies—'tis a god that makes us fools.
Enough! Fast round my temples the dark hair dwindles, wasted
  By silver threads, foretelling the years when folly cools.
We played while it was playtime. Now that the season brings
Farewell to that, we'll turn us to think of wiser things.

(v, 112.)

ZONAS OF SARDIS
(1st century B.C.)

Diodōrus Zōnas was an orator of repute at the time of Mithridates'
invasion of Rome's eastern provinces (88–7 B.C.).

' The Lip of this Poor Earthen Urn '

Hand me the sweet cup fashioned from that clay,
Whence I was born, where I shall lie one day.

(Anth. Pal., XI, 43.)

Harvest-Home

To the Winnowing Demeter, from his ploughland's scanty measure,
  To the Seasons, whose fair footsteps glide down the furrowed fields,
These motley seeds of pulse, these few ears from the thresher,
  Upon this three-legged table the poor Hērōnax yields,
The tiny tithe of a little. No broad lands his to till,
Heir of a narrow portion here on the barren hill.

(VI, 98.)

The Little Ghost

Ferryman that rowest the barge the buried fare on,
  With all its freight of anguish, across Death's reedy mere,
Give to the child of Cínyras, O gloomy Charon,
  A kindly hand for climbing to thy boat, as he draws near.
For the little one trips in his sandals; yet he will fear to tread,
Barefoot, the sandy beaches of the River of the Dead.

(VII, 365.)

The End of a Venture

I pile the chill sea-shingle with my hands above thee sleeping,
    A cold and breathless body, here upon the shore.
For the last rites to rest thee no mother renders weeping,
    These limbs that the waves have wasted *she* shall behold no more.
Only the lonely beaches in their friendless desolation,
    They were thy only welcome beside the Aegean Sea.
This little sand I give thee, and many a lamentation,
    Stranger. So bitter a bargain thy trading brought to thee.

(VII, 404)

THYILLUS
(mid 1st century B.C.?)

The Dead Dancer

Aristion, so swift once to toss her tresses curling
    And her castanets that rattled in praise of Cýbele,
Lightly beneath the pine-boughs to the horned flute's music whirling,
    She that would mix no water, as she quaffed her winecups three,
Rests here beneath the elmtree-shade; now no more lovers
    Gladden her heart, no vigils of maddened midnight hours.
A long farewell, all revels, all follies! Now earth covers
    The sacred head that, once, went bright with wreathéd flowers.

(Anth. Pal., VII, 223.)

ERYCIUS OF CYZICUS
(mid 1st century B.C.)

The Trophy

This horn of full two cubits from his bull that turned a rover
    And scorned the herd, its herdsman, the Ambraciot Saon, tore.
Long he tracked the truant the bushy gorges over,
    Up the glens, and found him on a torrent-shore,
Cooling hoof and flank there. Sideways from the river
    The beast charged at its master. But with a single blow
Of his club he dashed its horn off, and hung it here for ever,
    On the wild-pear by his steading, where sweet his heifers low.

(Anth. Pal., VI, 255.)

CRINAGORAS OF MYTILENE

(c. 70 B.C.–c. A.D. 18)

Crinágoras took part in an embassy from Lesbos to Julius Caesar at
Rome in 45 B.C.; and in another to Augustus at Tarraco in Spain in
26–5 B.C. He became a sort of court-poet to the imperial family, writing
poems for Octavia, Marcellus, Tiberius, and others.

Hunter's Thanksgiving

O caves of the Nymphs fresh-flowing, that scatter from your fountains
    Down this craggy hillside your brimming streams headlong;
O little shrine set at the feet of Bassae's mountains,
    That Pan with his crown of pine makes echo to his song;
Ye junipers honoured of hunters, of many a long year's growing,
    Ye cairns heaped high by the wayside for our Lord Hermes' grace,
Be kindly and receive these gifts of my bestowing,
    These spoils of the stag from Sōsander, since ye have blessed his chase.
                                  (*Anth. Pal.*, VI., 253.)

ANTIPATER OF THESSALONICA

(time of Augustus)

This poet and rhetorician was patronized by L. Calpurnius Piso
(Consul 15 B.C.), for whose sons Horace composed his *Ars Poetica*, and
wrote an epigram on Octavian's foundation of Nicópolis after the victory
of Actium (31 B.C.).

The Wife's Prayer

Cýthere the Bithynian in prayer sets me before Thee,
    Cypris—Thy marble image, wrought by the sculptor's art.
For this small gift grant a greater—Thou art kind when we implore Thee—
    She only prays that her husband be one with her in heart.
                                  (*Anth. Pal.*, VI, 209.)

The Desolation of the Cýclades

Ah lonely isles, fragments of earth, that with his thunder
   The wild Aegean girdles, like a belt about you thrown,
How have ye lost, unhappy, your splendour and your wonder,
    As desolate as Siphnos or Phŏlegandros grown!
It is Dēlos, once the dazzling, that has made you share her mood—
She that was first to suffer this doom of solitude.

(IX, 421.)

Hero's Tower

Here it was once Leander crossed; here beats the swelling
   Strait that brought a lover—and her he loved—to dust;
Here stands the ruined tower, that once was Hero's dwelling,
   Where of old she kindled the lamp that failed their trust.
Here, in one grave together, they lie—still crying in vain
Against the wind that grudged them to each other's arms again.

(VII, 666.)

POMPEIUS THE YOUNGER OF MYTILENE
(time of Augustus)

This is probably Marcus Pompeius Theóphanes, son of Theóphanes of Mytilene, historian and politician, who became an influential friend of Pompeius, Caesar's rival; persuaded him to restore the freedom of Mytilene; and wrote a history of his eastern campaigns. He was made a Roman citizen by Pompeius, taking the name Gnaeus Pompeius Theóphanes; and after his death received divine honours from his grateful country. His son, our poet, became in his turn procurator of Asia under Augustus, and a friend of the future emperor Tiberius; who, however, drove the poet's son and grandson to commit suicide in A.D. 33.

' In Fields where Roses Fade '

The peerless lass who gathered the lilies of the Graces,
   Herself, to all beholders, of flowers the loveliest,
Now Laïs sees no longer where high in Heaven races
   The Sun's team golden-bridled. She rests as all must rest.
Farewell, wan, jealous lovers; farewell now, feast and wine;
Farewell the lamp of midnight that watched Love's secret shrine!

(Anth. Pal., VII, 219.)

Mycenae Fallen

If I, Mycenae, moulder in dust and desolation,
  Humbler, to eyes that behold me, than a bare and barren stone,
Go, look on the towers of Troy that beneath my domination
  I trampled in their glory, and left Priam's palace lone.
Learn there my ancient greatness. If Time has worked his will,
Sufficient unto mine honour is Homer's witness still.

(IX, 28.)

ALPHEUS OF MYTILENE
(1st century A.D.—perhaps time of Augustus)

Homer

Still we behold Troy city from her foundations shaken,
  Still in our ears there echoes the wail of Andrómache,
And we watch the moiling Ajax, and Hector stripped, forsaken,
  Haled by the car of Achilles beneath Troy towers we see.
So mighty the Muse of Homer, not one land's pride alone,
To whom all Europe and Asia yield honour as their own.

(Anth. Pal., IX, 97.)

Mycenae Fallen

Lost now are the homes of the heroes. Scarce here and there a city
  From the dust lifts its head a little, where the sons of the gods were born.
And such wert thou, Mycenae, as I passed, a thing of pity—
  Even the goats of the mountain have pastures less forlorn.
The goatherds pointed towards thee. And I heard an old man say,
'The Giant-builded City, the Golden, here it lay.'

(IX, 101.)

DIODORUS OF SARDIS
(time of Augustus)

This Diodōrus, orator and historian, was a kinsman of Diodōrus
Zōnas (p. 182), and a friend of the geographer Strabo.

The Gods Forget

The poet Diodōrus has left these lines that cover
    A mother, dead untimely, who here for ever sleeps.
She died to bear her baby. And this stone mourns above her,
    Athenaïs, daughter of Mēlo; whom Jason her father weeps,
And all the women of Lesbos. But Thou upon that day,
O Artemis, didst hearken but to Thy bloodhounds' bay.

(Anth. Pal., VI, 348.)

SATYRUS
(1st century B.C.–1st century A.D.?)

The Voice of the Hills
(On a statue of Echo)

High up the mountain-meadow, Echo with never a tongue
Sings back to each bird in answer the song each bird hath sung.

(Anth. Pal., XVI, 153.)

MARCUS ARGENTARIUS
(early 1st century A.D.)

Serenade

Wake, Īsias, lips of fragrance, lips ten times sweeter, tasted,
    Than spikenard—see, this garland in your dear hands I lay,
Blooming tonight; but withered tomorrow morn, and wasted—
    Only too true a token of your fair flower's decay.

(Anth. Pal., V, 118.)

'For All the Saints and Sages . . .'

A fathom of earth shall be yours in death; no more thereafter
    To look on the sun in Heaven and the pleasant things of life.
Then crown the cup with wine unmixed, and drink with laughter,
    Clasping your arm, my Cincius, about your lovely wife.
If you deem that the sage's soul lives on, I bid you know
Both Zēno and Cleanthes passed to that deep night below.

(XI, 28.)

BIANOR
(early 1st century A.D.?)

' In Huts where Poor Men Lie '

This man that is mean, that is nothing, this drudge—he too is known
To Love; he too can call another's heart his own.

(Anth. Pal., XI, 364.)

MYRINUS
(1st century A.D.)

Love the Shepherd

Thyrsis the village⁄shepherd, with the flocks of the Nymphs in his keep⁄
   ing,
  Thyrsis that pipes as sweetly as Pan on the reedy stem,
Flushed with wine in the noontide, under the pine lies sleeping—
  But Love Himself has taken the crook, and shepherds them.

(Anth. Pal., VII, 703.)

ISIDORUS AEGEATES
(1st century A.D.?)

The Farmer Lost at Sea

To far⁄off shores as merchant the false sea's promise drew me,
  Éteocles, forsaking the fields I used to reap.
I rode the Tyrrhene surges. But they rose and overthrew me.
  My ship and I were swallowed, head foremost, in the deep
Under the thrust of the tempest—ah, different far the gale
That fans the floor of the thresher, and swells the seaman's sail!

(Anth. Pal., VII. 532.)

ANTIPHILUS OF BYZANTIUM
(mid 1st century A.D.)

Simple Pleasures

Give me a mattress aft and a good tarpaulin's shelter,
  A⁄thunder with the drumming of the inblown spray;
A roaring fire on the hearth⁄stones and, boiling helter⁄skelter,
  A pot with its rumble of bubbles that merrily dance away;

188

Let me watch the cook-boy cooking, and for my table clear me
  A rough ship's plank, and on it let a strip of canvas lie;
A game of pitch-and-toss, and the bo'sun's pipe to cheer me—
  Such luck I had just lately; hail-fellow-well-met am I!

(Anth. Pal., IX, 546.)

The Elms of Prōtesilāus

Long, O Prōtesilāus, long shall thy fame be chanted,
  Thou foremost in the onset that brought Troy's doomed wall down.
Deep-foliaged elms above thee long since the Nymphs have planted,
  Where thy grave lies facing, far off, the hated town.
Yet still thy trees are angered. For when they tower descrying
  With their tops the Trojan rampart, then fade and fall their leaves.
How deep that hate of the heroes, if passion so undying
  Even in senseless timber still lingers and still grieves!

(VII, 141.)

LUCILIUS
(mid 1st century A.D.)

A grammarian and satirist patronized by Nero. His numerous short pieces, mostly of a rather thin humour, influenced the Roman poet Martial and conform to our later idea of the 'epigram' as a brief, pointed poem.

The Champion's Statue

Apis his fellow-boxers here have set,
Because he never injured mortal yet.

(Anth. Pal., XI, 80.)

The Portraitist

Eutўchus paints: and twenty sons he's got—
And not a single likeness in the lot.

(XI, 215.)

The Miser's Entertainment

Asclēpĭădes the miser, about his chamber peering,
  Spied a mouse and asked it—'Dear mouse, what wilt with me?'
Sweetly the mouse smiled answer—'Good friend, no cause for fearing!
  We only look for lodging; not hospitality.'

(XI, 391.)

JULIUS POLYAENUS
(1st century A.D.)

Possibly C. Julius Polyaenus, duumvir of Corinth under Nero.

The Wanderer

Though Thine ears be filled with voices—voices that pray Thee fearing,
  Voices that praise Thee, thankful because their prayers were heard,
Lord of the sacred Schérian Plain, O Zeus, give hearing
  Unto me too, and grant me, with Thine unfailing word,
An end at last of exile—grant, in my native soil,
A home from all my wandering, a rest from all my toil.

(Anth. Pal., IX, 7.)

ARCHIAS
(1st–2nd century A.D.?)

Labour Lost

'Flee from Love', you warn me? Lost labour! How should I
Escape on foot, pursued by a creature than can fly?

(Anth. Pal., V. 59.)

ARCHIAS OF BYZANTIUM
(The same? 1st–2nd century A.D.?)

A Seaside Grave

Here lies the shipwrecked Thēris. Landward the rollers threw me,
  But my very dust cannot forget the sleepless sea.
Under the crags that the salt surf splits, by the deep that slew me,
  Here the hands of strangers have dug a grave for me.
Yet even among the perished, now and for evermore,
My sad soul listens loathing to the breakers' boom and roar.

(VII, 278.)

ARCHIAS OF MYTILENE
(The same? 1st–2nd century A.D.?)

' Ah, Poor Faun, Poor Faun!'

Alas, thy poor beast's body hangs for the winds to batter,
  Swinging aloft from the branch of the shaggy mountain‑pine,
High, high aloft. Ah to challenge Phoebus Himself, O Satyr,
  Child of the peak of Cĕlaenae—what fatal folly thine!
Never again shall we listen, we Nymphs, as thy fluting thrills,
With its wood‑notes sweeter than honey, across the Phrygian hills.

(Anth. Pal., VII, 696.)

GLAUCUS OF NICOPOLIS
(1st–2nd century A.D.)

Pan the Lover

'Now, all ye Nymphs, tell me truly of Daphnis—where shall I find him?
  Here has he been?—and rested his white kids by the way?'
'Yes, yes, O piping Pan. And letters here behind him,
  Cut in the bark of the poplar, he left for thee, that say:
"Pan, Pan, in Málea seek me—come, Pan, to Psōphis' hill;
Come, for I shall be there."' 'Farewell to you, Nymphs, I will.'

(Anth. Pal., IX, 341.)

On the Cenotaph of One Lost at Sea

Not a sod hath Erăsippus to entomb him, not a boulder;
  His grave is all this ocean outspread before thine eyes.
For ship and master perished. Far off his white bones moulder,
  Lost, and only the sea‑mews can utter where he lies.

(VII, 285.)

RUFINUS
(2nd century A.D.?)

The Happy Mean

I do not love a wanton, I do not love a prude.
One is too easy winning, and one too long pursued.

(Anth. Pal., V, 42.)

191

' This Same Flower that Smiles today '

I send thee, Rhŏdocleia, this garland's flowery splendour,
  That my own hands have gathered, to twine a crown for thee.
Here are violets purple-glancing, and rosebuds, and the slender
  Narcissus—here are lilies and the dewed anemone.
Wreathe them around thy temples, and cease from scorn, proud maid:
Like my wreath thou flowerest, and like my wreath shalt fade.

(v, 74.)

LUCIAN OF SAMOSATA
(c. A.D. 115–c. 185)

This Voltaire of antiquity was first apprenticed to a sculptor, then
became an advocate at Antioch, a disciple of the philosopher Dēmōnax
at Athens, an itinerant lecturer in Italy and Gaul. In his old age he was
made procurator of a district in Egypt. His fame rest on his satirical prose.

On a Child

Little Callímachus harsh Death bore hence
In his fifth summer's heedless innocence.
Yet do not weep for me. Of life I knew
Little; but little of life's sorrows too.

(Anth. Pal., VII, 308.)

PTOLEMAEUS OF ALEXANDRIA
(c. A.D. 100–178)

Claudius Ptolemaeus, who gave his name to the 'Ptolemaic system',
wrote not only on astronomy, but also on astrology, chronology, geography, and music.

The Scientist

I know well I am mortal, a feeble thing and fleeting;
  Yet when I watch the wheelings of myriad star on star,
My feet touch earth no longer. It is as I were eating,
  At the high God's own table, of Heaven's ambrosia.

(Anth. Pal., IX, 577.)

STRATO
(mid 2nd century A.D.)

' Gather ye Rosebuds '

Drink on, love on, not always lover by love reposes;
  Not for everlasting shall we drink, Dāmócrates.
Let us pour *ourselves* the perfume, let us wreathe *ourselves* with roses,
  Ere others come to carry to our graves such gifts as these.
Let my bones yet quick within me drink down the wine that's red—
Then all Deucálion's deluge may drown them lying dead!

(Anth. Pal., XI, 19.)

OPPIAN OF CILICIA
(2nd–3rd century A.D.)

Oppian of Cilícia wrote a poem on fishes and appears to be a different person from Oppian of Apămeia (in Syria) who about the same period wrote a poem, less good, on hunting. Fishes may seem a chilly theme for poetry (though Leigh Hunt and Rupert Brooke did brilliantly with them); but in fact much of the 3,500 lines of the *Halieutica* is interesting and amusing. These are not negligible qualities, even in poetry (though too many poets have seemed to regard themselves, in virtue of their lofty vocation, as licensed bores). Oppian knows something of his subject; and there is much to be said for sometimes writing objective verse even about fishes, which at least are real, rather than the type of lyric so super/ abundant during the last century and a half, which assumes it important to acquaint mankind with all the smallest private emotions of the writer's ego—'I and a thrush', 'I and the moon', 'I and she', 'I and God'. The best of Oppian, late and obscure as he is, shows both imagination and feeling—there are moments when this Greek Izaak Walton seems touched with all the tenderness of the Ancient Mariner towards the creatures of the deep.

Dolphin and Seal

Ah with what heart of wonder, on calm and windless days
Or when the breeze blows gently, thou mayest stand to gaze
Upon that gay and lovely sight, from thy ship's side,
Where gracefully flock the dolphins, the beauty of the tide!

Together in front the young ones come, like youths unwed,
As if in mazy circles of the whirling dance they sped;
Next, close behind their offspring, there swim, a guardian band,
The big ones and the leaders. As through spring meadowland
After the lambs the shepherds go, following as they graze;
Or as, when homeward children troop, from learning the Muses' ways,
After them come their tutors, watching from behind
Over the little ones' modesty, and guiding heart and mind
(For years bring man discretion); so the dolphin-parents all
Swim in the wake of their young, lest aught untoward befall.
    And no less love for her children the mother-seal shows.
For breasts she has, like the dolphin, whence milk for her infants flows,
And when the hour comes on her, to bear her travail-pain,
Landward she comes to be lightened—and not amid the main.
Twelve days in all on the beaches she hides with her young new-born;
Then, taking her whelps in her arms, upon the thirteenth morn
Seaward she goes, delighting in her children; as it were,
To show them the home of their fathers. So, if a woman bear
A babe in the land of strangers, then back to her own country
Returns, and the place where she was born, happy all day is she,
Nursing the child in her arms, bringing before its sight
The home that bred its mother—ever she hugs it tight
With a joy that nothing wearies; but the child—it stares at all,
With eyes uncomprehending, in its forbears' house and hall.
So that wild creature of the deep, she too displays
Before her young the waters and all their wondrous ways.
    Ah Gods above, we see, then, not only humankind
Loves, beyond all, its children, with a fondness that can bind
More dearly than life or the sunlight: even the savagery
Of beast, or bird, or the ravening fishes of the sea
Feels—wild, untaught, resistless—this passion too; and still
For their little ones—not grudging, but with an eager will—
They face death and the anguish of each extremest ill.

                  (*Halieutica*, I, 670–708.)

The Dolphin's Death

Now, of the ways of dolphins, this wonder too I hear,
For which I do them honour. When there at last draws near
The sickness that shall end them, unpitying, well they know
Their life is done; then coastward from the great deeps they go

And running themselves ashore on the beach's yielding sand,
There breathe their last; preferring to meet their doom on land,
In hope some man may find them and (still remembering
Their loving gentleness of heart) may stay to fling
A mound of shingle o'er them, feeling he honours so
The Earth-shaker's holy messenger; or else the flow
Of the wild-weltering surges may heap their sandy bed;
Lest the creatures of the waters should see their lord lie dead,
Or from some beast that hates them their bodies suffer shame.
So their virtue and their courage abide to the end the same,
Even in death; and they sully not the dolphin's ancient fame.

(II, 628–41.)

The Mullet and the Hook

But up soon swims our mullet, lured by the scent; the hook
He eyes at first from a distance, and with a sidelong look,
Searching the snare that waits him; as a stranger in the land,
Where three well-trodden trackways meet, comes to a stand
For all his haste, and sometimes to the leftward way his mind
Leans more—yet a moment later to the right he grows inclined.
Down each in turn he gazes, with thoughts like eddying tides,
Veering hither and thither—'tis long ere he decides.
So mix in the mind of our mullet endless perplexities,
Dreading a trap, yet drawn to the harmless food he sees.
At last temptation gains him, and near he swims to his fate—
Yet then starts frightened backward. Many a time the bait
He touches—then terror takes him, and off he darts in dismay.
As when some little girl, whose mother is gone away,
Seeing some thing she would touch or taste, yet does not dare,
For fear of her mother's anger. And yet she cannot bear,
Hard as she tries, to turn aside. But now she creeps
Towards it, and now draws backward; now through her heart there leaps
A sudden resolution—then panic! And evermore
She keeps her sharp-eyed glances turning towards the door.

(III, 499–519.)

QUINTUS SMYRNAEUS
(late 4th century A.D.?)

Even while the Roman Empire was falling before the barbarians, it
did not seem to its poets too late to retell the fall of Troy sixteen centuries

before. Quintus Smyrnaeus (also called Quintus Calaber because the MS. was found in Calabria) in his *Sequel to Homer* somewhat laboriously narrates the course of the struggle from Hector's death to the shipwreck of the Greek conquerors on their homeward voyage; this bridging the gap between *Iliad* and *Odyssey*. The episode of Oenone's death on her false lover's funeral pyre is perhaps the best part of his work, and not unworthy of comparison with the poems of Tennyson and Morris.

The Death of Oenone

Oenone, daughter of the River-god Cĕbrēn, was deserted by her husband Paris for the sake of Helen. Wounded by Philoctētes with one of the arrows of Hēracles, which were poisoned with the Hydra's blood, Paris came back to Oenone, begging to be cured; but she drove him away in scorn, and he died, little regretted by the city he had doomed.

One noble heart, one only, grieved in sincerity—
Oenone's. Not with the women that mourned in Troy was she;
But far away at home, in the bed where used to sleep,
In other days, her husband, she lay to moan and weep.
As when, high up the mountains, the woods stand mantled white
With snows that the western tempest has scattered in its flight
Across the glens—and now the east wind and the sun
Melt them once more—with torrents the long hill-ridges run
And in those swirling waters, chill though they be, the vast
Drifts that had choked the valleys, soften and thaw at last;
So now the heart of Oenone with intolerable pain
Melted, as she sorrowed for that husband loved in vain.
Then, as the sobs burst from her, to her own heart she said:
'Ah God, for my fatal folly! Ah God, that I were dead!
I loved my luckless husband—with him I dreamed to spend,
Even when years grew heavy, life to its honoured end,
In concord still unbroken. But the high Gods willed not so.
Ah, would the dark Fates had whirled me hence, long years ago,
The day that he was destined to leave me and forget!
But, though he lived to forsake me, I will dare one high deed yet—
To die with him, since the daylight is grown a hateful thing.'
  So saying, piteously she wept; remembering
Her husband, who had accomplished his bitter destiny.
Like wax before a flame, she wasted secretly,
Shunning the eyes of her father, her fair-robed handmaids' sight;
But when from the breadth of Ocean uprose the flooding Night

O'er this fair earth, to mortals bringing rest at last,
While sleeping lay her father, and the servants, like the blast
Of some wild storm through the doors she broke, and away she raced
On hurrying feet; as a heifer, high in the mountains, chased
By passion rushes headlong on her way to find her mate—
Losing all fear of the herdsman, she dashes desperate,
Searching the glades of the woodland for the lord she longs to meet.
So down the long track Oenone hurried on flying feet,
In frenzy to fling herself on the raging funeral-flame.
Weariness she felt not. Fast and more fast she came,
Hounded by Love and unpitying Fate. In the night-hung ways
She feared not the shagged wood-creatures—so feared in other days.
On, over rock and crag of the hill-thickets, she sped
Unfaltering; she battled through every torrent-bed;
While, looking down upon her, the fair Moon from above
Pitied her haste, still mindful of her own ancient love
For Endymion, the noble; and from the firmament,
Glittering in glory, lit the long road she went.

   And so at last, through that mountain-land, she came to where
The other nymphs round Paris stood wailing in despair.
There he lay wrapped in fervent flame; for, gathering
From every side, the shepherds for their comrade and their king
Had piled, as a last sad service of their sorrow, one vast heap
Of faggots from the mountain; and round they stood to weep.
But she—when she saw him lying there, no more she cried,
That broken heart; but, wrapping her mantle close to hide
Her lovely face, leapt headlong upon the blazing pyre.
Loud rose the wails of the watchers, as she clasped him in the fire;
Aghast the nymphs beheld her, flung on her husband's breast,
And low to her heart one whispered, as round the flame they pressed:
'Ah, mad indeed the folly of Paris that forsook
His own true wife and faithful, and a wanton mistress took—
Ruining himself, and his city, and all the Trojan folk.
Fool, that could care so little for the loyal heart he broke!
Yet she, though no more he loved her—nay, hated her to death,
Still loved him more than the sunlight!' So beneath her breath
Murmured a nymph. But there, amidst that blaze, to burn
They lay, henceforth for ever forgetting morn's return.
But the herdsmen stood in wonder, as wondered long ago
The Argive host, that day when they saw Evadne throw
Her arms about her husband, Cápaneus, by the fire
Of Zeus consumed. But when, within that raging pyre,

Both Paris and Oenone were both together made
One dust, they quenched the embers with wine at last, and laid
The bones within an urn of gold; and o'er the pair
They heaped a mighty burial-mound; and planted there
Two standing stones, with faces for ever turned apart—
Recalling, still, that ancient bitterness of heart.

(x, 411–89.)

NONNUS OF PANOPOLIS
(early 5th century A.D.)

With Nonnus of Panópolis in Egypt, who seems to have lived at
Alexandria, Antiquity can be seen merging into the Middle Ages. He
wrote both a poem on Christ, paraphrasing the Gospel of St John, and a
poem on Dionysus in no fewer than forty-eight books, for which his
name is at least remembered and by some has been admired. But his
poetry seems more remarkable for quantity than quality; this gigantic epic
recalls those prehistoric monsters that developed to colossal size on the eve
of extinction. The old sonority of the hexameter still echoes here; indeed
Nonnus himself introduced new refinements into its structure; but his
taste remains lamentable. Like Ovid, he is too clever; but he is not so
clever as Ovid. Writing a dozen centuries after Homer, he has not yet
learnt what Homer already knew—that an epic needs unity and is unlikely to obtain it merely by having a single dominant hero; especially
if it begins long before that hero's birth. Nonnus, however, starts with his
hero's grandfather—Cadmus. Eventually Dionysus is born, conquers
India, and ascends to Heaven. But he hardly takes the reader with him.
The extract which follows, describing Dionysus' view of Tyre, is an
example of that fanciful ingenuity which Nonnus did at least possess.

Tyre

With joy he saw that city which the Shaker of the Earth
Has girt with sea—though not wholly its waters ring her girth.
For such her shape as the Heavenly Moon's, what time she weaves
Almost her perfect round, yet one side still she leaves
Not wholly full. But his wonder redoubled as he gazed—
So linked in one were earth and sea. For wave-embraced
Lies Tyre; to the land united, yet by the waters bound
Upon three sides, as a girdle she gathers them around.

There in her poise unshaken, like a swimming girl lies she,
Her head and neck and bosom surrendered to the sea,
With arms submerged beneath the deep to left and right,
And body whereon the surges about her break in white.
Thrust against Earth, her mother, her two feet still remain;
But the great Earth-shaker holds her in his resistless chain,
A watery lover floating round—as if he grasped
His bride, with her neck beloved in his surging arms enclasped.

   So still at Tyre Bacchus marvelled. For nowhere save in her
The neatherd followed his calling beside the mariner,
Piping along the beaches; there at the goatherd's side
The fisherman hauled up his net; with oars the tide
Was sundered and, close beside it, the tilth by the ploughman's share;
Where the woodlands met the waters, woodmen and sailors there
Stood talking—boatmen and shepherds. Together he heard combine
The roar of waves, the lisp of leaves, the lowing of the kine.

                                        (*Dionysiaca*, XL, 311–34.)

GLYCON
(4th–5th century A.D.?)

Life's a Jest

All's dust, all's laughter, all's nonentity;
From blind unreason rise all things that be.

                                        (*Anth. Pal.*, X, 124.)

PALLADAS OF ALEXANDRIA
(*c.* 400 A.D.)

Fango è il mondo.
Leopardi.

   Pallădas is perhaps the most embittered writer of all antiquity. He hated
his marriage, his profession of schoolmaster, the monks now swarming
over Egypt, the Christian mob of Alexandria that hurled down its pagan
statues and later murdered Hypatia (A.D. 415); he hated life itself. Yet
his intensity has a certain ferocious power, recalling that greater figure of
Dean Swift who could find only in the tomb peace at last from 'the savage
indignation that lacerates the heart'. With him, night has almost fallen
on the ancient world.

Ballet

Memphis, the snub-nosed dancer, danced Daphne and Níobe:
Níobe, just like a stone; Daphne, just like a tree.

(Anth. Pal., XI, 255.)

'Tomorrow is a New Day'

Still, as each night dwindles, new-born each dawn we find us;
    All of our former lifetime is irrevocably past.
What we did yesterday, lies *now*, estranged, behind us;
    The life that still is left us, today begins at last.
Count not, you that are old, your long years passed away:
For all your years departed are yours no more today.

(x, 79.)

The World's Stage

Life's but a puppet-play. Play out your own,
Have done with earnest! Or—plod on and groan.

(x, 72.)

Vanity of Vanities

Naked I came on earth; naked to earth return:
Why toil in vain, when naked is the end mine eyes discern?

(x, 58.)

The Slaughter-house

For Death we all are nurtured, the greatest and the least,
Like fatted swine for the slaughter, to die as dies the beast.

(x, 85.)

Yahoo

O man, keep well in remembrance how thy father first begot thee,
    And let *that* memory put thy vanity to scorn.
Too much thou hast let the vapours of Plato's dreams besot thee,
    Calling thee 'immortal', calling thee 'Heaven-born'.
Of clay thou art. Why so proud, then? And even this too vainly
    Glozes the truth, and garbs it in a too presumptuous dress.
For indeed thou wast begotten, to put the matter plainly,
    Merely of wanton lust and a drop of filthiness.

(x, 45.)

Life is a voyage of peril. Before its tempests driven,
  Often we make worse shipwreck than ever ship at sea.
No pilot, except Fortune, to guide our helm is given,
  And none knows to what ending the course She sets shall be.
To some shall fall fair weather; for some shall ill winds blow;
Yet one for all is the harbour, deep in the night below.

(x, 65.)

The End

  We men of Hellas live now turned to dust,
  Feeding on naught but dead men's buried hopes;
  For all the world today's tossed upside down.

(x, 90, 5–8.)

MUSAEUS
(later 5th century A.D.)

By Sestos town, in Hero's tower,
  On Hero's heart Leander lies;
The signal torch has burned its hour
  And splutters as it dies.
Beneath him in the nighted firth,
  Between two continents complain
The seas he swam from earth to earth
  And he must swim again.

Housman.

I

None knows whence sprang the tale of Hero and Leander. Possibly it was a local legend, growing up round a tower at Sestos which may once have served as beacon for this crossing of the Dardanelles. It might, even, be partly founded on fact; it is well known that in May 1810 Byron swam from Sestos to Abydos. He took just over an hour. For though the distance for a crow is only a mile and a quarter, the two-knot current caused by the constant overflow of the Black Sea into the Mediterranean forced him to swim four. But Leander had to make the trip both ways.

According to Leaf (*Troy*, p. 382) this is normally impossible, unless by landing *ten* miles below Hero's Tower. In any case the feat could not become a habit, at all seasons, in water noted for its coldness and an area noted for its high winds. Besides, any young man in his senses would have found a boat.

In any case the theme of this ancient love-story is more ancient still; it occurs already in an Egyptian love-lyric:

> The love of my darling lies on the farther side,
> And between us the river rolls,
> And on a sandbank waits a crocodile.
> I go down to the water, I face the stream,
> My heart fails not amid its current,
> And under my feet the waves are like firm land.
> Her love it is that makes me strong,
> For me she is magic against the waters.

But it is in Latin literature that the legend of Leander first appears; Virgil cites him in the *Georgics* (III, 258–63) as an instance of the universal power of passion over man and beast:

And what of that youth also, whose soul was set alight
By Love that knows not pity, to swim at blind midnight
Seas tossing with the tempest? Above, great Heaven's door
Thundered, and loud the breakers along that rocky shore
Howled answer; yet nought could hold him—neither his parents' cry,
Nor that unhappy girl his death would doom to die.

A little later comes the first known allusion in Greek poetry—an epigram by Virgil's younger contemporary Antípater of Thessalonica, purporting to be written beside the lovers' grave (see p. 185).

On the other hand the tale seems unlikely to have been known to writers before (at earliest) the Alexandrian period. Its romantic tone is typically Hellenistic; and, were the tradition older, we should expect to find some reference to it before Virgil, seeing that we find so many after him—in Ovid, Strabo, Pomponius Mela, Lucan, Statius, Silius Italicus, Martial, under the early Empire; in Fronto in the second century, Ausonius in the fourth, Musaeus in the fifth, Agathias and Paulus Silentiarius in the sixth. The wide popularity of the story is also proved by frescoes at Pompeii; by a mosaic and a relief found at Zaghouan in North Africa; and by coins of Sestos and Abydos under the Roman Empire, which show the lover swimming and the maiden high on her tower.

Not even the Dark Ages could extinguish the memory of Hero's lamp.

The legend reappears in the twelfth-century Byzantine romance of Nicētas Eugenianus, *Drosilla and Charicles*; and in the thirteenth-century Provençal tale of *Flamenca*, where it forms part of the repertory of troubadours. Dante himself recalls it in Purgatory (XXVIIII, 71–5):

> Ma Ellesponto, là 've passò Serse,
> Ancora freno a tutti orgogli umani,
> Più odio da Leandro non sofferse,
> Per mareggiare intra Sesto ed Abido,
> Che quel da me, perch' allor non s'aperse.

Chaucer, too, planned to include in his *Legend of Good Women* the fate of 'Erro'.

With the Renaissance the old love-story renewed its youth. Aldus printed the poem of Musaeus at Venice in 1495. Scaliger thought it finer than Homer. Bernardo Tasso retold it in Italy; Boscán in Spain. In 1541 appeared Marot's French version; in 1598, Marlowe and Chapmans' English adaptation. There are four allusions to the tale in Shakespeare; more in Burton. Nash burlesqued it in his *Lenten Stuffe*, turning Leander into a ling, Hero into a herring. In the seventeenth century Scarron wrote another burlesque, slightly wittier; in the eighteenth, Voltaire's butt, Le Franc de Pompignan, turned the subject into a tragedy, and a curious German, Hermann von der Hardt, discovered in it a political allegory— Leander was Byzantium; Hero, Rome; her lamp, the minister Stilicho! Then the Romantics in their turn took up this ancient romance—Byron in the opening of *The Bride of Abydos*; Schiller, in his ballad; Grillparzer, in a play, *Des Meeres und der Liebe Wellen*, whose five laborious acts have perhaps less life in them now than the six simple lines of Leigh Hunt (who himself retold the story in not outstanding verse):

> I never think of poor Leander's fate
> And how he swam and how his bride sat late,
> And watched the dreadful dawning of the light,
> But as I would of two that died last night.
> So might they now have lived and so have died:
> The story's heart, to me, still beats against its side.

But it was not only to the hearts of the literary that the legend found its way. In the ballads of simple folk this memory of sorrow has spread through Piedmont, France, Catalonia, the Netherlands, Germany, Scandinavia, Carniola, Hungary, even the far-off Ukraine. Here the lovers' names are forgotten, their race, their time—all except that love strong as death which the waters could not drown:

Jadis, auprès d'Arles,
Vivaient deux amants.
Ce qu'est bien rare en France,
Ils étaient constants. . . .   (Metz district.)

'Bel amant, si vous y venez,
J'y mettrai flambeau pour enseigne.
Tant que le flambeau durera,
Jamais l'amour finira. . . .'   (Pays de Dôle.)

Es wirbt ein schöner Knabe
Da überm breiten See
Um eines Königs Tochter.
Nach Leid geschah ihm Weh. . . .

Hero becomes the nameless daughter of a castle in Bavaria—Leander turns knight and swims for her the Staffelsee. Hero takes the veil at a convent in the Chiemsee—Leander turns monk in the neighbouring monastery; but a jealous nun puts out the light. Hero is transformed to a princess of Hungry; Leander as a prince tries to swim to her across the Danube; and on their graves occurs a miracle familiar to readers of our own ballads of the Borderside:

Sur l'un on planta
Une tulipe blanche rayée;
Sur l'autre on planta
Une tulipe toute rouge.
Les âmes des amoureux
Devinrent des tulips vivantes,
Et elles croissaient, croissaient toujours,
Jusqu'à ce qu'elles purent s'embrasser.

Even the Punjab, it is said, can show the grave of two lovers who perished like Hero and Leander. This simple tale which (unless it too springs from some older *Märchen*) began on the narrow strait between Europe and Asia, was to travel eastward to the Indus and westward to the Atlantic.[1]

---

[1] For further details on the diffusion of the Leander legend see the edition of Musaeus by E. H. Blakeney (Oxford, 1935) and that by T. Sandre (Amiens, 1924), which very conveniently reprints many of the relevant texts.

Of Musaeus 'the Grammarian', as he is called, nothing is known; except that he seems to have lived in the later fifth century A.D., after Nonnus of Panópolis in Egypt, who was his main model, and in the days of Procópius of Gaza, who addresses two fulsome letters to a Musaeus that may be our poet. In other words, Musaeus was separated from Homer by a distance almost as great as separates Musaeus from us. Classical Greek poetry had already lived some thirteen or fourteen centuries; apart from a few epigrams, this poem is for us its dying utterance. But though Musaeus is one of the last Greek poets, he is not the least. He should not be underrated just because he is late, and simple, and not ashamed to borrow from the past. Those who think his subject easy may be advised to read the other poets who have tried it. The cure is not likely to need repeating.

Some five hundred years before Musaeus wrote, Ovid (unless it was a clever imitator) had already composed two imaginary letters between the lovers (*Heroïdes*, 18 and 19), which were to provide posterity with their other main source of the story. These verse-epistles are typical Ovid; neat, smooth, bright—and heartless. Not a tear stains his Muse's paint; not a sob cracks the enamel on her cheek. Leander's passion is so hot that he does not feel the coldness of the water; he has swum so often that there is almost a beaten track across the Hellespont. Hero, practical maiden, suggests that if he cannot swim so far as Sestos, they should at least meet and kiss on a wave-top. And both lovers keep under their pillows whole mythological dictionaries. Aeõlus, Daedalus, Endymion, Ceyx, Tithõnus, Phrixus, Andrómeda—the whole stage-army of gradus-figures dances dutiful attendance. And yet if it is epigrams one wants, perhaps there is more point—and truth—in four lines of Martial (*De Spectaculis*, 25), which Voltaire thought worth translating:

> They say the bold Leander, towards sweet Hero cleaving
> The waves that dragged already his tired body down,
> Cried, poor lad, to the surges high around him heaving:
> 'Spare me—I go to meet her: *returning*, let me drown.'

But paradox seldom makes poetry. The trouble with Ovid is that he really wants his reader, not to pity his lovers, but to admire the poet himself. That folly, throughout his career, was to stultify his gifts. A writer can sell himself to cleverness, as Faust sold himself to Mephisto-pheles; but a bout of tawdry brilliance in the world is a poor exchange for a soul.

Marlowe (though he wrote a tragedy on Dr Faustus) made this same mistake in his *Hero and Leander*. The poem has indeed been glorified by

Swinburne in one of his critical ecstasies as standing out 'alone amid all the wide and wild poetic wealth of its teeming and turbulent age as might a small shrine of Parian sculpture amid the rank splendour of a tropic jungle'. But Marlowe's poem seems more like the jungle than the shrine. He remains far closer to Ovid than to anything Greek. His poem, with Chapman's continuation, is seven times as long as Musaeus; but quantity is not quality. Every paragraph is bedizened with quips, quirks, and conceits. Pages are devoted to Hero's costume, which includes:

> Her kirtle blue, whereon was many a stain,
> Made with the blood of wretched lovers slain.

For Marlowe's Leander, the love of this fair murderess is not enough; Neptune too must be enamoured of him (for Marlowe could not resist exhibiting his own homosexuality); and even the waves of Hellespont: —

> mounted up intending to have kiss'd him,
> And fell in drops like tears because they miss'd him.

Chapman, when he took up the theme, was not to be outdone; he makes the drops of brine that trickle from Leander as he comes ashore die for love before the earth entombs them, leaving their souls behind them as froth upon the sea. Then descends the Goddess Ceremony:

> Her flaming hair to her bright feet extended,
> By which hung all the bench of deities;
> And in a chain, compact of ears and eyes,
> She led Religion. . . .

But let us leave Ceremony to comb the deities out of her hair. This curious poem has pleased; power of some sort it must therefore possess. Marlowe's part of it does offer moments of beauty, moments of genuine feeling; it is at least much superior, I think, to Chapman's continuation, which combines shuffling obscurity with snuffling morality; but it may be wondered whether the gift of sincerity is really so common in life that critics need to lavish eulogies on work so void of it.

Unfortunately even sincere work is no guarantee against boredom. That seems the trouble with Schiller's ballad and Grillparzer's play. The gaudy harlotries of Marlowe have at least a sort of life; but these later works, though noble, strike cold and dead as funeral monuments, with the stiff polished whiteness of Carrara marble. Similarly Leigh Hunt's poem on the subject, while it has feeling, lacks force—it is too much like Keats and water. Decidedly Hero and Leander do not make an easy subject. One returns with increased respect to the Greek of Musaeus, or even the simple, honest French into which Marot rendered him.

It is true that Musaeus himself has some discoloured patches of decadence. His brief narrative may invite comparison with the best of the Homeric Hymns or of Theócritus; but the comparison is often damaging. He too slips at times into Ovidian conceits. Leander stripping by the surf of Hellespont talks frigidly of the flames of love as being yet more terrible than the watery sea. And the poet's worldly-wise cynicism about a woman's 'No' being really 'Yes' is paraded till it grows a little tiresome. His style shows a curious carelessness about repetitions of phrase. He loves prettiness too much and restraint too little. Yet on the whole he remains wise enough not to spoil a good story with coxcombries. And after all how few poets of any race or time have known how to tell a story! Musaeus does keep his eye on the object. He retains some of the brevity and rapidity of Homer. Above all, as he nears the fatal ending, his pace smoothly quickens like a river as it nears a cataract. His characters may be simple outlines, like figures on a Greek vase; but the lines remain firm and clear. He is really moved by the passion of his lovers, by the loneliness of Hero's tower, by the beauty and terror of the sea. Romantic though Musaeus may be, he gives a saner answer to life than the charnel cynicism of Pallădas. After more than a thousand years of use, the Homeric hexameter still resounds and races in his hands, like the breakers on those beaches close to Troy where the long roll of its music first began.

> ἀεὶ δ'ἀνὰ νύκτα καὶ ἠῶ
> ἐξ ἁλὸς ἠνεμόεντος ἐπιβρέμει οὔασιν ἠχή.

> But in my ears alway
> Only the windy surges that thunder night and day.

And the climax of his eloquence comes, where it should, at the moment when Hero takes her wave-tossed lover to her arms and that brief union is sealed at last. Perhaps even the old Ionian master who sang of the happiness of Odysseus and Penelope joined again after their long years parted by the sea, would not have found his far-off descendant unworthy of him here. This night that curtains the doomed lovers recalls, no longer the garish glare of Marlowe, but that nobler mind which drew the last darkness round Romeo and Juliet.

Hero and Leander

Tell of the lamp that witnessed Love's secret, Goddess, tell
Of the youth that fared to his nightly tryst across the black sea-swell;
Of Sestos and Abydos, of Hero the midnight bride,
And that dark troth that never the deathless Dawn espied.
For I sing of Leander's swimming, of the lamp that faithfully

Served the Cytherēan and bore across the sea,
For Hero, bride of darkness, the message of her love—
That lamp which was Love's glory once; which Zeus above,
When its long task was over, should have hung in Heaven afar,
High in the constellations, and named 'Love's Pilot-star'.
For it shared the pain and passion of two lovers to the last,
A sure, unfailing herald of their sweet vigils passed
Together—till broke upon them the tempest's bitter blast.
O Goddess, sing Thou with me that final night that found
The lamp at last extinguished, Leander lost and drowned.

There stand two cities facing across the salt sea-flow—
Sestos and Abydos. Now Love once bent His bow
And shot against them both a shaft that set aflame
A young man and a maiden. 'Maid Hero' was her name,
And the name of the youth, Leander—by all men called 'the fair'.
The youth dwelt in Abydos, in Sestos she—a pair
In feature like each other, and each the brightest star
Of the cities that had bred them. If thou shouldst come so far
As Hellespont, look for that tower where, lamp in hand,
Hero of Sestos stood, to light her love to land;
Look for the ancient Abydos, whose sea-resounding strait
Mourns, methinks, still the passion of Leander and his fate.

How was it, then, that Leander, there in Abydos, fell
Deep in love with Hero, and won her love as well?
Hero the fair and lovely, of the race of Heaven bred,
Was Aphrodite's priestess, and dwelt, as yet unwed,
Far away from her parents, in a tower beside the sea—
Herself a second Cypris. But with maiden modesty
She took no part when gathered the women of the land,
Nor when the lasses of her age danced, graceful, hand in hand;
She dreaded women's gossip and their jealous-tongued surmise
(For women look on beauty, always, with jealous eyes),
And ever to Aphrodite she prayed with many a prayer,
Many an offering made to Love, that He might spare—
He and His Heavenly Mother—His quiver's dreaded fire.
In vain!—she could not shun those shafts where burns desire.

For now the holy feast of the Cytherēan came,
That Sestos holds in Adonis and Aphrodite's name;
And so in all their thousands the pilgrims flocked to keep
That festival—they gathered from the isles that fringe the deep,
From Thessaly, from Cyprus amid her seas embayed;
Through all Cythēra's cities there was no woman stayed,

Not a dancer left in the forest-glens of fragrant Lebanon.
All those, too, that dwelt nearer to that gathering were gone—
The Phrygians, the townsmen of Abydos o'er the strait,
And every youth that loved fair maids. For soon and late,
Whenever comes word of a festival, such youths it brings,
Not so eager to honour the Gods with offerings
As to eye the beauty of the young girls gathered there.
   Now Hero went her ways about the temple, fair
As is the bright-cheeked Moon, scaling the eastern skies—
So dazzling was her beauty, as it flashed on all men's eyes.
Like budding rose of double hue, those cheeks aglow
Against the whiteness of her skin; there seemed to blow
A meadow full of roses through all the loveliness
Of her young limbs; and under the pure white of her dress
Rosy shone her ankles, as she glided on her way,
Grace in her every motion. False are old tales that say
Three were the Heavenly Graces born—in Hero's eye,
In that sweet smile, men saw a hundred Graces lie.
Ay, here was a priestess worthy of Aphrodite found!
So, as she stood outshining every woman round,
And gave the Cyprian worship, the Cyprian's self she seemed.
Smitten was every young man's heart—not one but dreamed
How happy, could he hold her within his arms at last.
Wherever through that fair-built shrine her footsteps passed,
All eyes, all thoughts, all hearts pursued her as she went.
And one young man amidst them cried out in wonderment:
'I have been in Lacedaemon, I have seen the Spartan town,
Famed for its maids contending, that strive for beauty's crown;
But never I looked on lass like this, so fair, so fine—
Has Cypris found for servant some younger Grace divine?
I have strained my eyes with gazing, yet never gazed my fill—
Glad would I die, if only Hero would grant my will!
No God on high Olympus I envy for His bliss,
Were I but wed to Hero, were she but mine to kiss.
Yet, if I may not love a maid that served Thy sanctity,
Ah, grant me, Cytherēan, a bride as fair as she!'
   So cried one youth among them. But in silence and apart
Many another hid his pain, with frenzy in his heart.
Yet thou, ill-starred Leander, by her young glory stirred—
Thou couldst not hide, like them, thy wound without a word.
Once that fire-breathing arrow had struck thee unaware,
Without the beauty of Hero life seemed too poor to bear.

Higher the fire of Eros blazed, as her bright glances came,
Till his heart was grown one seething sea of quenchless flame.
For the perfect beauty of women, that gains their glory, stings
Man's heart with a keener anguish than wingéd arrow brings.
'Tis through the eye that shaft is shot—yea, eyes can dart
A pang that fast spreads downward, until it strikes the heart.
Fear seized on him and wonder, shamelessness and shame—
Hard beat his heart; he blushed, to find a girl could tame
His soul; yet her beauty dazed him—then passion conquered fear,
Joyful he felt his courage rise, and pressing near
With swift and noiseless footsteps, he stood before the maid;
Yet sidelong still his glances hither and thither played
And still his eyes, in silence, pleaded his cause. But she—
Soon as she had divined his passion's subtlety,
Her heart leapt at his beauty; and yet with tongue as tied,
Though secret signs betrayed her love, she turned to hide
Her lovely face from Leander—then she would turn again
To catch his look. Now clearly he saw her longing's pain—
And happy he at finding she did not scorn his heart!
But, while he sought occasion to speak with her apart,
Folding up all its splendour, to westward sank the day
And bright in the east rose Hesper, upon his twilit way.
Then, as he saw the mantling dark stride up the sky,
Leander followed Hero and drew more boldly nigh;
Gently his hand had taken her fingers rosy-red,
With a sigh drawn deep from his inmost heart. No word she said,
But back from him, as in anger, she plucked her rosy wrist.
Yet well divined Leander her heart could now resist
No more—he grasped undaunted her bright-embroidered dress
And drew her onward with him to that rich shrine's recess;
Then, with steps that faltered, after him Hero came,
As one still all unwilling; and with a woman's blame
Loud she cried to Leander—'Stranger, what violence!
To drag me!—a girl unmarried!—what, hast thou lost all sense!
Find someone else to bring here, but take thy hand from me!
I come of wealthy parents—how angry they would be!
I am the Cyprian's priestess—not for thy touch am I,
But maiden still. Nay, dream not within my bed to lie.'
So, as girls will, she threatened. But when Leander heard
This storm of woman's bluster, passionate word on word,
Well he knew that token of the yielding of the maid.
For when the tongue of woman grows loudest to upbraid

Some youth, it gives good warning that sweet love-talk is near.
So on her white and fragrant neck he kissed his dear
And cried, from a heart all flaming with passion through and through:
'O Love, O second Cypris, O second Pallas too!
For how should I liken *thee* to the daughters of the earth?—
Nay, to the daughters of Heaven, that from Zeus took their birth.
Happy the sire that begot thee, the mother that once bare—
Ay, blest the womb that carried thee! But hear my prayer,
Take pity on this passion that overmasters me.
Since thou art Love's own priestess—seek Love's reality!
Come to me and fulfil her law, perform her mystic rite—
What use has Aphrodite for a maiden acolyte?
It is not virgins Cypris loves. If thou wilt please
To learn her fair commandments, her faithful mysteries,
A bed of bridal waits for thee. Dost thou adore
The Cyprian?—then welcome Love's sweet, bewitching law.
Save me, thy suppliant now—thy lover, if I may—
Whom Love with His shafts has stricken, and made, for *thee*, His prey.
As Hermes, God of the Golden Wand, once brought and gave
Hēracles the dauntless to Omphăle for slave,
So me, not the subtle Hermes, but Love's own Queen has brought
To thee. By Atalanta, the Arcadian, be taught,
That loved her maidenhood too dear, and scorned the bed
Of Milánion her lover—yet, when upon her head
Fell Aphrodite's anger, to him she had loved not,
She gave herself. Then listen, love; lest Cypris' wrath grow hot.'
    So with love's soft beguilements he won her to his way,
So to his will he wrought her, loud as she said him nay.
Low on the ground she bent her eyes, no word she said,
But hid away her face, with shame flushed rosy-red,
And while with her foot she scraped the floor, in bashfulness
Often about her shoulders closer she drew her dress.
(For all such signs betoken that a maiden means to yield
And by her very silence a girl's 'Yes' is revealed.)
Already maiden Hero was stung with the desire
Of Love the bitter-sweet, and felt His gentle fire
Burn her, as she trembled before Leander's grace.
But while, in her confusion, earthward she bowed her face,
Leander's passion-drunken eyes were fastened still
Upon her delicate neck, yet could not gaze their fill;
And so at last, with cheeks aflush for lovely shame,
She gave Leander answer, and sweet her accents came:

'They would melt a stone, O stranger, the words that thou canst say.
Who was it taught thy tongue its sweet, seductive way?
Alas, who was it brought thee first to Sestos here?
Yet vain are all thy pleadings. For how should I hold dear
A dubious, wandering stranger? How yield my maidenhead?
With holy bonds before the world we may not wed—
That were against my parents' will. And shouldst thou make—
Thou but a strolling stranger—thy home here for my sake,
How couldst thou keep the secret of our passion hid?
Tongues are so full of slander; the thing a man once did
Most secretly, in the market he hears loud throats proclaim.
But tell me now, in frankness, thy country and thy name.
For thou hast mine already—to many is Hero known.
My home is a skiey tower, sea-beaten, where alone
I dwell with a single handmaid, there on the beach before
The wall of Sestos city, beside the breakers' roar,
With nought but the sea for neighbour—'twas my harsh parents' choice.
There are no young men's dances; *there* to me comes no voice
Of any girl-companion—but in my ears alway
Only the windy surges that thunder night and day.'
And again she hid her blushes deep within her cloak,
With shame renewed, and self-rebuke, for what she spoke.
    But, pierced to the quick, Leander set him to devise
How he should meet this challenge, and gain his passion's prize.
For cunning Love makes keener the hearts He takes in thrall,
Healing the hurt His own hand gave. He conquers all,
And yet to His own true servants wise counsellor is He.
So now He helped Leander with His own subtlety;
Hot with passion and quick of wit, the young man cried:
'For love of thee, dear girl, I will cross that angry tide—
Yes, though the deep be seething and never a ship dare sail,
I will not fear the weltering wave—I will not fail,
For all the surges' thunder, upon my way to thee.
Each night to thy arms thy lover shall come wet from the sea—
Ay, swim the racing Hellespont. Not far at all
My home is, but before thee—behind Abydos' wall.
Let but a single lamp, as darkness falls, be lit
Far off upon thy dizzy tower; that, watching it,
I may steer as Love's own vessel, thy lamp before my eyes
For pilot-star—not Boötes, late-lingering in the skies,
Nor bold Orion, nor yet the never-setting Wain.
So shall I come to harbour on Sestos shore again.

Only beware, belovéd, of the bitter winds of night,
Lest they blow out thy lantern, that is the beacon-light
Of all my life—and thus I cast my youth away.
But if indeed thou askest that I in turn should say
My name—it is Leander—to fair-crowned Hero wed.'

So when between the two these words of troth were said,
That they should love in secret, and that her lamp should be
The herald of their meeting, each night, across the sea,
That when she kindled it, then he should swim the deep,
They vowed themselves each other's, in a night that knew not sleep;
And yet at last must sever, reluctant—to her tower
Climbed Hero; but Leander, lest in the midnight hour
He lose his course, well noted the tower's landmarks, then
To the broad lands of Abydos and its great walls sailed again.

All day they sighed for Darkness, as their bridesmaid to bring
The sweet, hid strife of lovers, the nightlong whispering;
At last She rose, black-mantled, to all men bearing rest,
Save to passionate Leander. Then, while each breaker's crest
Broke thundering up the beaches, with straining eyes he sought
That far-seen sign of secret tryst, that lamp with sorrow fraught.
But Hero, as daylight faded and night's blue darkness came,
Set forth her lamp. And swiftly as Hero's lamp took flame,
Love kindled too Leander's impetuosity.
As blazed her lantern, blazed his love. He heard the sea
Boom with its maddened breakers along that echoing shore,
And for a moment trembled—then summoning once more
His courage, to his heart he cried with words of cheer:
'Ay, dread is Love, and fierce the sea. Yet shall I fear
The sea, that is but water, when Love flames wild in me?
Flinch from that flame, my heart, not from the watery sea.
On now, where Love is calling! What though the surges rave?
Hast thou forgot that Cypris Herself sprang from the wave,
And is mistress of the waters, as of thy own heart's need?'

Then bare he stripped his comely limbs, and bound with speed
His tunic hard about his head, and with a leap
Plunged from the shore, committing his body to the deep;
Then towards the lamp's far twinkle struck out with all his force,
With arms for oars, like vessel self-steered upon her course.
But Hero, lamp in hand upon her dizzy height,
Against the deadly veering gusts kept safe her light,
Shielding it with her mantle; till on the haven-strand
Of Sestos, spent with labour, her lover came to land.

On towards the tower her lantern led—there by its door,
Silent, she clasped him in her arms, still panting sore,
While fast from all his body the water dripped—then led
Into her maiden-chamber, where stood their bridal-bed.
His skin she bathed, and anointed his body fragrantly
With oil of roses, to take away the harsh tang of the sea;
Then in her bed, piled deep with rugs, laid him to rest,
Still breathing hard, and drew him with fond words to her breast—
'Ah love, so sorely tried as never lover yet,
O dear and sore-tried love, the bitter waves forget!
Forget the booming breakers, the harsh, fish-reeking brine,
And rest thy weary body within these arms of mine.'
He hearkened; then her girdle he loosened, and the will
Of glorious-hearted Cypris they turned them to fulfil.
A bridal it was where no man danced; no voice of minstrel praised
Hēra, Queen of Wedlock; no marriage-hymn was raised.
Round *that* bride-bed no torches filled the night with flame,
No revellers light-footed whirling about them came,
Their bridal-song no father and well-loved mother led—
Nay, in Love's crowning hour 'twas Silence strewed their bed
And shut their marriage-chamber; 'twas Darkness decked the bride,
And Night that gave them blessing. Nor by his true love's side
Did Dawn behold the bridegroom, in the happy sleep of home—
Back, by then, to Abydos he was plunging through the foam,
With passion all unsated still aching in his breast.

   Thus lived the long-robed Hero, though never her parents guessed,
A maid by day, by night a bride—how oft the twain
Sighed for the sun, impatient, to sink to the west again!
So, by Love's compelling, they tasted secretly
The joys of the Cytherēan, in trysts no man might see;
Yet but a little while they lived—soon passed away
The bliss they found together in their passion's stormy day.
For when the wintertide was come, and frosts lay white,
And the wild winds went shrieking across the heaven's height,
And ocean's depths were troubled, and gales with never a break
Lashed to fury the furthest seas, and made to quake
Their bottommost abysses; when, upon either strand
Of Hellespont, the sailors had hauled high up on land
Their black ships, out of reach of the treacherous winter sea—
Not even the seas of winter had power to frighten thee,
O gallant-souled Leander. Still from Hero's tower
Beamed the lamp to light thee, back to thy bridal-bower,

Urging thee on to defiance of the raging gulfs between.
Ah pitiless light and faithless! Far better had it been
If the unhappy Hero had borne those winter days
Apart from her Leander, and left unlit the rays
Of that brief star of bridal. But *too* strong was desire,
Too strong was fate. So tempted, once more she lit her fire—
A bridal-torch no longer—ah now the torch of doom!
  The night had come, when winds deep-breathing through the gloom,
Winds with their blasts like whistling spears, most furiously
Fall—and with fiercest onset—upon the surf-torn sea;
And now Leander, straining to reach his true love's breast,
Weltered amid those bellowing waves, from crest to crest;
Now mid the hurtling waters roller on roller dashed,
And sea and cloud were confounded, while all around him crashed
Blast against blast in battle—for now the east wind whirled
Against the west, the north wind on the south its fury hurled,
And infinite rose the tumult of that loud-thundering tide.
But from the pitiless surges ill-starred Leander cried
To sea-born Aphrodite, again and yet again,
And to the lord Poseidon, the master of the main,
And begged the North Wind's pity, for Oreithyia's sake.
In vain—what Doom had destined, not Love Himself could break.
This way and that, resistless, the raging breakers beat
Over his drifting body; faint grew his thrusting feet;
His tireless hands no longer could breast the surges—fast
Between his lips, despite him, the swirling waters passed
And a bitter draught he drank of the overmastering sea.
One ruthless gust extinguished that lamp of treachery,
And with it the doomed Leander's life, with it his passion died.
  Against the storm's blind fury bitterly Hero cried,
Already half foreboding her lost Leander's fate,
As hours passed, yet he came not. Still, as the night grew late,
Sleepless she stood there, weeping, in agony of thought.
Dawn lightened; yet no lover to Hero's eyes it brought.
She strained her sight, far scanning the league-long rollers' spray,
In case, when her lamp had failed him, he might have missed his way
And still she might see him drifting. But when, on the rocks below,
She saw the surges batter his body to and fro,
Rending the broidered robe upon her bosom's white,
Down she leapt, whirling headlong, sheer from her tower's height.
There on her true love's body, maid Hero's life was done:
Not Death Himself denied them the joy that made them one.

DAMASCIUS OF DAMASCUS
(earlier 6th century A.D.)

Damascius, last head of the Neo-Platonic school of Athens closed by Justinian in 529, took refuge with six fellow-philosophers at the court of Chosroës of Persia; but they found Persia, too, no Paradise; finally they were granted leave to return with an amnesty, by a clause in a treaty between Chosroës and Justinian (see Gibbon, XL).

' The Vasty Halls of Death'

In body alone was Zōsime
A slave. And now her body's free.

(Anth. Pal., VII, 553.)

JULIANUS PREFECT OF EGYPT
(mid 6th century A.D.)

On Anácreon

Oft and often I sang it, I will cry it yet from the tomb:
'Drink, ere ye wrap around you the mantling dust of doom!'

(Anth. Pal., VII, 32.)

The Bride of Sixteen

Anastasia, fair blossom of the Garden of the Graces,
  Betimes you came to the bride-bed, untimely to the tomb.
Sadly your sire, your husband, go now with tear-stained faces;
  For you weeps even, it may be, the Ferryman of Doom.
For here by his side that loved you, not twelve months you had seen,
And now the earth is o'er you, a bride of but sixteen.

(VII, 600.)

Her Picture

Just as she was, the painter has caught Theódote.
Would he had failed, and let us forget our misery!

(VII, 565.)

Laughter to the Last

Queen of the phantom faces that no smiles ever brighten,
  Yet give Demócritus welcome, as he comes, Persephone,
Though dead, still gaily laughing. Laughter alone could lighten
  Even thy mother's burden, what time she mourned for thee.

(VII, 58.)

MACEDONIUS THE CONSUL
(mid 6th century A.D.)

'The consular' would be more exact—it was a Byzantine rank or dig,
nity, which could be conferred on those who had not actually held the
office of consul.

Farewell to the Sea

Amyntichus the aged, when his fisher's days were ended,
  Swathing about his trident his leaden,weighted net,
Prayed to the Lord Poseidon, with his old arms extended
  Towards the salt,surging ocean, and eyes that glistened wet:
'Thou knowest, Lord, I am weary. Bitter the years that bow me,
  But young, and strong to break me, is my mate Poverty.
Now, for the old man's failing breath, bid earth allow me
  Bread, if Thou wilt, O Master alike of land and sea.'

(Anth. Pal., VI, 30.)

' Betwixt a Sleep and a Sleep '

Thou gavest me birth, Eileithyia; Earth, thou wilt hide me sleeping.
  Farewell to you both. I have finished the race you measured me.
I go, not knowing whither. For whence I came to your keeping,
  I know not, neither who made me, nor yet who I may be.

(VII, 566.)

PAULUS SILENTIARIUS
(died A.D. 575)

Paulus, called 'Silentiarius', as chief of the thirty Silentiarii or Gentle,
men of the Bedchamber at the Byzantine court, wrote also two poems on
Santa Sophia, one of which was recited at the reopening of the church

after an earthquake, in 563. It appears, however, from his verses (and those of his contemporaries) that both Christianity and marriage could still sit lightly on high officials in sixth-century Byzantium. Nor, contrary to the popular idea, do they seem a whit less pessimistic than their pagan forefathers.

Broken Tryst

Late lingers Cleophantis. And now begins to flicker
    The third lamp; now in silence falters and fails its fire.
Ah that the fever in my heart were quenched yet quicker,
    That my passion ceased its burning, sleepless with desire!
How oft by the Cytherēan she swore to come to me
Tonight!—but nothing, nothing for God nor man cares she.

(*Anth. Pal.*, v, 279.)

Love-Madness

They say that men whose veins with a mad dog's venom sicken,
    Everywhere see in the water the phantom beast they hate;
And mad was Love, it may be, when his fierce fangs left me stricken,
    Left me, soul and senses, maddened and desolate;
For in the whirling river, in the ocean wave I see,
Ay, in the brimming winecup, the lovely wraith of thee.

(v, 266.)

Stronger than Death

How long in stealthy silence must we watch with glances hidden?
    How long must our eyes encounter with looks of secret fire?
Enough, let us speak our anguish! And if we are still forbidden
    To find in each other's arms the sweet end of desire,
Then the sword shall cure our sorrows. Far better, side by side
To live one life together, or together to have died!

(v, 221.)

The Dead Ballet-dancer

Lips sealed in iron stillness, no more henceforth for ever
    Will you mime us, Chrȳseomallus, the men of olden days
With gestures of golden silence. Ah happy heart and clever,
    How bitter now your dumbness, that once we loved to praise!

(VII, 563.)

' The Rest is Silence '

'My name was—' 'Does it matter?' 'My country—' 'Can it profit?'
  'My lineage was splendid—' 'Though squalid, who cares now?'
'My days were full of honour—' 'Though base they were, what of it?'
  'Here rests at last my body—' 'Who heeds thee? What art *thou*?'

(VII, 307.)

AGATHIAS SCHOLASTICUS OF MYRINA
(A.D. 536–582)

Agathias, born at Myrīna in Aeŏlis, studied at Alexandria before
taking up a legal and official career at Constantinople, where he became
a Scholasticus (high legal functionary of the imperial court). He married
the daughter of his friend Paulus Silentiarius; wrote a history, continuing
Procópius, of the years 552–8; and made a collection of contemporary
epigrams which is one of the sources of our *Palatine Anthology*.

The Maid's Complaint

Ah, young men have less sorrow—a harder lot, and cheerless,
  Life has laid upon us, tender-hearted maids.
For *they* have young companions; and free of tongue and fearless
  Into his comrade's ear each lad his heart unlades.
They have sports to kill their troubles, they roam abroad unchidden,
  They can distract their longing with the hues of the painter's art.
But we are begrudged the very sun: alone and hidden,
  At home must we sit brooding in the darkness of our heart.

(Anth. Pal., v, 297.)

The Swallows

With sighing and with sorrow all my nights are bitter,
  And when at last comes dawning, to grant my grief some grace,
Then, breaking that sweet slumber, outside the swallows twitter
  And bring anew the teardrops hurrying down my face.
Once more my swollen eyes must watch; once more pursues me
  The memory of Rhŏdanthe; once more my heart is wrung.
Ah, envious chatterers, be still! Can ye accuse me
  That it was I who severed your Philomēla's tongue?

Go—cry among the mountains. There ye may settle, grieving
  For Ítylus, above the hoopoe's craggy nest.
Spare me a little slumber—maybe, some dream deceiving
  May lay me, for a moment, upon Rhŏdanthe's breast.

(v, 237.)

'A Kiss within the Cup'

I have no love for the winecup. If thou wouldst have me taste it
  And lose my wits, then pledge me—I take it from thy hand.
Hard indeed to be sober, when once thy lips have graced it.
  A cupbearer so lovely, how should my heart withstand?
For then the cup will carry a kiss to me from thee,
And low its lip shall whisper a tale of ecstasy.

(v, 261.)

'Here Lies a most Beautiful Lady'

I saw a tomb by the wayside, as I went towards Corinth city,
  The tomb of the ancient Laïs, for so its letters tell,
And wept. 'Though I never saw you, yet still', I said, 'I pity,
  Still for your story's sake, Lady, I greet you well.
Ah the young hearts that ached for you!—and lo, today
You dwell by Lethe, all your beauty turned to clay.'

(VII, 220.)

To Pan

These fields unsown the ploughman Stratonīcus hallows
  To Thee for all Thy goodness, O Pan that loves the hill.
Here feed thy flocks in gladness, rejoicing in these fallows,
  That from henceforth the ploughshare shall leave uncloven still—
Haunt for a happy lover. For joy in it thy bride
Shall Echo be and lay her, at last, her love beside.

(VI, 79.)

Spring Sailing

With calm the seas grow purple now. No storm-winds sunder
  Roller from furrowed roller, or toss their whitened mane;
No more around the headlands the surges crash in thunder,
  Then backward flung go swirling out to the deep again.

Now the west winds are blowing, and the swallow chirps preparing
  Once more her bridal-chamber, her wattled house of straw.
Grey mariner, take heart then, whether you go faring
  Past Syrtis, or the shingle of the far Sicilian shore.
Burn but a wrasse on my altar, or a gurnard red, and pray
To Priāpus, God of the Harbour, before you sail away.

(X, 14.)

ARABIUS SCHOLASTICUS
(mid 6th century A.D.)

A Byzantine lawyer under Justinian.

A Villa by the Bosphorus

With vineyards and with woodlands, with gardens and with rivers
  Filled am I, and gladdened by the neighbour sea;
And the fisher and the farmer from each side come as givers
  Of all the happy bounties of field and foam to me;
And for them that rest within me falls lulling on the ear
The fair cry of the ferry, or bird that carols clear.

(Anth. Pal., IX, 667.)

JOANNES BARBUCALLUS
(mid 6th century A.D.)

The Desolation of Bērytus

Stay not for *me*, O sailor, your vessel's swift careering;
  Shorten not sail for *me*. My haven's turned to sand;
Here lies a tomb. Some happier port shall hail you nearing,
  As, with her beat of oarblades, your galley makes to land.
Thus the Gods of the traveller, and Poseidon, bade it be:
Farewell, O men that wander alike by earth and sea.

(Anth. Pal., IX, 427.)

IV. ROMAN AND EARLY BYZANTINE PERIOD

MELEAGER

[p. 179] *Love for Sale.* Turned by Ronsard into a sonnet for Hélène (ed. Vaganay, II, 272):

> Qu'il me soit arraché des tetins de sa mere,
> Ce jeune enfant Amour, et qu'il me soit vendu.

But the epigram hardly gains by being stretched to fourteen lines.

[p. 179] *Brutal to his own mother.* Wounding her with his arrows; as when he made her fall in love with Adonis.

[p. 180] *His father's name.* Eros was credited with most various parentage—no parents at all; Chaos; Heaven and Earth; Heaven, or Zeus, or Ares, or Hermes, or Hephaestus, and Aphrodite; Hermes and Artemis; Aether and Night; Zephyr and Iris; Poros (Wealth) and Penia (Poverty), etc.

[p. 181] *The Bride of Death.* Imitated by Herrick, *Upon a maid that dyed the day she was marryed*:

> That Morne which saw me made a Bride,
> The Ev'ning witnest that I dy'd.
> Those holy lights, wherewith they guide
> Unto the bed the bashfull Bride,
> Serv'd but as Tapers, for to burne,
> And light my Reliques to their Urne.
> This *Epitaph*, which here you see,
> Supply'd the *Epithalamie.*

Pretty; but the tragedy is gone.

PHILODEMUS

[p. 181] *Endymion.* A young king, shepherd, or hunter, of Elis or Caria, loved by Selēne, the Moon; who, by one account, bore him a liberal progeny of fifty children. He was granted eternal sleep and eternal youth, either at his own desire or from Selēne's wish to have him always hers.

ZONAS

[p. 183] *The End of a Venture.* With poems on drowned mariners such at this and those on pp. 76, 77, etc., compare what is perhaps the finest of Heredia's imitations of the Greek Anthology—*Le Naufragé*:

Avec la brise en poupe et par un ciel serein,
Voyant le Phare fuir à travers la mâture,
Il est parti d'Égypte au lever de l'Arcture,
Fier de sa nef rapide aux flancs doublés d'airain.

Il ne reverra plus le môle Alexandrin.
Dans le sable où pas même un chevreau ne pâture
La tempête a creusé sa triste sépulture;
Le vent du large y tord quelque arbuste marin.

Au pli le plus profond de la mouvante dune,
En la nuit sans aurore et sans astre et sans lune,
Que le navigateur trouve enfin le repos.

O Terre, ô Mer, pitié pour son Ombre anxieuse!
Et sur la rive hellène où sont venus ses os,
Soyez-lui, toi, légère, et toi, silencieuse.

From Egypt, with clear sky, breeze following free,
While in his wake the Pharos' fires grew pale,
At the rising of Arcturus he set sail
In his swift bronze-beaked ship, triumphantly.

Alexandria's Mole no more his eyes shall see.
In sands ungrazed by even a kid, the gale
Dug his sad sepulchre; there, as they wail,
Winds of the deep twist some sea-withered tree.

In the darkest hollow of the shifting dune,
In the night where gleams nor morn, nor star, nor moon,
Let the tired mariner sleep now at will.

O Earth, O Sea, pity his troubled shade,
And on that Greek shore where his bones are laid,
Be light above him, thou; and thou, be still.

THYILLUS

[p. 183] *Cýbele.* The Asiatic Mother-goddess. For her orgiastic worship, see Catullus, *Attis*; Frazer, *Golden Bough*, v, 278.

[p. 183] *Horned flute.* Made of boxwood, but curved like a horn.

CRINAGORAS

[p. 184] *Bassae.* In Arcadia, with one of the loveliest of all ruined temples.

[p. 184] *Cairns.* 'Hermes' may be connected with *herma*, 'a heap of stones' and was perhaps originally a daemon inhabiting a sacred stone or cairn.

ANTIPATER OF THESSALONICA

[p. 184] *Thy marble image.* As it is a 'small gift', doubtless a statuette.

[p. 185] *Siphnos, Phólegandros.* Small islands in the Cýclades. Cf. p. 60.

[p. 185] *Dēlos.* In the second century B.C. the sacred island became a prosperous port. Rome made it a free harbour (166), so ruining Rhodes; twenty years later the destruction of Corinth removed another rival. In Dēlos market 10,000 slaves are said to have changed hands in a single day. But about 87 B.C. the island was plundered by a general of Mithridates, and 20,000 massacred. It suffered further from pirates, then from Caesar's refounding of Corinth (46 B.C.). Pausanias (2nd century A.D.) speaks of it as deserted, but for its temple-attendants. It is even told that Athens, trying to sell it, could find no buyer.

POMPEIUS

[p. 185] *Laïs.* See pp. 95, 114, 220.

[p. 186] *Mycenae.* Destroyed by Argos in 468. Diodōrus Sículus, under Augustus, says it had lain desolate ever since. But there must be some exaggeration here; for it had some inhabitants in the Macedonian period, and its youth were carried off by Nabis tyrant of Sparta (early 2nd century B.C.). See Frazer, *Pausanias*, III, p. 97.

DIODORUS

[p. 187] *Artemis.* Goddess both of hunting and of childbirth.

MARCUS ARGENTARIUS

[p. 187] *Zēno, Cleanthes*. The first and second heads of the Stoic School.

ANTIPHILUS

[p. 189] *Prōtesilāus*. A Thessalian hero, killed in the first landing at Troy; according to one version, because he knew the first ashore was doomed, he deliberately sacrificed himself. The Gods allowed him to revisit for three hours his young wife Laodameia; after which she pined away, or killed herself (cf. Wordsworth's priggish poem on her). The story of the withering of the branches of the trees on his grave in the Thracian Chersonese (Gallipoli), whenever they grew tall enough to see Troy, recurs in Pliny (*Nat. Hist.*, XVI, 88).

JULIUS POLYAENUS

[p. 190] *Schérian*. The Schéria, where reigned Alcínoüs in the *Odyssey*, was identified with Corcȳra (Corfu).

ARCHIAS OF MYTILENE

[p. 191] *Poor beast's body*. Athene invented the flute but, disgusted by her own grotesque appearance when playing, flung it away. It was picked up and mastered by the Phrygian Satyr Marsÿas, who in his vain-glory challenged the harper Apollo himself. The victor was to do what he would with the vanquished. Apollo, who sang while he played, was judged victor (except by Midas, who thus earned his ass's ears); and Marsÿas was hung on a pine and flayed. Even in historic times his skin was on view at Cĕlaenae in South Phrygia (70 miles E. of Laodicea); if you played a Phrygian tune, it would quiver with emotion; but a strain in praise of Apollo left it sullenly unmoved.

The River Marsÿas, said to have sprung from the satyr's blood, rises in a reedy lake on the mountain above Cĕlaenae, the supposed scene of the contest. The story is sung by Callicles in Arnold's *Empedocles*.

GLAUCUS OF NICOPOLIS

[p. 191] *Daphnis*. See p. 163.
[p. 191] *Málea*. Here an Arcadian city, not the cape in Peloponnese.
[p. 191] *Psōphis*. Also in Arcadia, now the village of Tripótamo.

RUFINUS

[p. 192] *Violets purple-glancing, etc.* It was a clever lover that found all these flowers in bloom at the same time. But, after all, the botany of *Lycidas* itself is equally poetic. For, as pointed out by A. Sidgwick, Milton strews the hearse with three kinds of berries, none of which would have appeared when King was drowned on 10th August, and with eleven kinds of flowers, nine of which would then be over.

PTOLEMAEUS

[p. 192] There is a not untypical contrast between this scientific modesty and the artist's arrogance of Parrhasius, p. 96.

STRATO

[p. 193] *Deucálion.* See p. 169.

OPPIAN

[p. 194] *The mother-seal.* Cf. Buffon and Daubenton, *Histoire Naturelle*, XIII: 'Les femelles mettent bas en hiver; elles font leurs petits à terre sur un banc de sable, sur un rocher, ou dans une petite île et à quelque distance du continent; elles se tiennent assises pour les allaiter, et les nourissent ainsi pendant douze ou quinze jours dans l'endroit où ils sont nés, après quoi la mère emmène ses petits avec elle à la mer, où elle les apprend à nager et à chercher à vivre; elle les prend sur son dos lorsqu'ils sont fatigués.' For the seal's human ways, cf. a Welsh poem of Gwilym Dyved (E. Rhys, *South Wales Coast*, 296):

> Bald-head, bald-tail—see him rise!
> Ware him: he hath woman's eyes;
> Ware him, where he lies asleep.
> Years before he knew the deep,
> Three salt tears his change began,
> When he changed from mortal man.

See too the ballad of *The Great Silkie o' Sule Skerrie.*

QUINTUS SMYRNAEUS

[p. 196] *Quintus Calaber.* Cf. Tennyson, *To the Master of Balliol* (dedication of *The Death of Oenone*):

226

> a Grecian tale re-told
> Which, cast in later Grecian mould,
> Quintus Calaber
> Somewhat lazily handled of old.

[p. 197] *Endymion.* See p. 222.

[p. 197] *Cápaneus,* one of the seven heroes who marched against Thebes, had boasted that not even the fire of Zeus should keep him from scaling its wall; as he scaled it, the lightning blasted him. His wife Evadne burnt herself with his body on the pyre.

NONNUS

[p. 199] *Neatherd . . . mariner.* Cf. p 221.

PALLADAS

[p. 200] *Níobe.* Usually described as daughter of Tantalus, sister of Pĕlops, and wife of Amphīon, who built Thebes with the music of his lyre. She boasted of having six sons and six daughters, whereas Lēto had only Apollo and Artemis. In revenge, Apollo and Artemis slew all her children; and Níobe herself was changed by grief to a stone. Pausanias says that on Mt Sípylus (5,000 feet), near Smyrna, there was a rock shaped like a mourning woman, whence in summer dropped water like tears (see Frazer, *Pausanias,* III, 552 ff.).

[p. 200] *Daphne.* Turned into a laurel-tree when pursued by Apollo.

[p. 200] *The World's Stage.* Cf. the dying Augustus: 'Do you think I have played well?' After which he quoted a Greek comic epilogue:

> If any worth you found in this poor play,
> Clap now!—and send us gaily on our way.
>
> (Suetonius, *Augustus,* 99.)

Similarly Beethoven in his last illness: 'Plaudite, amici, finita est comoedia'; while Berlioz put at the beginning of his Memoirs, in French, and at the end of them in English, the words of Macbeth (v, v, 24):

> Life's but a walking shadow, a poor player
> That struts and frets his hour upon the stage,
> And then is heard no more.

[p. 200] *Vanity of Vanities.* Cf. *Job,* i. 21, 'Naked came I out of my mother's womb, and naked shall I return thither' (on which the dying

Friedrich Wilhelm I, father of Frederick the Great, made the perfect Prussian comment: 'No, not quite naked, I shall have my uniform on').

[p. 201] *Life is a voyage of peril.* Cf. Swinburne, *Erechtheus*:

> Death at last for all men is a harbour; yet they flee from it,
> Set sails to the storm-wind and again to sea;
> Yet for all their labour no whit further shall they be from it,
> Nor longer but wearier shall their life's work be.

And contrast Tennyson's *Crossing the Bar*.

MUSAEUS

[p. 207] *Sestos*. On the coast of Gallipoli, opposite Abydos on the Asiatic shore. Here crossed Darīus, to invade Scythia; here Xerxes built his two bridges, to invade Greece; here Alexander in his turn invaded Asia.

[p. 211] *Omphăle*. Daughter of Iardănus, King of Lydia. When Hēracles was stricken with sickness for his murder of Iphĭtus, an oracle revealed that to be cured he must serve three years as a slave. Hermes then let him away and sold him to Omphăle.

[p. 211] *Atalanta*. Daughter of Iăsus or Schoenus. Her jealous father made all her suitors run a race against her; the defeated were put to death. But Aphrodite gave Milánion three golden apples so beautiful that Atalanta stopped to pick them up and her lover won.

[p. 212] *Boötes*. The constellation containing Arcturus. It has been suggested that the description 'late-lingering', which is taken from *Odyssey*, V, 272, is due to the brilliance of Arcturus, which keeps it visible for some time after dawn.

[p. 215] *Oreithyia*. Daughter of Erechtheus, King of Athens, carried off by Boreas the North Wind.

DAMASCIUS

[p. 216] *In body alone. . . .* This epigram, with slight variations, recurs in an inscription found at Homs in Syria and dated A.D. 537.

JULIANUS

[p. 217] *Demócritus* (c. 460–370). One of the founders of atomism, made the basis of his ethics *euthymia*, 'cheerfulness'; later tradition contrasted him and Heraclītus as the Laughing and Weeping Philosophers.

[p. 217] *Laughter alone could lighten Even thy mother's burden.* The Homeric Hymn to Demeter tells how the Goddess, in search of her daughter Persephone carried off by Pluto, came to Eleusis and was at last brought to laugh and take food again by the jests of the serving-maid Iambe. Allen, Halliday, and Sikes in their edition of the Hymns compare a Sardinian story that the Virgin, inconsolable after the Crucifixion, was at last moved to smile by a frog who told how seven of her children had been killed at one fell swoop by a cartwheel.

MACEDONIUS

[p. 217] *Master alike of land and sea.* As giver of springs, Poseidon the Earth-shaker was also its fertilizer.

[p. 217] *Eileithyia.* See p. 20.

PAULUS SILENTIARIUS

[p. 218] *Mad dog's venom.* Actually human beings suffering from rabies feel thirst and long to drink; but the attempt (sometimes even the sound, or the thought, of water) may bring on choking spasms of the throat-muscles.

Ronsard has adopted the idea in one of his sonnets to Hélène (ed. Vaganay, II, 257):

> Je voyois, me couchant, s'esteindre une chandelle,
> Et je disois au lict bassement à-par-moy,
> Pleust à Dieu que le soin, que la peine et l'esmoy,
> Que'Amour m'engrave au cœur, s'esteignissent comme elle.
>   Un mastin enragé, qui de sa dent cruelle
> Mord un homme, il luy laisse une image de soy
> Qu'il voit tousjours en l'eau: Ainsi tousjours je voy,
> Soit veillant ou dormant, le portrait de ma belle.

But the Greek seems more intense in its brevity. Indeed few Greek poems are so passionately romantic as this, and the next.

AGATHIAS

[p. 219] *Philomēla's tongue.* The Thracian king, Tēreus, wedded to Procne, daughter of Pandīon, King of Athens, ravished her sister Philomēla and, for secrecy, cut out her tongue. In revenge the two sisters fed Tēreus on the flesh of his own son, Procne's child Ítylus. When Tēreus pursued the murderesses, he was changed into a hoopoe, Procne into a nightingale, Philomēla into a swallow. The hoopoe with his golden crown of feathers is still one of the most spectacular of Greek birds, wintering in Africa and returning in spring. It nests in holes in walls or trees.

[p. 220] '*A Kiss within the Cup.*' Cf. Ben Jonson, *The Forrest*, 'To Celia' (based on Philóstratus, *Love-letters*, 355, c. A.D. 200):

> Drinke to me, onely, with thine eyes,
>   And I will pledge with mine;
> Or leave a kisse but in the cup,
>   And Ile not looke for wine.
> The thirst, that from the soule doth rise,
>   Doth aske a drinke divine;
> But might I of Jove's *Nectar* sup,
>   I would not change for thine.

[p. 220] *Laïs*. See p. 114.

[p. 221] *Syrtis*. The Syrtes were the dangerously shoaling waters off Tripolitania and Cyrenaica—the Greater Syrtis being the Gulf of Sidra, SW. of Benghazi; the Lesser, the Gulf of Gabes, NW. of Tripoli.

[p. 221] *Priăpus*. See p. 164.

ARABIUS

[p. 221] *Villa by the Bosphorus*. Cf. Nonnus on Tyre, p. 198; also the Delphic oracle to the Megarians, which bade them colonize the mouth of the Euxine 'where the red deer and the fishes go feeding side by side'. (They then founded Byzantium.)

BARBUCALLUS

[p. 221] *Bērytus* (Beirut) in Phoenicia, on St George's Bay (where he slew the dragon), was destroyed by earthquake in A.D. 551. Gibbon (ch. xliii) speaks of the city as 'illustrated by the study of civil law, which opened the surest road to wealth and dignity; the schools of Berytus were filled with the rising spirits of the age; and many a youth was lost in the earthquake, who might have lived to be the scourge or the guardian of his country'. ('Scourge' is, perhaps, a little hard on the legal profession.)

[p. 221] *Poseidon*. The Earth-shaker, from whom earthquakes come.

APPENDIX I

PIECES OF UNKNOWN DATE, OR AUTHORSHIP

Hymn to Ares

THIS is included among the Homeric Hymns; but is thought to belong
to the imperial period, perhaps to the fourth or fifth century A.D.

Ares, in might surpassing, gold-helmeted charioteer,
Shielded warder of cities, bronze-armoured lord of the spear,
Whose strong hand wearies never, nor the great heart in thee;
Stay of Olympus, fighter for Right, father of Victory,
Terror of all that withstand thee, champion of the leal,
Sovereign lord of valour, thy red orb thou dost wheel
Through the sevenfold paths of Heaven, above whose third great sphere
Thy fiery-breathing horses still whirl thee, year on year.
Saviour of men, and giver of gallant youth, O shine
Upon our life from above with thy own calm light divine,
Thy fortitude in battle. Oh might I shake from me
The bitterness of evil, and bend obediently
My heart's deceiving passions, its violence control,
That drives me to hideous conflict. Give courage to my soul,
Thou Blessed One, and the kindly reign of Peace for evermore,
Away from the clash of battle and the brutal dooms of war.

PHILITAS OF SAMOS

' Man is Born to Sorrow'

Says this gravestone sorrow-laden: 'Death has taken to his keeping,
In the first flower of her springtime, little Theódotē.'
But the little one makes answer to her father: 'Cease from weeping,
Theódotus. Unhappy all men must often be.'

(*Anth. Pal.,* VII, 481.)

DIOSCORIDES OF NICOPOLIS
The Old Slave

A Lydian I, a Lydian slave; and yet, O master,
  To Tīmanthes, your old fosterer, a freeman's tomb you gave.
Long be your life, dear lord, fair days without disaster;
  And if, grey-haired, you follow, I am yours yet in the grave.

(*Anth. Pal.,* VII, 178.)

ANON
The Young Bride

Timárete, ere she wedded, gave the coif that tamed her tresses,
  To Thee, O Lady of Limnae, and her drums and her lovely ball;
To Thee her dolls, as is Thy due, and her dolls' dresses,
  O Artemis the Maiden, maiden she gave them all.
Stretch out, dear daughter of Lēto, above Tīmárete
Thine hand, and the pure in heart guard with Thy purity.

(*Anth. Pal.,* VI, 280.)

The Secret

I loved, I kissed, I was happy, I conquered, her love is mine;
But *her* name, and mine, and our story shall Love alone divine.

(V, 51.)

My Lady Wine-pot

You with the smooth round belly, and lofty neck ascendant,
  One-eared, lank-throated creature, with bubbling mouth and small,
Handmaid of Love and the Muses, Lord Bacchus' gay attendant,
  Lightly laughing hostess, when revel's in the hall,
Why are you full of liquor, when no drop's passed my lip;
Then dry, when I am drunken? You wrong good-fellowship.

(V, 135.)

On an old Tippleress

By the vats of Dionysus, where the sacred vine-juice splashes,
  Many a cup I emptied, with no water mixed at all.
No dusty grave for Myrtas! This wine-jar crowns my ashes,
  Symbol of merrymaking, and my gay memorial.

(VII, 329.)

Siesta

(On a statue of Pan)

Fling yourself here, O traveller, in the lush meadow-grasses
    And rest your limbs, aweary from the road that seemed so long;
Here Zephyr's breath shall soothe you, as soughing low it passes
    Through the pines, and round you cicadas chirp their song;
Here the shepherd of the uplands shall pipe beside the fountain
    His noontide song, where shady the plane-tree coppice grows.
Shun for today the Dog-star's glare; and cross the mountain
    Tomorrow. Trust the counsel that Pan himself bestows.

(XVI, 227.)

Hermes the Hermit

(On a statue of Hermes)

Desolate is my station here on the height, O stranger.
    No choice of mine. Archélochus has set me here.
No mountain-lover is Hermes, nor ever a hilltop-ranger—
    To me, my friend, the trodden thoroughfare is dear.
Yet since he loves not neighbours, but only solitude,
Hither Archélochus brought me, me too, to share his mood.

(XVI, 256.)

The Dead Child

So young, the little Callaeschrus—ah, Death, why must thou take him,
    Thou heart that no pity softens, ear that no prayers placate?
Now in the House of Hades the Queen of Death shall make him
    Her little page to play with.

                But his home lies desolate.

(VII, 483.)

Death in Boyhood

It is not death that is bitter—*that* for all men stands fated—
    But when, before his parents, a boy's young life has fled.
No bride I had, no bridal-song. I died unmated,
    In life beloved of many, dear now to the myriad dead.

(Kaibel, *Epigr. Graec.*, 373.)

' The Hunter Home from the Hill '

Here I stand, the gravestone that tells where you are lying,
   Pericles, son of Archias, and how you loved the chase;
And all about your tomb horses and hounds a-crying
   And hunting-spears stand ready, and stakes with nets in place—
But, ah, in stone! And around you lightly the wild things leap,
While you lie here, but twenty, lost in the last long sleep.

(Anth. Pal., VII, 338.)

' The Whole World Kin '

Hades laid hand upon me while yet my years were blooming,
   Aethérius' son, Rūfīnus; and here within this earth
That held my sires before me, they laid me for entombing,
   Son of a noble mother, yet brought in vain to birth.
To the flower of youth I ripened; of lore I learnt the rarest:
   Ah, for the grave my youth was; my learning, for the pyre.
Weep o'er these lines, O stranger, ere on thy road thou farest;
   Surely among the living thou too hast son or sire.

(VII, 558.)

On a Stone at Corinth

O noble heart, Sabīnus, of the great love we cherished
   Only this little stone keeps now the memory.
But always I shall miss you. I beg you, among the perished
   Drink never a drop of Lethe, to dim your thought of me.

(VII, 346.)

Harvest Home

Dear Earth, within Thy bosom grant rest and long forgetting
   To old Amyntĭchus, for all his toil for Thee;
So many a wreath of vine-leaves Thou wearest of his setting,
   So many a grove of olives, green eternally.
With garden and with orchard, with Demeter's golden glory
   He gladdened Thee, with channels of water murmuring.
Therefore, O Earth, lie gently upon those temples hoary,
   And make the grass above him grow fair with flowers of spring.

(VII, 321.)

The Old Bee-master

Ye Naiads, ye high pastures, where the cold gusts go sweeping,
  Tell to the bees returning upon their springtide way,
That on a night of winter, while for the hares light-leaping
  The old Leucippus waited with his snares, he passed away.
No more shall he tend his bee-hives, so lovingly; yet still
The glens of the shepherds mourn him, who dwelt high up the hill.

(VII, 717.)

The Dead Fowler

Once with his sling Ariston, poor weapon of the lowly,
  To gain himself a living would hunt the flying geese,
Nearer and ever nearer he stalked them, softly, slowly,
  As they fed, their sharp eyes glancing sideways without cease.
Now he is dead. And idle his whizzing sling must lie,
While, over the grave of their hunter, onward the wild geese fly.

(VII, 546.)

The Blessing of the Dead

Mariner, ask not whose these ashes be,
But chance thyself upon a kindlier sea.

(VII, 350.)

' He Fell Among Thieves '

If ever you come to Phthīa, with her vineyards greenly growing,
  And to Thaumácia, stranger, that ancient city, tell
How upward through the woodlands of desolate Málea going
  You found this stone that marks where the son of Lampon fell—
Derxias, slain by robbers upon his lonely way
To glorious Lacedaemon; by stealth, not open fray.

(VII, 544.)

Heraclītus to his Popular Crtics

The voice of Heraclītus—'Why fret me with disputations,
  Fools? Not for you I laboured, but for those that understand.
One man to me is a million, to me unnumbered nations
  Nothing. This is my answer, still, from the dead man's land.'

(VII, 128.)

235

The Sage

I, Epictētus, was a slave; a cripple, I;
And poor as Irus the beggar; and dear to the Gods on high.

(VII, 676.)

Fortune's Freehold

Achaeménides once, Menippus now they call him
    That holds my acres; soon, another's I shall be.
My old lord thought he owned me; the new, whatever befall him,
    Dreams I am *his*. I am only—Fortune's property.

(IX, 74.)

The Common End

I am dead, but I wait your coming. For another you shall wait.
Alike for all men living, wide stands the Dead Man's Gate.

(VII, 342.)

All Roads Lead to Death

To Hades' gate the road runs straight, with never a turning,
    Whether you go from Athens, or from Méroë.
Though far from home you perished, nothing is here for yearning:
    Fair sets the wind for Hades from all the lands there be.

(X, 3.)

Better Unborn

Dionysius, of Tarsus, here doth rot,
Sixty, ne'er wed. Would God my sire had not!

(VII, 309.)

'And in the Grave we're Safe, surely'

Farewell now, Hope and Fortune. You get no more of me.
I am come home to harbour. Go, fool posterity!

(IX, 49.)

'Après Moi le Déluge'

Once I am dead, let earth go up in flame.
My cares are done. To me 'tis all the same.

(VII, 704.)

NOTES

APPENDIX I

Hymn to Ares

[p. 231] *Red orb.* This allusion to Mars as a planet is one sign of the poem's lateness.

[p. 231] *Third great sphere.* Sun, moon, and planets were thought to revolve round the earth in the following order of nearness—moon, sun, Venus, Mercury, Mars, Jupiter, Saturn. Thus Mars is 'third' from outside.

DIOSCORIDES

[p. 232] *Your old fosterer.* The dead man had been a *paidagōgos* (whence our 'pedagogue'), that is, a trusty slave looking after his young master from six or seven till puberty and attending him to school and gymnasium. (Cf. p.194.)

ANON

[p. 232] *Limnae* ('the Lakes'), on the border of Sparta and Messēnia, in a glen 6 miles north of Kalamáta, had a famous temple of Artemis (Frazer, *Pausanias*, III, p. 427). In its girlish simplicity this seems to me one of the most moving of ancient (or modern) short poems.

[p. 233] *Death in Boyhood.* From a tomb near Aezani in Phrygia.

[p. 234] *Aethérius.* Perhaps the so-named brother of the Neo-Platonist Simplicius (time of Justinian).

[p. 234] *Son of a noble mother.* Or possibly 'son of Agathe'.

[p. 234] *Lethe.* The infernal river of forgetfulness.

[p. 235] *Tell to the bees.* Brand, *Popular Antiquities* (1913), p. 480, mentions various similar superstitions about bees—that, if master or mistress dies, they will die too, unless moved away; or that their hives must be turned round as the body is borne from the house. *The Oxford Book of Greek Verse in Translation* (p. 760) gives a still closer parallel from Mark Twain's *Huckleberry Finn*, where the bees must be told of a death before next sunrise, or die themselves.

[p. 235] *Thaumácia* ('Wonderful'). Now Dhomokó, a township north of Lāmia, where the mountain wall suddenly opens before the traveller from the south and reveals the great peak-encircled amphitheatre of the Thessalian Plain. The view is 'wonderful' indeed; though not more so than the number of biting creatures when I once passed a sleepless night in a house there.

[p. 235] *Málea.* Easternmost of the three southward prongs of Peloponnese.

[p. 235] *Heraclītus* of Ephesus (*c.* 500 B.C.). Famous alike for his view of the universe as ceaseless flux, for his pride, and for his obscurity of language.

[p. 236] *Epictētus* (*c.* A.D. 55–135), a Phrygian slave of one of Nero's freedmen, was converted at Rome to Stoicism and, when Domitian expelled philosophers, retired to Nicópolis in Greece, where his teachings were taken down by his disciple Arrian.

[p. 236] *Irus.* The sturdy beggar who quarrels with the disguised Odysseus at the palace in Ithaca.

[p. 236] *Fortune's Freehold.* Cf. the Chinese poem quoted by Lin Yutang (*The Importance of Living,* 1938, p. 41):

> What pretty, golden fields against a hill!
> Newcomers harvest crops that others till.
> Rejoice not, O newcomers, at your harvest;
> One waits behind—a new newcomer still!

[p. 236] *Méroë.* On the E. bank of the Nile, between Atbara and Khartoum.

[p. 236] *Better Unborn.* Cf. Hardy, *Human Shows, Far Phantasies,* 'Epitaph on a Pessimist (from the French)':

> I'm Smith of Stoke, aged sixty-odd,
>   I've lived without a dame
> From youth-time on; and would to God
>   My dad had done the same.

[p. 236] *Farewell now, Hope and Fortune.* Famous especially in its Latin form, which may, indeed, be the original and was put on Petrarch's tomb at Arqua. Gil Blas inscribed it on his cottage near Valencia (Book IX, ch. x.); Lord Brougham, on the portal of his château at Cannes. Dumouriez adopted it as his motto from *Gil Blas*; and Goldsmith has it in Greek at the end of the preface to his *Citizen of the World.* Benserade set an adaptation on a tree in his garden at Gentilly:

> Adieu, Fortune, Espoir! adieu, vous et les vôtres!
>   Je viens ici vous oublier.
> Adieu toi-même, Amour, bien plus que tous les autres
>   Difficile à congédier!

(See J. Hutton, *The Greek Anthology in France,* p. 514.)

[p. 236] *Après moi le Déluge.* Apparently a tragic fragment. The first line was a favourite quotation of Tiberius. Nero, says Suetonius, went one better and, when the line was quoted to him, replied: 'No; while I am still *alive.*'

APPENDIX II

THE PALATINE ANTHOLOGY

NEARLY a hundred and fifty of the short poems in this book (some arranged under their authors; some, anonymous) are taken from the *Anthologia Palatina*. A brief note on that classic collection may help.

About the time when Caesar and Cicero were boys in Italy, some ninety years before Christ, a selection of short Greek poems was made by a man of Syrian Gadara, soon to be more famous for its swine. This selection covered half a hundred authors, and its compiler, the gay philosopher-poet Meleāger, likened it in an introductory poem to a 'Garland' (*stephanos*) of diverse flowers—the lilies, for example, of Anyte, the ivy-clusters of Leōnidas, the honeysuckle of Anácreon, the golden bough of Plato, and of Sappho 'few, but roses'. From this metaphor of a 'garland' all 'anthologies'—'flower-gatherings' (a word first found in the first century A.D.)—ultimately take their name.

Under the early Caesars, about A.D. 40, a sequel was produced by Philippus of Thessalonica.

A century or so later, probably under Hadrian, builder of our Roman Wall (A.D. 117–38), further collections were made by Străto of Sardis and Diogenianus of Heraclea.

Some four hundred years later still, towards the end of Justinian's reign (A.D. 517–65), when Roman Law had been codified and Alboin's Lombards were menacing Italy, while at Mecca was soon to be born the Founder of Islam, a new anthology of contemporary verse was edited by the Byzantine scholar and historian Agathias.

After some three hundred and fifty years more, probably, in the early tenth century, when Constantine Porphyrogenitus was Emperor of the East, and Alfred the Great had been laid to his rest at Winchester, another Byzantine scholar, Constantinus Cephalas, assembled a more extensive work from earlier collections and elsewhere.

Another four centuries passed. Round the beginning of the fourteenth century, when Edward I was busy hammering the Scots, and Dante had reached his prime, an encyclopedic Byzantine monk, Maximus Planudes, reshaped and expurgated the Anthology of Cephalas. It will be seen that many of its poetic flowers were by now extremely ancient—some of them nearly 2,000 years old. It is as if some modern anthologist edited a collection of verse ranging from Virgil's time to Shakespeare's.

Planudes chopped and garbled. Yet his work elbowed that of Cephalas into obscurity. Nearly two centuries later, in 1494, it was edited and printed at Florence by Janus Lascaris, who found refuge in Italy after the fall of Constantinople, as the protégé of Lorenzo de' Medici and Leo X. Numerous other editions followed.

But there still survived in secret one solitary manuscript containing nearly all the Anthology of Cephalas. In 1606–7 this was discovered in the library of the Elector Palatine at Heidelberg (whence the name 'Palatine Anthology') by the young Salmasius—Claude de Saumaise, 'miracle of the world, most learned of mortals', and later opponent of John Milton, who ridiculed him as a hen-pecked cur, and a counterpart of Judas Iscariot. The boy of eighteen recognized that here was something quite distinct from the now familiar Anthology of Planudes. But it was not till 1776 that the fruits of his discovery reached print. Meanwhile in 1622–3, during the Thirty Years War, the Heidelberg manuscript was captured and presented to the Pope. In 1797 the French Directory carried it off to Paris; after Waterloo, most of it (for, by oversight, part was left in Paris) came home once more to Heidelberg. With such strange vicissitudes have these relics of the ancient dead, these epitaphs on men lost in battles or shipwrecks of twenty-five centuries ago, continued to be tossed this way and that by the earthquakes of European history.

Between them the anthologies of Cephalas and Planudes contain some 3,700 epigrams. Many of these, inevitably, are poor stuff—rubbish from the long decadence of Greece, marred by futile cleverness, agonizing witticisms, novelty-mongering, vulgarity, pornography. But a few hundred pieces remain of lasting worth.

Indeed if one had, in half an hour and a hundred lines, to try to convey to a modern reader the essential qualities of the Hellenic mind, one might easily do worse than take as text some of the finest things in the *Palatine Anthology*; so vivid, like illuminations in the margin of a medieval manuscript, is the vision they give of a vanished world and of the poetry which that great race could put even into little things.

History is largely preoccupied with crises and cataclysms; but the daily life of ordinary men and women remains harder to recall. Towering masterpieces like Homer's epics, or the Parthenon, or the pediments of Olympia are, of their nature, exceptional and rare; far more light may be thrown on the common folk of Hellas by the delicacy of some painted vase, the grace of a Tanagra statuette, the quiet sorrow of a grave-relief from the Cerameicus, or by small and unpretending poems such as these.

> And still the grass eternal springs,
> Where castles stood and grandeur died.

After wind and earthquake, the still small voices. These can tell us of a people's simple yet enduring joys and sorrows, hopes and fears.

A girl mourns for the pet rabbit, or cricket, she has loved and lost; or is mourned herself by the playmates her gay stories will never gladden again. A young bride offers the dolls and drums of her childish years to the Maiden-Goddess who has watched over her maidenhood; or is lit to her own untimely tomb by the same torches as made gay her marriage-feast. Lovers warn their coy mistresses how fast a rose must fall; or curse their fickleness; or chide their own despair. Of Love's goddess a wife begs only that her husband be always one with her in heart; a courtesan prays to the same Aphrodite, whom, according to her lights, she also has always truly served; or puts aside the too truthful mirror in which it has grown terrible to look. A young hunter lies, his hunting ended, among the wild creatures that now leap heedlessly across his grave. The tired traveller plunges his parched face in the cool of the wayside spring, or sprawls, relaxed at last, under its plane-trees' shade. A shepherd listens to Pan piping among his nymphs in the windless silence of the hills; or prays still to hear, even in his grave, the flocks quietly nibbling at the turf above him. A ploughman turns out his faithful ox to grass for its few remaining years; or recalls his own lifelong warfare with the briars and brambles that now triumphantly invade his final resting-place. The sailor lies happily lazy beside the bubble of his cooking-pot; or finds a friendless grave in some grey, surf-pounded shingle, or amid the waste seas of the Levant. The old man, life's journey done, passes to his rest with quiet resignation, or a smile of irony.

Century after century, while politicians schemed, armies tramped, empires rose and fell, such obscure lives still went their unnoticed ways. Their thoughts and feelings remain so widely human that they are still easy for us to share; and yet about them clings, also, something essentially Greek. The tone of these poems may subtly change, as the great age of Hellas grows overshadowed by the power and glory of Alexandria, of Rome, of Byzantium; yet they still retain certain qualities that mark the Hellene—the flexible strength of their language; their sense of a noble tradition; their care for grace and form, brevity and artistic economy; their hatred for the exaggerated, the extreme, the unmeasured; their compassion for human fate; their clear-eyed acceptance and endurance of life's relentlessness, without any drugs of frenzy, fanaticism, or dream. At moments one may be reminded of Chinese poetry, or Persian, or (not by chance) of writers like Ronsard, Herrick, or Landor. At their best, the epigrams of the *Palatine Anthology* seem to me unaffectedly natural, yet also deeply civilized—qualities not always very conspicuous in the literature of our world today.

APPENDIX III

THE ORACLE OF DELPHI [1]

'The Oracles are dumm,
No voice or hideous humm
   Runs through the archèd roof in words deceiving.
Apollo from his shrine
Can no more divine
   With hollow shreik the steep of *Delphos* leaving.'

DELPHI lies at the heart of Greece. Indeed ancient legend put it at the navel of the earth itself—so Zeus had found, by releasing simultaneously from the eastern and western verges of the world two eagles which met at Delphi. Even today its landscape remains typically Greek in beauty of colour and splendour of form. In the words of the 'Homeric Hymn' to Apollo:

> Towards the West wind its face is turned; above it lean
> The mountain-crags; and beneath it there runs a rough ravine.

Northward rises the 8,000-foot wall of Parnassus; southward, Mount Kirphis; west and south-west the valley opens to reveal the snow-crowned peaks of Aetōlia and the Peloponnese. Delphi itself clings perched on a mountain-ledge; overhead tower the red-brown and slate-green of the Phaedriad crags; beneath, the grey-green olives of the Pleistus gorge tumble steeply towards the vaster olive-groves of the Vale of Sálona, flanked on their left by the blue Bay of Itéa, 2,000 feet below. As Flaubert says, it was a stroke of genius to choose such a site for Apollo's oracle. That choice seems to have been already made in Minoan days (*c.* 1500 B.C.).

Naturally (like most religious centres) Delphi became the seat of imposture as well as faith; but though its priests were often cunning,

---

[1] See H. W. Parke, *History of the Delphic Oracle*, 1939; P. Amandry, *La Mantique Apollinienne à Delphes*, 1950; and the chapter on Delphi in my *From Olympus to the Styx*.

often corrupt, in the earlier centuries of Greek history they did their part to civilize their world. Less idealistic than the prophets of Israel, they were also less ferocious. The maxims they carved upon their shrine—'Nothing too much', 'Know thyself'—may not seem highly inspired or inspiring: but they expressed a fundamental sanity that can outlast much inspiration. And so it has seemed worth giving here, as epilogue, a brief selection from the hexameters into which the Delphic prophets were wont to turn the incoherent utterances of their priestesses, supposedly intoxicated by vapours imagined rising from the sacred chasm—a typical example of the Greek way of imposing conscious control even on raptures from the Unconscious. For some of these oracles are linked with the finest or most typical memories of the Greek race. That some of them were fabricated after the event may be likely enough; but even if fabricated they remain *ben trovati* and psychologically interesting. And some are memorable poetry. Indeed legend told that the magnificent roll of the hexameter was first heard in the divine summons for bird and bee to come and build the God, with wax and feathers, the earliest of his Delphic shrines:

Ye birds, bring hither your feathers: bring hither your wax, O bees.

First, then, some instances of the moral teaching of Delphi. Here, for example, is an utterance recalling more than one passage of the Bible that sets righteousness above the fat of rams:

Draw near with heart unsullied to the pure house of Apollo,
  O stranger; sprinkled only with water from the spring.
For the good, one drop suffices; but he whom ill deeds follow,
  Though all great Ocean cleanse him, shall find his guilt still cling.
                                        (*Anth. Pal.*, XIV, 71.)

It was long remembered, too, at Sparta how one Glaucus, being summoned by certain Milesians to repay a sum deposited with him by their father, asked the God if he should dare deny the trust on oath. The reply was grim:

Son of Epicÿdes, well indeed—for a while—
Thus to win thee a windfall by perjury and guile.
Swear then! Since even for honest men Death waiting stands.
Yet Oath has a child, that bears no name, and wears no hands,
No feet—yet fleet to pursue the trail of treachery,
To reach and ruin the guilty, and all his race to be.
Better the lot that the loyal leaves to *his* posterity.

243

The frightened Glaucus begged the God's forgiveness, and duly paid his debt. Yet his race died out of the land (Herodotus, VI, 86). Aelian, again (*Var. Hist.*, III, 44) tells how three youths bound for Delphi were attacked by robbers. One was hard-pressed; the second fled; the third, running to help his comrade, by mischance killed him. To the coward, as he entered the shrine, the Pythia cried:

Thou hast left the friend forsaken they were slaying before thy face:
I will tell thee naught. Begone now, from my fair and holy place!

But to the other survivor:

Thou didst slay thy friend in helping. His blood lies not on thee.
For this, only the whiter thine innocence shall be.

Again, Apollo is said to have snubbed Gyges, the rich lord of Lydia, by answering that an obscure peasant of Psōphis in Arcadia was a happier man than he; and to have told a wealthy Magnesian from Asia that all his lavish sacrifice was less welcome than the cake and incense offered by a poor pilgrim from Arcadian Methydrium. But one of the noblest of these utterances, however apocryphal, is the counsel supposed to have been given by Apollo to Lycurgus, the law-giver of Sparta (which might well be remembered by some modern politicians):

Two roads there lie before thee, that issue diversely.
One leads to the home of Honour, the house of Liberty,
And one to the gate of Bondage—*that* is the path to flee.
The first way, it is trodden by brave men hand in hand,
That fear not, and that hate not. By *this* lead on your land.
The second, it is followed by the fool who cannot dare,
And the frenzied heart of faction. Of *that*, before all, beware.
(Diodōrus Sículus, VII, 12.)

For a time, indeed, Delphi was able to render practical service also, as the eighth, seventh, and sixth centuries B.C. saw white sail after white sail vanish over the blue horizons of Greek seas, bearing colonists to Africa and the Euxine, to Thrace, Italy, and Sicily. For, as a centre of pilgrim-age, Delphi became also a centre of information and initiative. Battus of Thera, for example, consulting Delphi about his stammer, was told to his astonishment to colonize Libya. Reluctantly sailing with two ships, he settled in an island off its coast; after two years of hardship he and his men returned and complained to Apollo—only to be met with the withering retort:

If thou, that hast never been to Libya rich in sheep,
Knowest it better than I that *have*, indeed thy wit is deep.
(Herodotus, IV, 157.)

So the weary Battus sailed back, settled in Libya proper, and there flourished; even to having his stammer duly cured by the shock of meeting a lion.

But it was naturally in the politics between state and state that the interventions of Delphi became most memorable and called for the greatest astuteness. Thus the Spartans coveted Arcadia; and with one of his famous ambiguities the God replied:

> For Arcadia ye ask me. 'Tis much—ye ask in vain.
> In Arcadia too many stout acorn-eaters live
> Who shall beat back your onset. And yet this gift I give—
> For your stamping feet to dance in, I grant ye Tégea's plain,
> I grant, for your rods to measure, all Tégea's fair domain.

But the Spartans were worsted even by the men of Tégea; it was as prisoners-of-war that they measured its fields and hopped among its clods (Herodotus, I, 66). Yet in the Greek mind, with its admiration for subtlety and wit, this divine Machiavellianism seems to have roused no resentment. Those who read the riddle wrong felt they had been fairly caught.

But as the world widened for Hellas, this game grew more complex, even with the adroitest ambiguities. The story is familiar how Croesus King of Lydia set a scientific test for the various Greek oracles by sending envoys to ask what he was doing on the hundredth day from their departure. Proudly Apollo replied:

> I know the deep sea's measures, I know the count of its sand,
> And him I hear that speaks not and the dumb I understand;
> And now to me, in spirit, of lamb's flesh comes the smell,
> Broiled in a brazen vessel with a tortoise hard of shell;
> Yea, brass is laid beneath it and brass above as well.

> (Herodotus, I, 47.)

This convinced Croesus, who had in fact been boiling a lamb and a tortoise together in a brazen cauldron, that at least Delphi could be relied on; so he now asked his real question—should he attack the rising power of Cyrus the Persian? And there came the famous equivocating answer:

> If Croesus crosses the Hălys, he shall ruin a mighty realm.

> (Aristotle, Rhetoric, III, 5.)

When Croesus had thereby ruined his own country and became a Persian captive, tradition told that the fallen king sent his own chains as an ironic offering to the God who had so ill repaid his past munificence; but Apollo replied that, though even he could not alter what had been doomed for Lydia, he had at least saved the king's life. Yet even if this answer satisfied Croesus, Delphi was soon to make a far more serious blunder, as the Persian turned on Greece itself. Perhaps the priests had been taught respect for Persia by the fate of Lydia; perhaps with their wider knowledge they were too well informed about the terrible resources of this new empire; in any case, as Xerxes mustered his armies, Delphi spread only alarm and despondency. It frightened the Cretans into an ignoble neutrality; it gave the like advice to Argos:

Deep though thy neighbours hate thee, the high Gods hold thee dear.
Abide behind thy rampart and ready grip thy spear
And guard thy head—the headpiece shall bring the body clear.[1]

(Herodotus, VII, 148.)

The Spartans on the other hand were menaced by the oracle with only a choice between calamities:

Dwellers in wide-walled Sparta, before the Persian horde
Your great and glorious city is doomed to sack and sword;
Or the land of Lacedaemon, if *this* be spared, instead
From the house of the Heraclīdae must mourn a monarch dead.
Not the strength of bulls nor lions shall force your foe away;
For in his arm is the might of Zeus. He shall not stay,
Till either your king or your country is fallen for his prey.

(Herodotus, VII, 220.)

With those words ringing in his ears King Leōnidas marched out to die at Thermópylae. But it was above all in his answer to Athens that Apollo piled horror upon horror, with the grim eloquence of another Isaiah:

Ah wretches, for what do ye linger? From your homes to the end of earth
Flee!—from your craggy hilltop, from the circling walls of your birth.
For the head and the body of Athens are tottering to their fall,
Her hands and her feet wax feeble, her reins grow faint, and all
Darkens with doom; upon her, to ruin and to break,
Come fire and the edge of Ares, in the Syrian chariot's wake.
Many another towered town—not only thine—
He shall sack; to the flame devouring he shall give many a shrine,
Where the images of the Immortals now stand and drip with sweat,
Quaking for dread, and the walls with dark blood glisten wet,
As it runs from the roof, presaging the doom that cometh sure.
Hence from my holy place, and steel ye to endure.

(Herodotus, VII, 140.)

---

[1] Perhaps the head is the ruling class, the body the masses.

In their despair at a denunciation so frightful the Athenian envoys, by the counsel of a friendly Delphian, returned as suppliants to the temple and threatened, unless they could be vouchsafed at least some glimmer of hope, to stay there till they starved. Then the God relented a little:

In vain with her prayers, her wisdom, Athene labours still
To move the Lord of Olympus and turn Him from His will.
But one thing more I will tell thee—yea, it shall stand as fast
As adamant—when conquered lie all thy lands at last,
Far as the march of Cĕcrops and divine Cïthaeron's glen,
The Thunderer shall grant to Tritogĕneia then
A wooden wall, that shall not fall, to save thy race.
Yet, when they march against thee, by land do thou not face
The horsemen and the footmen in their thousands—turn away
And give them ground—to meet them shall come another day.
Ay, Salamis divine, full many a mother's son
Thou shalt slay, at Demeter's seedtime, or when her harvest's done.

(Herodotus, VII, 141.)

The reference to Salamis remains curious. If the Delphians had falsified their oracle in retrospect, they would have wished to falsify it much more. It seems a not inconceivable guess that some mind like Themistocles, shrewdly awake to the importance of sea-power and to the strategic value of Salamis in conjunction with a land-defence of the Isthmus of Corinth, might have deliberately prompted the allusions to 'wooden walls' and to Salamis itself.[1] In any case Greece was saved by men who kept their courage when even Gods, and experts, despaired. And yet, when the victory was won, the Greeks forgave the defeatism of Delphi (which at least claimed the miraculous repulse of a Persian detachment sent against the holy place) and offered there part of their booty. None the less the glory of the shrine never quite recovered. It could still utter in the centuries that followed oracles that became memorable, such as its mysterious praise of Socrates—that no man was wiser than he [2]—and its supposed predictions of the victories of Epaminondas, of the murder of Philip of Macedon, of the fall of Pyrrhus, of the rise of Rome. But it was to be ironically discounted by Thucydides, seized by the Phocians, plundered

---

[1] A similar explanation, I find, has been put forward by Prof. Parke in his history of the oracle.

[2] Later amplified and distorted into the form:

Wise, Sophocles; wiser, Euripides;
But Socrates is wiser yet than these.

again by Sulla. Under the Empire, Nero slighted it, Hadrian patronized it. Indeed there is still a sort of faded charm about the reply Delphi is related to have given to Hadrian's inquiry about the birth and descent of Homer:

> Thou askest what the country and what the family
> Of that immortal Siren? From Ithaca was he;
> Polycaste, daughter of Nestor, was she that gave him birth,
> And Telémachus the father of that wisest bard on earth.
>
> (*Anth. Pal.*, XIV, 102.)

There are Homeric scholars who have done far worse. But by now the oracle was mostly reduced to giving prose answers to trivial domestic inquiries; and Plutarch describes the Pythia of his day as a simple peasant-girl. Yet long verse-utterances still occur also, even when the rise of Christianity was bringing the close of a thousand years of Delphic fame—for example the long piece of verse on Plotīnus finely, though too freely, translated by F. W. H. Myers in his essay on 'Greek Oracles'. And, whatever their authenticity, Apollo was never credited with lines of more poetic sorrow than those with which he is supposed to have replied to Julian the Apostate, before that last champion of dying paganism marched to his own death beyond the Euphrates:

> Say ye to Caesar: 'Fallen our fair-built columns lie.
> Phoebus hath left his temple, his laurel of prophecy,
> His speaking spring—yea, even the spring that spake is dry.'

But even today the spirit of Ancient Greece can be felt, perhaps, more intensely at Delphi than anywhere else. The snows of the long-ridged Olympus still tower, indeed, in snowy splendour or roseate flush above the long Thessalian plain; yet Thessaly, after the legendary glories of Jason and Achilles, soon declined into a backward part of Greece, and it does not hold the enchanted associations of the south. The Acropolis of Athens, again remains, incomparable; yet round it stretch the glare and clatter of a modern city. But at Delphi, as one sits among the white and yellow flowers of one more spring, with the bees humming over them and the wild birds whistling among the rocks, as in the distant days when they built Apollo's shrine of wax and feathers, while the Gulf of Corinth turns a deeper azure and a white cloud-fleece trails along Mount Kirphis and Apollo sinks again westward towards Aetōlia, there still breathes the essential Hellas. Here are only the ancient crags of Parnassus and the ruins of Apollo's holy place—little modern but the humble village-roofs of Kastrí. And yet it is not merely a matter of futile brooding over a vanished past. Apollo is dead; but part of the ideal he symbolized is not. 'Nothing too much'—'Know thyself'—these have not lost their meaning; modern politics, modern psychology have only deepened it. In this rocky valley the God of reason and control long ago yielded a place beside him to his ecstatic and untamed younger brother Dionysus; and that myth can still symbolize the eternal need for balance in the human soul—the danger alike of crushing the primitive and unconscious within us, or of blindly surrendering to it. And here where dwelt the God of so many poets who died 'leaving great verse unto a little clan', one remembers by contrast our own overcrowded modern world, tormented by the problems which that overcrowding brings to a humanity that risks losing in quality what it gains in quantity. (How much better if, like Apollo's Daphne, nine-tenths of us were changed to trees!) And one may be allowed to dream that mankind in centuries to come, learning the lesson of our fate and living in the natural beauty of a less populated earth, as an aristocracy of human beings with machines for slaves, might turn once more towards that ideal of free and sane individuality which Hellas, with all its many faults, has left as its unique bequest to a world that has never wholly forgotten it.

INDEX OF POETS

Addaeus, 97
Agathias Scholasticus, 219
Alcaeus, 54
Alcman, 48
Alphēus, 186
Anácreon, 70
Anacreontea, 156
Antípater of Sidon, 151
Antípater of Thessalonica, 184
Antíphilus, 188
Ányte, 141
Apollonius Rhodius, 142
Arabius Scholasticus, 221
Arātus, 117
Archias, 190
Archílochus, 45
Asclēpiădes, 140
Autómedon, 137

Bacchýlides, 84
Barbucallus, Joannes, 221
Biānor, 188
Bion, 152
Bion, Lament for, 153

Callímachus, 118
Cleanthes, 97
Cleobūlus?, 54
Crinágoras, 184

Dāmāgētus, 149
Damascius, 216
Delphi, Oracle of, 242
Diodōrus, 186
Dionysius the Sophist, 150

Dioscórides, 232
Diotīmus, 138
Empédocles, 92
Erinna, 96
Erȳcius, 183

Glaucus, 191
Glȳcon, 199

Hēsiod, 3
Hippōnax, 69
Homeric Hymns. See *Hymns*
Hybrias, 72
Hymn to Aphrodite, 22
Hymn to Apollo, 16
Hymn to Ares, 231
Hymn to Dionysus, 50
Hymn to Pan, 73

Íbycus, 68
Ísidōrus Aegeates, 188

Joannes Barbucallus, 221
Julianus, 216
Julius Polyaenus, 190

Lament for Bion, 153
Leōnidas, 138
Lucian, 192
Lucílius, 189

Macedonius, 217
Marcus Argentarius, 187
Meleāger, 179
Mimnermus, 48
Musaeus, 201
Myrīnus, 188

Nīcias, 137
Nonnus, 198
Nossis, 141

Oppian, 193

Pallădas, 199
Parrhasius, 96
Paulus Silentiarius, 217
Perses, 97
Phaedimus, 150
Philētas, 117
Philītas, 231
Philodemus, 181
Phocýlides, 69
Pindar, 78
Plato, 93
Polyaenus, Julius, 190
Pompeius, 185
Poseidippus, 139
Praxilla, 92
Ptolemaeus, 192

Quintus Smyrnaeus, 195

Rufīnus, 191

Sappho, 55
Sátyrus, 187
Semōnides, 51
Simōnides, 75
Solon, 60
Străto, 193

Theócritus, 124
Theodōridas, 149
Theognis, 61
Thyillus, 183
Thȳmocles, 150
Timótheüs, 95
Tyrtaeus, 47

Xenóphanes, 71

Zōnas, 182